D1824455

Still the Real
LAKELAND

A. H. GRIFFIN

I dream that heaven is very like this land,
Mountains and lakes and rivers undecaying,
And simple woodlands and wild cherry flowers. . . .

EDMUND CASSON

Photographs by G. V. Berry

50026 GRE
914.28

ROBERT HALE & COMPANY

© *A. H. Griffin 1970*
First published in Great Britain 1970

ISBN 0 7091 1870 8

Robert Hale & Company
63 Old Brompton Road
London S.W.7

THATTO HEATH
BRANCH LIBRARY

PRINTED IN GREAT BRITAIN BY RICHARD CLAY
(THE CHAUCER PRESS), LTD.,
BUNGAY, SUFFOLK

Contents

Illustrations

Foreword

This is a book about the English Lake District that looks back to quieter, less crowded days, but it is also a book of hope for the future. Much has happened to the district since I wrote my first Lakeland book ten years ago—the growing menace of mass tourism, new roads and reservoirs, and the shrinking of times and distances from the cities and the towns—and there are those who fear that the least-spoiled corner of England could some day be ruined for ever. Undoubtedly, Lakeland is changing—this is the way of life—and in places some of the old flavour has already disappeared; but the message of this book is that the best is by no means lost, and will always be there. The real Lakeland is still to be found by those with the enterprise and energy to seek it out, but much of it is hidden and—fortunately—beyond the easy reach of the casual motorist speeding along the fast, new highways.

Here I have tried to picture some of these places, to revive memories of quiet days on lonely hills, to look back on some of the lesser-known characters of the district, old ways through the fells, and ancient crafts, and to grasp something of the genuine atmosphere of the dales. Familiar places—so well documented for more than a hundred years—have been mainly avoided, but little things that seem to me to matter more than well-worn guide-book facts have crept in. This is, I hope, a book for the enthusiast and the connoisseur—ideally, the energetic on foot, but also the exploring motorist who really wants to discover unspoiled beauty and feel the real spirit of lonely places.

This fifth Lakeland book is a companion to the first, where I wrote of my great good fortune to live within the shadow of the fells. And, after nearly fifty years in exploring these delectable places and despite a lifetime of sometimes disturbing change, I can still find something new every day and still catch my breath at the beauty of it all.

Some of the material, although considerably altered and enlarged, is based on writings of mine that have appeared in *The Guardian* and the *Lancashire Evening Post* during the past quarter of a century. I would like to thank Mr. G. V. Berry, secretary of the Friends of the Lake District, for providing me with so many of his splendid photographs, and I am deeply grateful to my wife for her long hours of work in typing and proof-reading.

Cunswick End near Kendal　　　　　　　　　　　　A.H.G.
April 1970

THATTO HEATH
BRANCH LIBRARY

I

The Unspoiled Sanctuary

On a bright April day when there were said to be more motor cars crowding through the Lake District than ever before and the popular routes across the fells were 'wick wi' foak', as we say, two of us sat in a corner of rock high above the Lingcove Beck and looked out at the wild, tumbled landscape. And, incredibly, there was just nobody to be seen—nobody, so far as we could see, in upper Eskdale or in Moasdale or in Green Hole or on any of the fellsides, and not even the glint of a car windscreen down in Dunnerdale. Here we were, perhaps only half a mile away from one of the best-known mountain tracks in the district on the most crowded day that anybody could remember, and yet we seemed to have the fells absolutely to ourselves. For half an hour or so we sat, peering up each valley in turn and systematically sweeping every square mile of fellside and crag, but not a sign of movement anywhere, except, now and again, a distant grazing sheep and the ravens quartering the sky. But then, as we got up to wander down the valley, we spied tiny dots on Slight Side moving along the snow-covered summit ridge of Scafell, nearly 3 miles away, and realised we were not quite alone, after all. Others, besides ourselves, were about in the sanctuary. Not all the thousands were sitting in cars creeping along the Kendal-to-Keswick highway or in procession on the well-worn tracks to Gable and Helvellyn.

For those who seek peace and solitude in the hills this, surely, is the saving grace—that on days when the roads and the villages are chockful of traffic, with cars bumper to bumper over the passes and noble fells alive with winding caravans or brightly coloured anoraks, you can still find quiet places by getting off the tracks and exploring new ways across the hills. Hundreds of places, if you know where to look, with rich discoveries round every corner.

And even the motorist with a real interest in the Lake District, and not merely in the area because the run there and back represents a convenient day's motoring, can escape from the queues and see something of the unspoiled charm of the fell country—if he knows the district or can use a map. Good Friday 1970—the first outdoor holiday of the year—was a sunny day of almost unbroken blue skies, remarkably clear distant views and a fresh north wind. Warm enough to sunbathe if you could find a corner out of the wind, but with snow on the high fells and big breakers down on the beach at Silecroft. I drove through the quiet lanes of Underbarrow and Crosthwaite and over the side of Gummer's How to the toe of Windermere, took the side roads through wooded foothills to the lovely sweep of Gawthwaite Moor and worked my way through the lower reaches of Dunnerdale and the fell road across Birker Moor to the unmatched glory of early spring in Eskdale. And perhaps a quarter of an hour later I was lunching by the shore of Wastwater with the Screes towering above the lake and the familiar shapes of Gable and Scafell—the finest view in England—straight ahead.

No need to describe my clamberings on dry rock in the sunshine, but I returned over the superb Bootle Fell road and eventually through the woodlands around Rusland and Finsthwaite to the Leven and then back home over Cartmel Fell and the Winster valley. And in a low-raftered room in an old farmhouse two of us— the only visitors—ate ham and eggs and listened to the sad story of Good Friday in the Lake District. Seven-mile-long traffic queues at Levens Bridge, they said, and somewhere or another they'd run out of beer and had to call in the police. Another pub, it was strongly rumoured, had had to be closed because of the fighting. And yet we'd seen no traffic queues, nor more than a dozen or so cars, and only a few handfuls of people quietly enjoying the open air in their own different ways—this and the unspoiled charms of places like Bowland Bridge, Bouth and Eskdale Green, and the soaring majesty of the fells, the smell of woodsmoke and the gulls wheeling above the stubble in a field at Santon Bridge. I remember noticing only one alien note—not the distant towers at Windscale nor the new forests in the Furness fells, but an ugly new house near Lakeside. Much had changed along the quiet byways I had known so well as a boy, but the best was still there—in this part of Lakeland, at least. The popular places, the trippers' haunts, are now lost areas to the connoisseur, but the real Lakeland—if you know where to seek it out—is still there. And you can find it—even on a busy Bank Holiday.

I have been on Pillar Rock on one of the hottest days of the year and had the whole of this splendid crag completely to myself—mainly because it is a long walk, of about two hours, from anywhere except Ennerdale, to get to the climbs. And I have walked the fells alone on high days and holidays, bathing in hidden pools or scrambling up unmarked rock, and never seen a soul. The old days with perhaps only two or three parties on Dow or Gimmer on a summer Sunday are over, but you can still find uncluttered climbing in Eskdale or Buttermere or on the eastern crags, or even on Scafell when they are queueing up to climb the Needle. And although a fine weekend will nearly always attract strings of walkers on to Striding Edge or the popular routes up Great Gable and Scafell Pike, you can always find hills to yourself round Riggindale, on the Dodds or in many on the western dales. While the 'back ways' up even the best-known hills are relatively unexplored.

Lakeland is not so much Dove Cottage and the Bowder Stone, Tarn Hows and Lodore Falls, Grasmere sports and knick-knack shops, nor even sheepdog trials and the Eskdale railway. Rather is it the untracked fells where the crowds don't go, shepherds searching for sheep in a steep ravine, foresters and quarrymen working in the woods or in stone huts, or perhaps an old man plaiting baskets in the sunshine or a village lad trolling for char. The tourists' Lakeland is not always—in fact, rarely—the real Lakeland, for to get the real feel of the fell country you have to get away from the highways and the popular tracks and go exploring. Some of it you may discover by car, and I have the utmost respect and admiration for those elderly or infirm people who deliberately seek out the quiet places so that they can taste once again the genuine flavour of the district and be reminded of the more active days of their youth.

But, ideally, the district should be combed on foot—perhaps

from a strategically placed vehicle—with the map as your guide, and there should be an element of adventure in your explorations. Mountain country presents the twin rewards of beauty and adventure, but you are not likely to achieve the latter by following the crowds along tracks cairned every few yards, nor by driving, bumper to bumper, along the high roads. But once away from the clustered road signs the motorist can discover quaint villages and hamlets where country life has changed very little in the past fifty years, while for the walker and climber three-quarters of the fells still remain largely unvisited. Thousands go up Skiddaw every year to every handful who penetrate the lonely country immediately to the north of the mountain, while the splendid Eskdale side of the Scafell range can be as quiet and empty as the hills above Loch Hourn when there are processions going over the Pike. And you can even find lonely corries on Helvellyn, the most popular mountain in the Lake District, or have the Ennerdale side of Great Gable to yourself when the Wasdale crags and screes are alive with people. While the possibilities for quiet enjoyment of the hills around the less frequented fells are even greater and, provided you are prepared to use your legs, the rewards unlimited.

The inability or disinclination of people to use their legs is, of course, one of the growing diseases of the age, and the revelation, in a recent official survey, that only a very small percentage of weekend visitors achieve more than a mile on foot in their journeyings from the car came as no great surprise. Only a modest proportion of Lakeland visitors apparently come into the country's finest national park for open-air exercise. Many of the remainder, of course, come to enjoy the Lake District in their own way, sitting by the lake shore or admiring the hills from a convenient lay-by or the top of a pass, but to thousands, I am afraid, the area is no more than the turning-point in a motor-run, and the glories of the unidentified hills no more than distant shapes barely noticed through the car windows. These people go to 'the Lakes' but do not find the real Lakeland, and, in most cases, are perhaps not seeking it. But for those who take the trouble to seek it out it is still to be found, despite the immaculate new roads, the reservoirs, the new forests, the widespread building, the disappearing hedgerows, the caravan and car-parks, the viewpoints and the sweep of the motorway along the eastern fringe.

Tomorrow, and next week, and next year and, I believe, for many years to come, connoisseurs of beauty and adventure will still be able to find the real spirit of the fell country. Our heritage is still there—not perhaps so obvious as in the days of our parents and grandparents, but therefore even more precious. Despite everything, the real Lake District will not be ruined in our lifetime, but it will only survive into the next century by national concern and the determination of tens of thousands of dedicated people that at least one corner of England must be left untrammelled by the march of civilisation, the passion for uniformity and the urge to develop and commercialise. The future of the best bit of wild, mountain country that still remains south of the Border rests with all those who see beauty in nature and whose hearts are stirred by the pattern of cloud shadows on a hill or the sight of mists suddenly swept from some lonely ridge and the dale leaping upwards from below their feet.

A REMOTE PERCH

There's a couple of hours' hard walking from almost any-where to get to Pillar Rock, which makes it a different sort of climbing ground than these 'modern' crags within handy reach of the main roads and hotel bars. Climbers met on the Rock, therefore, tend to be determined devotees quite prepared to walk up mountains to find their cliffs, rather than single-minded gymnasts for whom an urban quarry face would serve equally well. They are also likely to be much thinner on the ground, and one summer day, with the crags in superb condition, there were only six people besides myself on the biggest lump of rock in England. The walk from Buttermere in August can be long and hot, but the steep scramble up from the Liza and the massed conifers was made enjoyable by the sight of the heather in bloom and the refreshing taste of the bilberries which grow here-abouts in great profusion. While the real lodestone of this walk is always the sight, high up and straight ahead, of the great bulk of the Rock—rather like two cathedrals piled on top of each other, but bigger than any cathedrals in the world. I reached the top of the Rock by a route befitting a lone and slightly decrepit climber and joined the others in leisurely contemplation of the scenery. Strings of walkers, looking, from High Man, like moving matchsticks were crossing the roof-tree of Pillar mountain, but there was no other move-ment, save for the clouds, over the whole tumbled landscape. No sound, either, with the becks stilled by the long, dry summer—not even a slither of sliding scree from sheep on the fellside far below. Westwards towards the lake, the sea and the sunset stretched the dark carpet of conifers, and northwards rose the blue evening hills around Buttermere as we smoked in silence on our steeple top, oblivious of the busy world so far away.

2

Forty Years Back

'THE MOST WONDERFUL PLACE'

Forty years or more ago some Lakeland farmers drove to market on Saturday mornings in two-wheel, horse-drawn gigs, and four-in-hands were still going over the passes. The roads were nothing like so good as they are today, for I have a particularly clear memory of cycling down the Cumberland side of Dunmail Raise in the twenties and finding it so bumpy that in an unguarded moment I hit a stone and went over the handlebars, landing in knee-scratching gravel. There were no double-decker buses in Lakeland in those days, and the danger on the roads was caused not so much by cars and coaches as by flocks of sheep. Driving over Hardknott and Wrynose passes was something of an adventure, for the road was little better than a dried-up watercourse, and the road over Birker Moor was quite a sporting route, too. I remember, however, round about that time, a car being driven over the Walna Scar track between Coniston and the Duddon.

There were nothing like the present-day crowds at holiday time. Most visitors came to the district by train, and charabancs—as we called them in those days—were rarely seen. There were no youth hostels, only one climbers' hut that I can remember, and probably not one-half of the existing private hotels. Many of the present-day private hotels and boarding houses were private residences. 'The Old England' at Bowness was renowned as a honeymoon hotel.

Keswick and Ambleside were fairly quiet places—even on a Saturday night in summertime—and I can only remember two

B

cafés in each of these towns. There were no juke boxes, no fish and chip shops, no crowds of rucksack-laden youngsters in the streets, no caravans and few tents in the valleys. The more affluent visitors stayed in the hotels, the less wealthy in the farms and the occasional boarding-house. There were no 'hikers' in those days. The word had not been invented, and the masses had not yet discovered the hills. There were a number of serious-minded walkers on the fells, but not the weekend exodus from the towns which we know today. I used to go rock climbing on the crags each weekend from Barrow, and so far as I know there were only two other people from Barrow regularly doing the same thing.

There were little coteries of rock climbers in the Furness area and in Kendal, Penrith and Keswick, and we used to meet on the crags each weekend. We all knew each other, and the only other climbers we saw were the better-known mountaineers from the few well-known clubs and a few university people during the vacations. If we saw strange faces on the crags we wondered who they could be. There were two climbing guides for the few who paid for their rock work—Stanley Watson and J. E. B. Wright. A bearded 'Professor of Adventure', the late Millican Dalton, who lived in a cave in Borrowdale, occasionally took people on the crags. There was hardly any rock climbing in the Borrowdale area, none to speak of on the eastern crags, and none on the lower crags in Langdale, many of these cliffs, now honeycombed with routes, not having been 'discovered'. Very few skiers went on the fells in winter, and the Lake District Ski Club had not been formed. There was no water ski-ing, very few speedboats on Windermere and no yachts on either Ullswater or Bassenthwaite.

If you wanted to build a house in Borrowdale or Langdale you could do so without having to seek planning permission. There was no electricity in the valleys and no telephone at Wasdale Head. Few people had wireless sets, and the dalesfolk had comparatively little contact with the outside world. An old shepherd I knew in Wasdale was said never to have travelled farther than Gosforth, and never to have seen a train or a bus. Almost all the dalesfolk spoke in a rich dialect, which varied from valley to valley. You could recognise a man from Eskdale—or from Kendal, for that matter—by his speech. Farmers engaged their men at hiring fairs held in the principal towns, and few of them had their own cars.

Visitors did the 'Round of the Lakes' in a four-in-hand coach, and you had to walk up the steep bits on Honister and Kirkstone. I remember more than once going to Grasmere sports in an open, horse-drawn vehicle. In the shops you saw the same, rather dreary picture-postcards—no colour photographs. Kendal mint cake was hardly known and Grasmere gingerbread was much more famous. The multiple shops had not come into the Lakeland towns, and the names over the shops were the local names. Each town and village had its own separate and distinct atmosphere. There were very few petrol filling stations, and none of those that I can recall were in any way ornate.

There was little or no afforestation, and Ennerdale was a wild naked valley. The paths over the fells were nothing like as prominent as they are today, and many of the hills—Glaramara was one of them—were practically trackless. Very few cars ever went to Seathwaite in Borrowdale, and Nicholas Size wrote a book describing Buttermere as 'The Secret Valley'. Most of the sheep on the fells were Herdwicks, and nobody in Seascale had ever heard of atomic energy.

The Lake District was a precious corner of England—a little too precious some people might say today—inhabited by dalesfolk whose families had lived there for generations, the hoteliers and tradesfolk, a number of wealthy people and a few who had chosen to make it their home. Its visitors were the discerning seekers after beauty or adventure in the hills and, at holiday times, the comparatively few trippers on the Windermere steamers, the Eskdale railway and other innocent amusements. But the caravanners, the picnickers, the weekend motorists, the hitch-hikers, the rope-carrying youths from the cities, the coach parties and the litter louts had not yet arrived. A dreary, boring place it might have seemed to many of the visitors who come today, but to those of us who grew up in or around the Lakeland of forty years ago it seemed the most wonderful place in the world.

THE WASDALE HILLS

The emblem of the Lake District National Park is the ring of fells at the head of Wasdale, with the beautifully symmetrical shape of Great Gable in the centre and the lake in the foreground. It was chosen because this view seemed to typify the very best of Lakeland—the lake, the dale, the mountains and the sky—and for thousands of people the Wasdale hills together form the finest piece of wild scenery in England. 'There are no hills like the Wasdale hills when spring comes up the dale,' sang one of our local poets—and he was right.

Almost as if it was last year I remember my own first close-up view of these magic hills. As a boy I had seen Great Gable and its neighbours from afar on many occasions, and we youngsters came to know the southern Lakeland fells quite well, but Wasdale Head seemed outside easy cycling range. We'd read all about the place and knew the shape of the Wasdale hills from a distance, but we wanted to see them near at hand and to look down into the valley. There was no place like Wasdale Head, we were told, and the mountains there were far better than our 'own' hills around Coniston and Langdale. Wasdale seemed almost a holy place— remote and indescribable—and we resolved that one day we would go and explore the place and see whether these were really the finest hills of all.

It was in the 1920s and I remember it all very clearly, for this was the very first time I was struck by the actual beauty of the mountains. Before then the hills were friendly, but the principal attraction was the adventure they provided. As youngsters we were looking for excitement in a mild sort of way—not mountain beauty. But we set off on the Wasdale trip as if we were off on a big adventure. There were two of us—schoolboys in short trousers—and we had with us a tiny, cheap tent, a couple of blankets apiece, a dangerous petrol stove in a tin, a big packet of oats, a lot of bread and some candles. The loads, carried in old-fashioned knapsacks, were bulky and heavy on shoulders un-accustomed to the work, but our spirits were high and we had no doubt that we would reach the Promised Land. We went by train to Foxfield, I remember, and walked the rest of the way—to

Broughton-in-Furness, through Dunnerdale to Ulpha and over Birker Moor to Eskdale, where we established a base camp, first near Stanley Force and then in a field near The Hows above Boot.

Two little memories of the walk come winging back over the years. The first is of enquiring the price of bed and breakfast at the inn at High Cross beyond Broughton, and of being staggered to discover it was 6s. I can't remember why we were considering abandoning our tent so early in the expedition, but, at all events, we decided the price demanded was extortionate and trudged on through the downpour. It seemed to rain on most days that holiday, but I don't think it bothered us a great deal. We were already well accustomed to getting wet through. A couple of miles farther on—and nearly a lifetime later I could pinpoint the exact spot—we brewed some tea in the lee of a tumbledown wall near the Duddon, and in the process set fire to a corner of one of our blankets. And that's all I remember about the walk from Foxfield to Eskdale.

The camps at Eskdale were not a great success. It rained most of the time, we spent half the nights holding down the miserable tent against gusty winds and much of the daytime burning wet grass in unsatisfactory attempts to control the midges. After a time, too, our diet of tea, porridge and bread fried on a bit of tin with lard bought from the village store at Boot became a little unappetising. But this was only a staging-post, and after a couple of days we set off over Burnmoor to look at the real mountains.

It was, for a change, a glorious morning, and I remember walking up the Whillan Beck past Gill Bank and on to Burnmoor and feeling strangely excited that at last we were drawing near to the real thing. We trotted down to the tarn, sat on the shore in the sunlight eating our stodgy sandwiches and viewed the dull slopes of Scafell, rising on our right, with some disappointment. Our packs felt heavy as we trudged up the rise beyond the tarn, but at the top of the pass we forgot our aching shoulders and our chafed ankles and toes and the discomforts of camping on empty stomachs. For the fields of Wasdale had suddenly opened up below our feet and the most noble ring of mountains in England rose up to greet us.

These were the hills we had come so far to see, and they did not disappoint us. They looked shapelier than our own familiar

Coniston and Langdale hills, and yet more rugged and massive. There seemed something exciting about the way they were grouped together around the level fields of Wasdale Head, and as we watched the cloud shadows chasing one another across the rocky slopes I think we both realised these were the best mountains we had yet seen. And the little dale head between the lake and the winding track over the Sty seemed a wonderful, almost magical place. Today, nearly a lifetime later, I see no reason to alter that early opinion, and I still think this corner the very best of Lakeland.

We walked down into the valley and up to the inn, where we bought lemonade. Although only youngsters, we already knew quite a bit about this inn, but it was to be a few years before I came to know this birthplace of British mountaineering really well. John Ritson Whiting, a descendant of the famous Will Ritson, was the landlord, and the place hadn't changed very much since the days when the first climbers were scrambling about the crags. But for many years now the old billiards room where the guests used to climb round the walls and play 'billiards fives' has been a drawing-room, and the barn-door traverse in the courtyard outside is now forgotten.

We went back to our camp well satisfied with what we had seen, and a couple of nights later went up Scafell and sat shivering in a huddle of boulders just below the summit while we waited for the dawn. Before the darkness came down we enjoyed the wonderful sight of the mountain-tops apparently floating in a sea of white mist, and later we saw summer lightning over Great Gable. It was a perfect dawn—my first on a mountain-top—and we quickly forgot the long, cold night hours as we tripped about the summit rocks in the morning sunlight. This was the time, as a youngster, that I first discovered mountain beauty, and I found it in the Wasdale hills. Looking back on that holiday so long ago, I cannot remember seeing anyone else in the hills except two people who came on to Scafell just as we were leaving.

Our homeland hills were the Coniston fells. They had been 'discovered' 150 years earlier by the very first tourists, but that did not spoil our own explorations, and there seemed something new round every corner. At first the principal enjoyment lay in the physical satisfaction of getting to the top—a feat which had to be achieved at the end of a 25-mile bicycle ride, with the ride home in the evening, perhaps after too much lemonade, to be tackled later. But later there came—quite subconsciously—the search for mountain beauty, although as youngsters we probably never realised this.

After all, anybody, provided he is reasonably fit, can get to the top of any Lake District mountain, and our scramblings had no merit of any kind. But although the walk up Coniston Old Man or Bowfell or Harrison Stickle was nothing for healthy boys, there was nevertheless considerable satisfaction to be won. It came, I remember, from the changing views, the play of sunlight across the fellsides, the wonderful sense of spaciousness and the feeling— quite strong in those days—that these kindly, old fells made up a very special countryside that not very many people knew really well. After all, this was long before the days of mass tourism, and even before the opening of the very first youth hostel in the Lakeland area in June 1931. People went fell walking in those days, but not in shoals, while the crags were rarely crowded, and a man with a rope was an uncommon sight. Dozens of times I have come down from the fells in the evening as a youngster immeasurably sad that I would not see them again for at least a week, but immensely grateful that I lived so near to all this quiet beauty. Perhaps we didn't look upon the mountains and crags, or even the lakes and valleys, as particularly beautiful at first, but the friendliness of the kindly old hills seemed almost overpowering at times, even to a youngster.

And that first close-up view of the Wasdale hills was, for me, the real beginning of a long search for mountain beauty that has remained with me all my life.

TORVER MEMORIES

In Coniston when I was a lad they used to say that Torver, 2 or 3 miles away, was a strange place, full of rather odd folk, and that almost anything could happen there. They never went so far as to tell you that it wasn't safe to be out alone in Torver at night, but you would have thought they were talking about some wild place beyond the Hindu Kush, instead of the next sleepy little village down the road. Many of the stories, of course, were grossly exaggerated. For instance, the Torver quarrymen were alleged to work for a month and then spend the next month drinking their pay, and there was one strange tale about a quarryman who didn't bother to bury his father after he had died until the neighbours insisted. In the meantime, so it was claimed, he had, with apparent unconcern, continued to live with the corpse.

But, certainly, there were some unusual characters living around Torver in those days, and the village was very far from being a typical bit of Lancashire. There was, for example, the red-bearded giant who kept the Church House Inn, sometimes terrifying us youngsters but on other occasions keeping us fascinated by his wild stories. He smoked cheroots which sometimes singed his beard and in the summertime wore a huge haymaker hat and sloppy carpet slippers. Motorists might be welcomed with old-world curtesy, cursed for disturbing him or threatened with physical assault, depending on his mood. Then there was the little man who lived at Tranearth, a mile up the rough fell road, and used to drag his coal up there in sacks. Sometimes we gave him a hand, and now and again, after a convivial Saturday evening had left him marooned by the side of the track, we steered him up the rocky slope. And on another social level there was an expert on the Lakeland dialect in the vicarage and an internationally famous scientist living down the road.

Nowadays Torver is not really much more than a scattered community on one of the main highways into Lancashire Lakeland, but many, many years ago it was probably a much larger village. You can still see some of the ruins of the old farms and, higher up the fellside, archaeologists have traced remnants of a civilisation dating back to the days before history. Most of the names around this part of Lakeland come from Old Norse, but there were people living on the moor between the mountains and the lake many hundreds of years, perhaps thousands of years, before the Vikings came. Several stone circles, prehistoric mounds and burial places have been found on the moor, as well as the sites of ancient hutments and cairns covering old treasures, tools and weapons. There were also mineral workings on the moor long before the German miners came to start the industry that led, more than 100 years ago, to the coming of the railway and the beginnings of modern Coniston. Now the railway is closed and the copper mines derelict, while the slate industry, once depressed, is in the midst of new-found prosperity.

For centuries this moorland shelf below the slopes of the Coniston fells and overlooking the lake has been said to be haunted, and people will sometimes tell you they have had the feeling they were being watched when they walked across the moor above Torver. And it was in this same place several years ago that a doctor's son living near Torver claimed to have seen a flying saucer, and indeed, has a remarkable photograph, taken by his young companion at the time, clearly showing the circular shape associated with these strange objects. Just the place you could say—out of all Lakeland—for this sort of sighting.

As youngsters we used to go to Torver on the early morning 'workmen's' train—it was cheaper—and many early memories are of rattling along this picturesque line and under the bridges to the little station behind the pub and almost in the shadow of the fells. The only 'shop' in the village was the pub itself. You knocked at a little window fronting the road, and if you were lucky you were served. Then up the lane past Tranearth—now a climbing hut— to the crags. The road up to Broughton Moor Quarries—it used to be the old post-chaise road—was no more than a track in those days. There were all sorts of minerals and stones to be found in the deserted quarry workings above the village, and char to be fished for in Goats Water under Dow Crag.

It was also said that there were wild goats about if you knew where to look for them, but I've never seen them in the Coniston fells. Sometimes I believe the farmers used to put the goats into the crags so that they could eat up the grass off the dangerous ledges and remove the temptation from the Herdwick sheep. There are several tarns within easy distance of Torver, and we bathed in all of them, including Beacon Tarn, just below the little hill, where fires were once lit to arouse the countryside. All this area used to be thickly wooded, and you can still see the stumps of oak, ash and beech in the peat mosses. Many of the woodlands were cut down for iron bloomeries, and there were charcoal burners at work among the lower woods earlier this century. The church of Torver stands on the site of one conse-crated by licence from Archbishop Cranmer more than 400 years ago. More than one close friend of mine now lies buried in the churchyard. From the moor above the village you look along the whole length of Coniston Water and—nowadays—across to the forestry plantations on the other side. Torver undoubtedly has an atmosphere of the past, the very ancient past, for those who feel these things. In fifty years it has not changed very much, and I don't suppose it will alter a great deal in the immediate future, but a thousand years ago it could have been an important place. Scattered all round the village are some of the most hospitable farmsteads in Lakeland—places where I have enjoyed wonderful farmhouse food and friendly company.

For me Torver is not a strange place full of odd people but a village of happy memories—a little bit of Lancashire quite unlike any other part of the county, with enough history behind every stone to excite anybody who likes to dip into ancient days. I hope it never becomes commercialised and built up and that it will always remain the sleepy sort of place it still is today, but perhaps this is asking too much.

THE EAGLE'S NEST

When I started rock climbing more than forty years ago I used to be fascinated by a large photograph that hung, along with scores of others, on the wall of the dining-room at the Wastwater Hotel. This showed a man, wearing old-fashioned tweeds and nailed boots, poised on the edge of space on a steep rock ridge on the side of Great Gable. His position seemed precarious in the extreme, for the footholds looked small, smooth and sloping, while the climber appeared very lonely and a long way up, but, at the same time, remarkably composed. I greatly admired his sang-froid and obvious skill, and wondered whether I would ever be able to get up the same place without dying of fright. The climber was the late A. E. Field, the photograph was taken by the late George D. Abraham, of Keswick, and the climb was the Eagle's Nest Arête on the Napes. When the picture was taken—probably towards the end of the last century—it was one of the hardest climbs in England.

I am reminded of all this by the realisation that it is nearly eighty years since this ridge was first climbed. Now, this mere fact, the first ascent of a well-known climb in the Lake District, may be of little or no interest to many people, but I have long considered that this particular feat has its own special historical importance in the growth of the sport, and also in the story of our great outdoors. For this was the most exposed climb done in England—or perhaps anywhere else in Britain—up to that time, and it was the most significant route in the transition between the gully epoch and the ridge-and-wall era. Before that date climbers, for the most part, confined their attention to the gullies on the crags—often dark, damp and even slimy places, but relatively safe. But now they were to launch out on to the ridges and buttresses of the precipices, where the sense of danger was more apparent and an ill-chosen step could have more serious consequences. A sport which had been feeling its way with some caution now began to flex its wings.

The Eagle's Nest Arête lies just to the left of the Napes Needle, if you are standing below the crags looking up Needle Gully, which nestles between the two. At the foot of Eagle's Nest is a roomy ledge known as the 'Dress Circle', from which walkers and scramblers can have an excellent view of climbers on the Needle. When one is seated on the 'Dress Circle' the ridge or arête rises steeply at one's back, soaring impressively skywards, and two narrow, parallel cracks will be noticed about 50 feet up. The climber goes up the wall to a ledge just below these cracks and then crosses them to the skyline on the left, which he follows to the top. On the second 70 feet pitch he first reaches a tiny platform on the ridge—the Eagle's Nest—and, about 15 feet higher, there is a second ledge known as the Crow's Nest. Elsewhere on the ascent, which has a considerable amount of fresh air below and to either side, there are some small, slightly downward-sloping footholds.

The first ascent of this rather intimidating route was made on a cold April day in 1892 by Godfrey Allan Solly, a 34-year-old solicitor from Birkenhead, who was to become a notable Alpine mountaineer. His second on the rope was W. Cecil Slingsby, the pioneer of climbs in many parts of the world, notably Norway, who lived in the Lake District area at one time; and with them were G. P. Baker and W. A. Brigg. At that time the only climbs that had been done on the Napes Ridges were the Needle itself, the Needle Ridge behind and the easy Sphinx Ridge, but Solly and his party immediately launched out on the steepest and most intimidating of all the ridges, in clumsy, nailed boots on a bitterly cold day. Six years earlier W. P. Haskett Smith had made climbing history by his lone ascent of the Napes Needle, but this lead of Solly's up a much more difficult climb, harder than anything else in the country at that time, was at least as courageous and demanding of much more skill.

It is said that the name for the Eagle's Nest was given after Solly, sitting on one of the little platforms with his back to the ridge, and his legs hanging down on either side, was told by the others that he looked just like the bird in its eyrie. In a description of the climb, Solly afterwards wrote: 'Standing up, I found that the first steps up the next pitch were very difficult and that the rock rather pushed one out. The others got out of the rope, and Slingsby, climbing up as far as possible, stood on a little step far below, with his hands on the platform. I put one foot on his shoulder, and as I climbed up, making room for him, he raised himself and finally stood on the platform, helping me as far as possible.' Nowadays, these sort of combined tactics are quite unnecessary, and the climb is regarded as a fairly ordinary sort of route; but it is still steep and exposed, and the holds small enough to make one realise that these old pioneers in their clumsy nails must have been exceptionally daring men.

I remember meeting Solly in Borrowdale either just before the war or perhaps when on leave in the war's early stages, for he died in 1942. He was a solemn-looking, rather austere gentleman with a big white beard, and although he was then about 80, he was still climbing. At the age of 75 he had climbed the Strahlhorn in the Alps, and Lord Chorley has written that a day or two after his (Solly's) eightieth birthday the old man led him up one of the climbs on Pillar Rock. I believe it was on the occasion of this weekend visit that I met Mr. Solly, and I remember feeling that I was in the presence of a great man. He must have been a remarkable man in other ways, too, for he was clerk to the Wirral justices for fifty years and became Mayor and Honorary Freeman of Birkenhead. Perhaps he was one of the last of the old school of Lakeland pioneers to go, and he provided an interesting link between the earliest days of the sport and much more recent times.

The last link with the early days, Mr. George D. Abraham of Keswick, who died in 1965 at the age of 93, took the photograph of the Eagle's Nest that inspired so many of us to climb it. Mr. Abraham was one of the most notable of the climbing pioneers, making history on the crags as well as with his pictures. I believe he took the photograph from the neighbouring Abbey Buttress, and it is certainly one of his best-known and most famous climbing pictures. Round about the time I first became attracted to this photograph, I met the late Mr. A. E. Field, then an old man, at the Wastwater Hotel, but never realised that he might have been the man in the picture. Field was, I think, a professor at one of the universities, and had climbed a great deal with the legendary Owen Glyn Jones, being with him on the first ascent of the redoubtable Walker's Gully on Pillar Rock. And with them on this famous occasion in 1899 was the ubiquitous Mr. George Abraham.

I was lucky the first time I went up Eagle's Nest, for I had with me the man who taught me most of my climbing, the late George Basterfield of Barrow. George, always anxious to encourage youngsters, insisted that I should lead, which I did, but it was difficult to do anything wrong with him behind me on the rope. I remember that when I reached the parallel cracks he told me the exact sequence of hand and foot holds, and the whole thing went quite easily. And once on the ridge, his voice came up calmly from below: 'Now step up easily. Don't try to pull. Use your hands to balance. There's nothing to it.'

Perhaps there wasn't, with a man like that behind me, but then, it was a warm sunny day, and I was in rubber plimsolls—a very different state of affairs from nailed boots on cold rock, half-way up a frightful looking place which nobody had climbed before. I am glad to have known, however slightly, the man who, nearly eighty years ago, had the courage to step up into the unknown, and to become such an inspiration to the thousands of us who came later.

A GOOD DAY ON DOW

Rock-climbers rarely go to the top of their mountain, contenting themselves with their chosen route on some fellside crag and then sliding down at the side to find another way up the same precipice, or perhaps several if they feel fit enough. But whenever we climb Dow Crag, above Coniston, we have always reckoned to go to the top of the mountain at least once during the day, and the crag is conveniently equipped with routes that take you most of the way up. The attraction is partly, I suppose, because we consider ourselves mountaineers first, and climbers second, but there is also the superb view. Surely this must be the most exciting and comprehensive view in Lancashire. Six or 7 miles away to the north-west, beyond the Hardknott track, the notched line of the Scafells stretches across the sky; south-west through the woodlands and past old stone farmsteads winds Wordsworth's Dunnerdale all the way to the sea; while south, stretched out like a map, is the whole of Furness with Morecambe Bay beyond. It is a view that has everything—sea, sky and mountains, islands, valleys and lakes—and by turning your head you can switch from the contemplation of the highest land in England to the sight of sailing craft on Coniston Water, ships far out in the Irish Sea, walkers smaller than tin-tacks on Brim Fell, the dome of Ingleborough and the glint of a car windscreen somewhere Morecambe way. This is the ideal ending to a good day on Dow—to emerge from the darkness of the shadowed crag into the summit sunshine with the swifts shooting out of the gullies and a fresh breeze blowing out of Eskdale. And then the walk quietly down the fellside in the evening, with the blue hills for company, the larks still singing and the shadows lengthening across the close-cropped turf.

3

Beauty and Adventure

USING OUR EYES

When the stage coaches were rattling over the rather bumpy Lakeland roads the coachmen often used to play a game with the passengers sitting on top with them in much the same way that bored youngsters on a family car outing nowadays will spot car numbers or count beards. The players would toss a coin to decide which side of the road they would take, and the game consisted of calling out numbers which represented animals and birds and other things spotted from the coach, the winner being the player with the highest total. In one game a donkey, being slightly unusual, might count for, say, six or seven, whereas a pig would rate only two and a black sheep or a dog no more than one. A magpie, too, might only be one with a hawk several more, while a grey horse counted for five. On the other hand, a cat would also be worth five, and a cat in a window ten at least. It was all very simple, and you could make your own rules, but it passed on the time and it meant the players were at least using their eyes.

And this is where I believe some visitors are not making the most of their visits to Lakeland; they don't use their eyes nearly enough. I remember a few years ago two young campers being lost in the Lakeland hills during Easter, and search teams spending an anxious time until they were found. And when questionned afterwards the youngsters admitted they had no idea where they had been camping, did not know the name of the valley and could not even describe the area. It was the same weekend that the leader of a party of young people lost when walking in the hills had to tell his rescuers that he simply did not know how to get over the passes from Langdale to Borrowdale.

There are so many things to see and to do in Lakeland and so much to learn that a lifetime can be too short for fitting them all in, but this is no reason why we should not look around us and do out best to find out what it is all about. For, by making the conscious effort we can add immeasurably to our enjoyment and build up a permanent interest. Too many people taken into a Lakeland dale or half-way up a fellside will glance casually at the scenery, exclaim, 'How lovely'—as if admiring a new dress—and take the matter no further. In effect, they have looked out at the view with unseeing eyes, and most of the magic and the wonder and the reason for it all will have escaped them. But if they took just a little trouble it could be all so much more exciting and rewarding. Forcing facts down people's throats is no way of getting them to enjoy the countryside, but a few suggestions about the sort of things that visitors to the district might pursue could perhaps be of some use. Admittedly, you can't do much on a day trip or even during a long weekend, but you can at least make a start.

Much may be learned from books, especially when you are longing for the hills from far away, but a good map is, I suggest, an essential. Every time I go into a part of the world which is strange to me, either in this country or abroad, I buy a map before anything else and familiarise myself, roughly speaking, with the lie of the land. A good map is a thing of beauty in itself, and the best Lake District maps will tell you not only the shape of the mountains and the valleys but, if you look closely, something of its history and romance. However well you think you know an area, you can always learn something more from the map. In time, you should be able to recapture much of your joy in the hills by half an hour with your old Ordnance Survey sheet as familiar place-names are noted and interesting contours followed. In the mountains the map should be your constant companion, and you should be constantly checking up the hills on the skyline—not so much in case you get lost but to add to your enjoyment. The fells will soon become familiar, and later you will be rewarded by the thrill of identifying a shoulder of Glaramara, perhaps peeping round the side of the Langdale Pikes or a bit of Pillar, almost

The Wasdale Hills

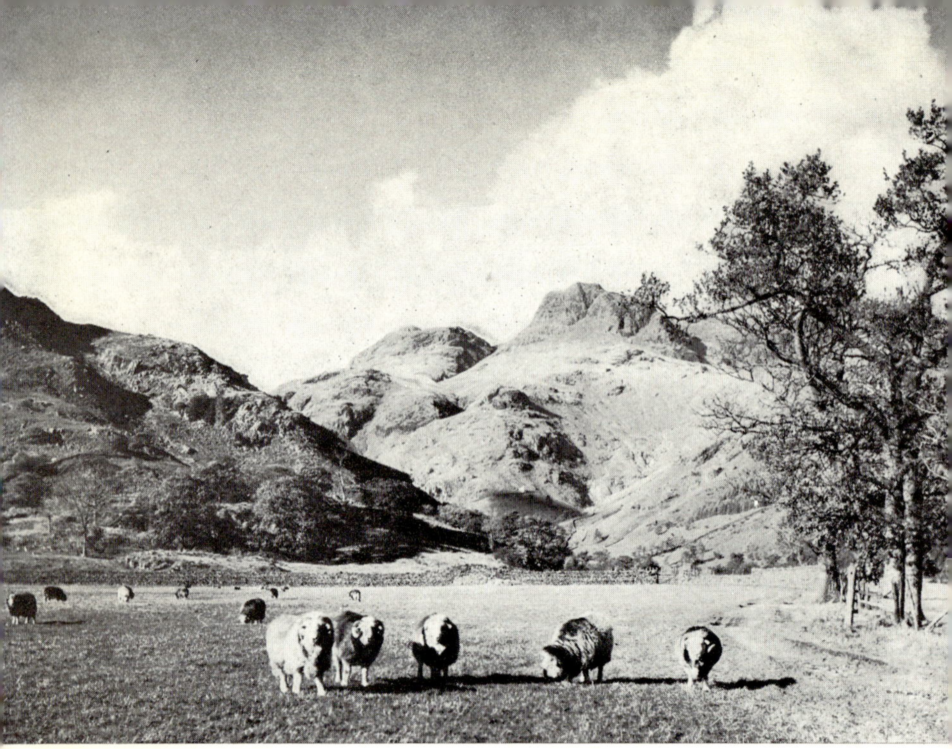

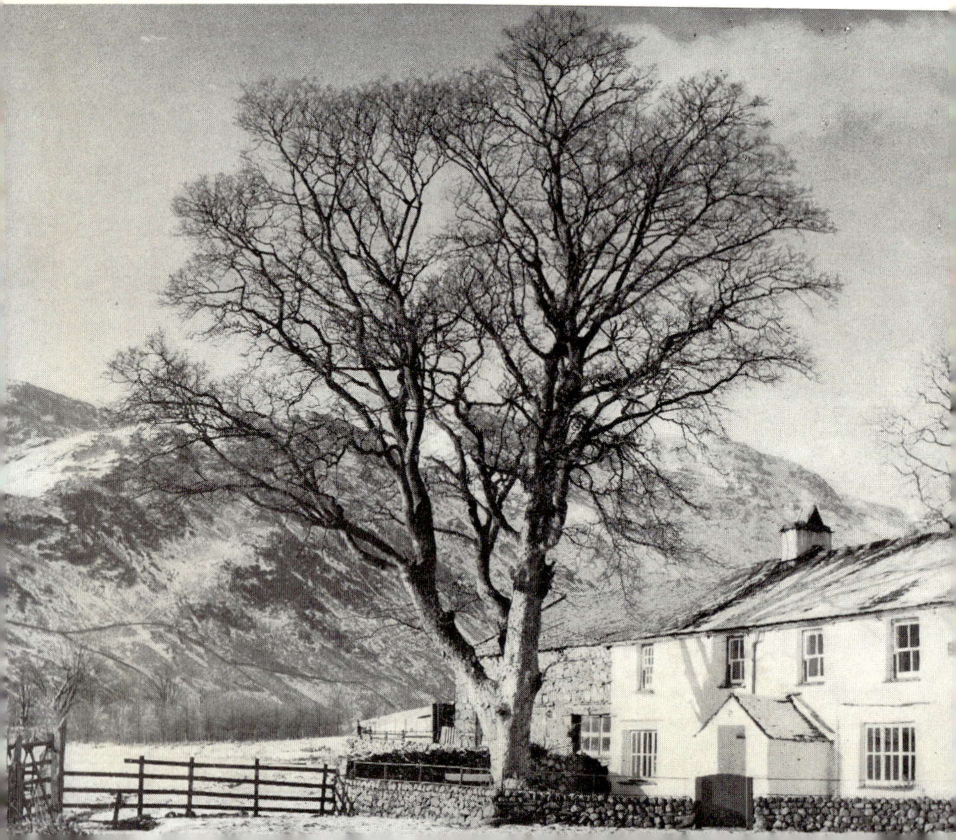

hidden by the Buttermere fells, or the discovery that Grasmoor or Great End can, from certain angles, be fine-looking mountains. And when you have got to know the shape of the best-known mountains from their popular sides you will have to learn what they look like from the other way—which may not be easy.

As you study the mountains you will notice they have no particularly regular shape, some being rounded and grassy and others steep and craggy, and you will learn that these differing shapes and the way the valleys are carved out and even the type of trees or the ground cover—grass, screes, heather, bracken, scrubland—are governed entirely by the rock underneath. You can get hold of a geological map of Lakeland and trace the different types of rock as they cross and circle the district, but you can also easily study them on the ground, and gradually get to know the different types and the shapes they form. For instance, where I live on the edge of the Lake District is limestone country, but half a mile up the lane the walls change from light grey to the greens and browns of volcanic rock, some dark and rounded, others glinting in the sunshine and jagged to the touch. And in that half mile you pass, in effect, out of one country into another.

Besides the shape of the mountains and the crags, and their names and the reasons for their names, there is the colour of the fells to be investigated. Much of the colour comes from the sunshine, but an important factor is the presence of clouds. In the towns or cities clouds are rarely noticed, and in any case, are most often associated with rain, but in the Lake District they fill most of the view, as often as not, and affect the whole picture. Most of us know very little indeed about clouds and their meanings, and we thus miss a great deal of beauty. Frequently the whole pattern of a view is controlled by the cloud shadows, and the sight of these shadows chasing across the sunlit side of a mountain can be among the finest in Lakeland.

The varying types of tracks, such as the paths for sledging down quarry stone, walkers' tracks and the tracks made for the ponies of the Victorian visitors are interesting. Many of them you will be able to trace on a map: others you will not find there, but you can try to discover their reason. Perhaps they lead to a viewpoint or to a rock-climb. And just as interesting are the little 'trods' of the sheep winding along the contours. We know almost nothing

c

Great Langdale
Middlefell Farm, Great Langdale

about these, but much can be learned by following them—why they go across the fellside instead of down, and why they never seem to start nor finish anywhere. And then there are the sheep themselves—the different types, for by no means all mountain sheep are Herdwicks—their lives on the mountains and how often they are brought down. And when you see the shepherd and his dog listen to his whistles and watch the dog and you will get to know the language he is using.

But all this is just a start—the mountains, the crags, the clouds and the sheep. There's the wild life—foxes, red deer, fell ponies, mountain birds and so on, each with their own long story—and the trees and flowers. Worthy of the very closest study are the miles of dry-stone walls climbing over the fells—their history (up to 1,000 years in places), the way they are made, the different types of stone, their varied uses. Many are no longer used and left derelict, but at one time all were boundaries of one sort or another. And sit down on a fellside in midsummer and try—with the aid of a flora, if necessary—to identify all the plants you see growing around you. Or walk through the valley and see how many trees you can name. Daily we are missing beauty because we don't use our eyes.

Several years ago I moved a few miles farther into the Lake District and built a bungalow on a corner of hillside from which I could see the Coniston fells, Bowfell, the Crinkles, Great End and the whole skyline from Red Screes to Harter Fell, while from another window I could see the Howgills and even some of the Yorkshire fells. Every day, except when the mists were low, I could see nearly a score of mountains and, naturally, I knew—or thought I knew—every hump, nick or hollow in the view. But it was a year or two before I discovered, one exceptionally clear morning, that I could see Thornthwaite Crag peeping behind Ill Bell and even spot the 15-feet-high cairn on top—about 10 miles away. I just hadn't been looking hard enough before. And all climbers know the story of the late Professor Norman Collie, one of the pioneers of climbing in Skye, who discovered the famous Cioch on the great crag of Sron na Ciche by noticing a strange shadow on a photograph of the cliff and then going up to investigate.

Nobody has ever known the whole of Lakeland, so there is

always something new to discover. The district contains something like 1,000 different flowers, plants and mosses, while nearly 300 species of birds have been seen in the fell country. And how many of us can identify every tree—even in wintertime? Every day the wild life of the area, the red deer, foxes and badgers, and the now-tamed fell ponies are moving about the district and may often be seen if you keep your eyes open. And so much more—old smugglers' ways and the remains of the old mine workings, the leavings of the Romans, the garnets in the rocks, the pools and springs, the remnants of long-forgotten civilisations, the meaning of the clouds and the flight of a curlew. All to be seen at all seasons of the year and at all hours of the day. A lifetime of study and observation for people who keep their eyes open.

LESS FAMILIAR HILLS

Seatallan, 3 miles away from Wasdale Head as the raven flies and less than a mile from the well-trodden track around the Mosedale fells, is one of the neglected and least-known mountains of Lakeland. Some years ago a young Wasdale shepherd taking part in a race over the mountains in mist failed to find the check-point on the summit and confessed to me afterwards: 'It's strange country to me, over there. Our sheep don't go much beyond Red Pike.' Probably it is the very popularity of the surrounding heights of the Scafells, Great Gable, the Pillar range and even Yewbarrow which makes Seatallan almost an 'unknown mountain'. Nobody is going to bother very much with an ordinary sort of mountain 2,266 feet above sea-level, without any great crags or particularly tremendous views, when there are so many more worthwhile peaks all round it. It is just off all the recognised walking routes, does not fit into a round of fells, has no attraction for the rock climber and is not even mentioned in any of the better-known guide books. At the same time, it is a pleasant enough hill set among the finest scenery in England, and merely owes its comparative immunity from the footprints of man to its situation so close to even better things.

Of course, Seatallan is not alone among the relatively unknown mountains of Lakeland. Many others, perhaps only a mile or so away from the over-cairned tracks, the orange peel, the rusty tins and the empty beer bottles, are equally 'unknown'. Some years ago the late Nicholas Size wrote a book called *The Secret Valley*. It was a good title, but he was only writing about Buttermere, which now has a youth hostel, a climbing hut, a holiday guest house, camping sites, car parks and, of course, hotels along its 2 miles or so of unsurpassed beauty. Although Mr. Size's secret valley might have been unknown when long-forgotten battles were fought out there, its surrounding fells have been familiar for very many years, but travel just a few miles to the north, and you are in fine mountain country which is very little visited by the tourist.

For instance, Grasmoor is perhaps the least visited of all the big mountains of Lakeland, and yet it presents a most challenging side above Crummock Water and is at the end of a particularly attractive set of ridges. And around it there are other fine summits —Whiteside, Hopegill Head, Crag Hill and Whiteless Pike, which if they were in Langdale or Borrowdale would be swarming with people every weekend, but as it is are nearly always deserted.

Great End, the highest mountain in Lakeland below the magic 3,000-feet contour, is comparatively seldom climbed, when you remember it is on the highest ridge in England, and I doubt if one in every twenty of the hordes who tread the well-marked route to Scafell Pike troubles to make the necessary detour from the broad track. Yet Great End is a mountain of character and a particularly fine viewpoint, as winter mountaineers who hack up its ice-filled gullies to the summit well know. Another example of a comparatively unknown mountain is Seat Sandal, less than a mile away from popular Fairfield. Tens of thousands of motorists see it every year as they climb over Dunmail Raise—the great whale-backed shape on the right when travelling north from Grasmere—but how many of them have ever been on its summit? Thousands of walkers go along its shoulder as they traverse the old packhorse route from Grasmere to Grisedale Tarn, but few of them turn aside to admire the view from the top. For W. T. Palmer, the Lakeland writer who died several years ago, it was one of the unknown mountains of Lakeland. He had been on it many times, but had never seen anybody else there.

I am as guilty as others in my neglect of many of these summits.

As I made a point of ascending all the 'two-thousanders' in Lakeland when I was young, I know I have been on top of all of them, but it is sometimes difficult to remember much about them. Seatallan I vaguely remember because of a bathe in Greendale Tarn on the way down, and Seat Sandal is fairly clear in my memory because we went on to the summit after exploring the little crags above the Green Tongue track. But Great Calva, the mountain north-east of Skiddaw, has no memories for me, although my old records show I have been to the top. The mountain is hardly part of Lakeland, but the late Eustace Thomas incurred the wrath of many would-be fell record aspirants by including it in his record round of the Lakeland peaks. It is not a very interesting mountain, and it must be a big strain on these runners to have to run out of Lakeland into the John Peel country and scramble up and down its dull slopes. But few other people, apart from shepherds, ever go there.

In the familiar Coniston fells it is remarkable how seldom Grey Friar—a shapely peak with a lovely name—is climbed, while in the neighbouring Langdale area High Raise, which has been described as the central mountain in the Lake District, is not often visited. Ullscarf, 2 miles or so to the north, is another fairly unpopular summit, but there is ample reason for this—the dreariness of its upper slopes. Its lower slopes are ringed with promising crags, but above them there is nothing but boring grass slopes, not unlike the worst parts of Yorkshire.

A few years ago I would have written of the neglect of Glaramara, a fine, straggling mountain of considerable character, and named this as the least visited of the fells in that area, but since the establishment of the guest house at Seatoller, this mountain has been 'discovered' anew. Not so many years ago there was no track across its undulating ridges; now there are several, and a fine mountain has come into its own. Bowscale Fell, north of Blencathra, is not very well known, but this is not greatly to be wondered at, for, although a much finer summit than Great Calva, it is a little outside the tourist area. But Hart Side, less than 3 miles from Helvellyn, is close to many well-tracked haunts, yet is ignored by almost everybody except skiers. Here again, the reason, I would suggest, is that there are so many other good things to go for not far away. Two other little-visited summits are

Branstree—not named on the Ordnance Survey map although 2,333 feet high—and Selside Pike. These peaks lie north-east of Gatescarth Pass between Longsleddale and Mardale, but have little to commend them, while the several 'unknown' peaks of more than 2,000 feet in height that lie between the Shap Fells road and Longsleddale have even less.

The neglect of some of these mountains is perhaps understandable, but it is remarkable that so few people bother to take the trouble to go up Lingmell, which has from its summit one of the most magnificent views in England. Nearly 100 years ago the Westmorland brothers decided the finest mountain view in Lakeland was the view of Wasdale and the surrounding fells from the crags just below the summit of Great Gable. In 1876 they built a fine cairn at this point—still known as the Westmorland Cairn—and for generations most people have been content to agree with them. But splendid though this well-photographed view undoubtedly is, I think it could be claimed that the view from the summit of Lingmell is equally good, and in some circumstances even better.

Lingmell is a remarkably neglected mountain because it lies too close to so many better things—just off the beaten track to the Scafells and across the valley from Gable and the Mosedale fells—but it is this very proximity to the finest mountains in England that makes it such a superb grandstand. No other mountain in the Lake District is so closely ringed with mountain, rock and scree, and the view, from just north of the summit, of Great Gable, only a mile away across the great trough of Wasdale and the Lingmell Beck, must be the most detailed view of one mountain's architecture in the country. The rather more distant view of the south face of Gable seen from the Scafell range or from the Corridor Route is familiar enough, but when you see it from the top of Lingmell it is as though you were looking at Lakeland's most shapely mountain through a telephoto lens or a zoom camera. You have nearly halved the distance so that, on a clear day, every feature of the mountain leaps into sharp focus and, in addition, you have the impression of tremendous depths dropping below your feet.

One autumn day from the top of Lingmell I could plainly see the Napes Needle, identify a dozen climbs on the ridges and even pick out the position of the Westmorland Cairn and every well-known corner on the whole south face of the mountain. In the Gable view there are also the Mosedale fells, backed by the great bulk of Pillar, to the right the long reaches of Borrowdale with Blencathra and Skiddaw on the horizon, and to the left the length of Wastwater and, far beyond, the sea. All round the compass the mountains of Lakeland, from Haycock to Helvellyn crowd the horizon, while to the south, just over the Lingmell col, rise the rocky ramparts of the highest peaks in England. This southern view provides the finest close-up of the Scafells from any mountain top. You see the whole line of the Pikes from Great End to the highest summit and then, just round the corner, the end-on view of Pikes Crag and the great precipices of Scafell Crag, the biggest wall of rock in the country. This day the mists were swirling round this jagged skyline, making it appear even more impressive, while the whole front of Gable was bathed in sunlight.

All this tumbled panorama of peaks would be enough to justify the top of Lingmell as an outstanding viewpoint, but the mountain also happens to boast, sliced into its eastern flank, the most tremendous ravine in Lakeland—the dog leg-shaped Piers Gill, big enough to hide an army. And from the summit cairn you look straight down into the depths of this enormous chasm, below a decaying confusion of crags and rickety towers This is one of the big crags of Lakeland, but it is too broken and rotten to be worthy of the close attention of cragsmen. Even so, it can claim the longest rock climb in the district—I can't think of anything longer. This is the 2,000-feet-high Pilgrim's Progress which leads out of Piers Gill to the top of the mountain—not very difficult, but an interesting expedition for those seeking something a little unusual.

Lingmell can also boast one of the most splendidly sited and beautifully built summit cairns in Lakeland. It is a graceful obelisk about 10 feet high, perched right on the edge of the crags and obviously the work of somebody devoted to mountains and having a craftsman's eye. At one time it suffered the fate of most well-built cairns, being decapitated by vandals, but this day it was standing proud and complete, and completely putting to shame the rather ugly and ruinous heap that indicates the highest land in England. But this is the only evidence of the hand of man on Lingmell—no survey column or concreted shelter, no pile of old tins and orange peel, not even a track across the summit. Perhaps the best grandstand in the district and yet hardly anybody ever goes there, although it lies only an easy quarter of an hour's walk away from the Corridor Route—one of the mountain highways of the district.

On my last visit, a perfect autumn day with just enough mist on the tops to make them interesting and the valleys full of sunlight, there were processions going over the Pike but nobody on Lingmell, and I don't ever remember seeing anybody up there. Lingmell is rarely an end in itself. People don't say they are going up Lingmell as they might say they were going up Scafell or Gable. It is rather a mountain to be ascended as an afterthought or as an incident in the day, and therein lies some of its charm. You just go up there—on your way to or from somewhere else—because you feel like it, because the time and the weather and the position of the sun and many other things are just right. Lingmell is therefore a mountain for the connoisseur—the mountain the crowds don't notice.

LOVELY VILLAGES

Which is the loveliest village in the Lake District? Not long ago a member of the Lake District Planning Board said there were many 'five star' villages and hamlets in the National Park, but that if there were a 'six star' classification he believed that Strands, near the toe of Wastwater, was one of the places that would qualify. It was, he said, a little corner of incomparable beauty, and completely unspoiled—and he was right. Strands is a cluster of houses and farms set in glorious woodland and close to one of the most dramatic viewpoints in England—the first sight of the length of Wastwater, with the Screes towering up on the right and, straight ahead, the shapely peak of Great Gable and the Wasdale hills. When the sun is slanting through the woodlands, rimming each branch in gold, and the morning mists are just rising in the fields, this can be a place of magic, where anything might happen. See it in the evening with long shadows across the floor of the dale and the westering sun glinting on the lake waters, and it is no less perfect, and on a calm, winter's day the quiet, still beauty of the scene can make a man feel at peace with the world.

Many years ago, when people were talking and writing about lovely, unspoiled Lakeland villages, they would think of places like Hawkshead and Grasmere, but, unfortunately, these tourist centres, although still attractive, have lost some of their quaint charm in trying to meet popular demand. The places that now come to mind as examples of more or less unspoiled Lakeland beauty are villages and hamlets a little removed from the main roads, where the life of the countryside has gone on quietly down the centuries and 'progress' seems to have passed by. This is not to say that these dalesfolk and new residents from the towns are still living in the last century, with poor amenities and out-dated ideas. In fact, very much the reverse. These houses and cottages and village inns may look, from the outside, much the same as they did 100 years ago, but inside you will find their deep-freezes, hi-fis, concealed lighting, under-floor heating and the very latest in cookers and washers. These people, locals and 'off-comers', are leading busy, civilised lives, and they are not part of a museum. They have been lucky enough to escape both commercialisation and the over-neat strictures of suburbia, so that their hamlets don't look like photogenic garden-villages, but unspoiled corners of genuine Lakeland.

Many of these naturally beautiful retreats come readily to mind —delightfully quaint houses, still with their own spinning galleries, at Low Hartsop, the perfection of Winster at daffodil-time, a still evening in Easdale under Helm Crag, the superb siting of Applethwaite under Skiddaw, and the white-washed cluster of cottages around the inn at Bowland Bridge. I live close to a village—Crook, on the Kendal-to-Bowness road—that is making the most of the past, but at the same time planning intelligently for the future. The old cottages are still there, white and shining in the sunshine, with banks of flowers growing by the roadside and jealously tended by the residents because they are proud of their hamlet. While up the hill are the new houses, nestling into the fellside, each one individualistic but traditional in design. No ribbon development here nor rows of neat bungalows such as you see within twenty minutes' drive of every city.

It is difficult to list the 'five star' places—or better—for personal preferences will be different, but many could claim inclusion. The village of Eskdale Green, for instance, has changed little in my lifetime and is a good example of a straggling Lakeland community that has preserved the best of the past, maintained a sturdy independence and kept a charm uncluttered by commercial demands. Little Langdale is another example. Here there has been some recent building, but the place still remains a mountain village, typical of Cumbria but of nowhere else. It is this sense of unmistakeably belonging to Lakeland that matters. The larger villages are constantly at risk because of development, the random growth of tourist facilities, traffic problems and commercialisation. Coniston was the pretty little mountain village of my youth, but it has altered considerably during the last generation, and now has urban features that tend to spoil its former image. Villages such as Braithwaite and perhaps Threlkeld have altered, too, but Grange in Borrowdale has not greatly changed, nor have the Sawreys and Kentmere.

Sometimes the circumstances or the time of the year, or even the day, colour our impressions of beautiful places. I remember as a boy often coming down from the fells to little places such as Woodland or Broughton Mills and being completely fascinated by their peaceful, old-world atmosphere, and even now when I sniff woodsmoke I think of evenings in those parts. I can remember, too, deciding many years ago that the most wonderful place to which to retire would be somewhere in the Vale of Newlands, beyond Stair, and perhaps I was right, but there are places in Dunnerdale, around Seathwaite, just as peaceful and unspoiled.

As a boy I used to go nutting and blackberrying around Bouth and Rusland and accepting that this was thickly wooded country, but little else. But when I go that way nowadays I see neat little hamlets and remarkably fine property conversions; if you like woodland country this is a superbly beautiful area. Seen on the right sort of day, hamlets like Scales under Blencathra or Mungrisdale have their appeal, while Dockray and Watermillock near Ullswater are beautifully sited communities. Some of the villages in north and east Westmorland—for instance, Dufton, Milburn, Temple Sowerby and so on, with their sandstone buildings—have a charm of their own, and the Lowther village of Askham is an architectural gem, well supplied with magnificent country inns.

I have mentioned a handful of places at random, and one could easily add to the list, for we are fortunate in the Lake District in our villages and hamlets, even though some of our towns have lost much of their atmosphere and appeal. Buttermere was once the 'secret valley' and you can still catch the magic of early summer mornings in the village between the lakes or farther down the dale at Loweswater or High Lorton. Wasdale Head was once the most wonderful place in the world to me, and the atmosphere is still there on the right day or in the right sort of company, for there's not been much change in the shadow of the Scafells.

But Strands, the place you'll hardly find in the guidebooks, hasn't changed at all in a lifetime. Auld Will Ritson who kept the Wastwater Hotel last century and, as much as any other man, was responsible for the old image of Lakeland, died at Strands almost 100 years ago. They say he was babbling until the very last about the local hunt, and perhaps as he looked out towards the fells and the lake the old man realised he was going to his rest in one of the loveliest corners in England. But he would not know that it would be just as perfect 100 years later.

A PERFECT DALE

One glorious, sunny Sunday before the opening of the new motorway through Westmorland cars returning southwards from the Lakes were jammed in long queues for miles before the Lancaster by-pass—the normal occurrence on a busy weekend at the height of the season, although this was only late spring. And earlier in the day families were out, as usual, on the roadside verges in Lakeland with their portable tables and chairs, their washing-up bowls, their inflatable rubber mattresses, their Sunday newspapers and their wireless sets. Years ago, you did this sort of thing in your back garden; today, with no more initiative and much less comfort, it is apparently done by driving 50 or 100 miles on crowded roads, setting up camp on some dusty, grass verge within petrol fumes range and then joining the queue for home. Still, everyone to his own taste.

Mercifully, however, it is still possible to get away from this sort of thing, and my notes remind me of how two of us spent that particular day. I will not mention where we went, for these things are better discovered for oneself—but those who are sufficiently interested should be able to guess, and if not, they may enjoy the mental exercise of working it out. We left the car up a rocky farm road perhaps half a mile beyond the last of the car picnic parties, and followed a glorious winding uphill track through a wood of newly sprouting hazels, birch and holly. Ahead of us stretched a valley which is one of the least-visited in Lakeland, but is everything a valley ought to be. Indeed, it is one of the finest of the smaller dales in the National Park. It is ringed with fells rising steeply on all sides, threaded by twin becks which splash and gurgle down through the gorges or slide along white pebbles in the shallows, and several great crags frown down into rocky coves. At its entrance the dale is as flat as a dancing floor, and in the evening, with the shadows lengthening across the turf, there is magic in the peace of these lovely, level acres between the winding becks and their deep, dark pools.

This is a countryside—at the entrance to the dramatic, tumbled, upper dale—which has been made by centuries of husbandry. The two or three scattered farmsteads squat inconspicuously, each within its little grove of trees, and it is plain that the meadows were once part of the lake lower down the valley which the motorists fly past in their thousands each summer. Through generations of hard work these fields have been won from the scrub and the marshland, until now, I am sure, there are no more productive acres in Lakeland and no more delightful picture of pastoral simplicity when seen from the fells above. The patchwork-quilt fields of Wasdale Head are a well-known feature of the view from Great Gable, but the meadows we admired that Sunday have a different sort of beauty. There was something in the shape of the enclosing stone walls—here a straight line, here a graceful curve—which gave them their charm—that and their flatness, their green, sunlit splendour, and the winding river, with its banks of shingle, threading through their midst. There is no finer camping site in Lakeland if you go there in April when you might have the valley to yourself.

From leaving the car until our return six or seven hours later, we saw no one, apart from two or three specks on distant ridges, but now and again, from some high point on crag or fell, we saw

the sun glint on the windscreens of motor cars, passing in a procession along the main road a couple of miles away. In their own
way, perhaps, the motorists were seeing Lakeland, but hardly the
real Lakeland that stretched out below our feet. But although there
were no people about on the tops, there were sounds, and all of
them pleasant sounds. We did two rock climbs on one of the crags,
and even at that height there was the noise of the waterfalls far
down in the valley always in our ears. Later there was the croaking
of an old raven who kept darting in and out of the crag, furious at
our presence, and as we came down a long sunlit ridge towards
the end of the day the larks were singing high above our heads.
Then there was the sad bleating of the lambs down by the river,
both at the beginning and end of our day, and the clatter of pails
in a farmhouse dairy, but no other sounds all day, except now and
again, the sighing of the warm wind in the crags.

I had expected to see a peregrine in one crag, but he did not
appear. There used to be one there, I know, and once I saw him
sitting in the crag—a splash of white on a dark precipice. But that
Sunday only the raven who lives near a cave at the top of the crag
went into the air. From the tops the views were not particularly
extensive because of the heat haze, but we could see all the
mountains of eastern Lakeland and now and again a stretch of
lake or a distant tarn. From one of our climbs we looked across
at a distant summit and saw one tiny speck, and then two or three
more, reach the topmost cairn and then disappear down the other
side. Whoever they were, I'm sure they were getting more out
of their day than the people listening to 'Family Favourites' down
by the roadside, but, of course, it takes all sorts to make a world.

The main crag visited on our little expedition faces north-east
and so does not get the sun, but towards the evening the topmost
blocks were full in the sunlight, so that we came up out of the
comparative darkness into the brightness of a perfect Lakeland
evening. The Herdwicks nosing about for herbs among the
boulders cast long shadows across the rocks, but the young lambs
were more than 2,000 feet lower down the fellside, skipping about
near the beck. Not far below one of the summits we found a patch
of rather dirty snow—the only snow we could see in Lakeland—
and we glissaded down the disappointing remnants of the Lakeland
winter sports season.

Our way down from the tops took us through a fine, rocky ravine, which not one in a thousand visitors ever sees, but which is one of the wildest and most impressive bits of rough country in Lakeland, and then along a sunny shoulder of fell, and down to the valley floor and the farms. The wireless was going full blast by the lake shore, and some youths were kicking a football about at the side of the road. Whether or not they will remember the day, I cannot say, but although for us it was just another Lakeland day like hundreds before it, it had for me something of a special quality. I think it was the feeling that despite all the bustling crowds on the main roads, we had a lovely valley almost to ourselves all day, for the expenditure of comparatively little effort.

I had not seen my peregrine, we had not done anything remarkable on our rock climbs and we have often seen much more extensive views, but for seven hours we had been high up in the hills, listening to the lovely sounds of nature, marvelling, as we looked down into the dale, that so much unspoiled beauty could be crammed into so small a space, and watching the clouds sail by. And we could still hear the larks singing and the sad bleating of the lambs as we threw the rucksacks into the car and set off to join the procession towards Kendal and the south.

OTHER WAYS UP

However much of an adventure walking in the Lakeland fells in good weather might have been a hundred years ago, it is rarely a real challenge nowadays. All the navigational problems have long since disappeared, most of the tracks are well marked and graded and there are illustrated guidebooks to point out every step. In bad weather or in wintertime, of course, a walk over the tops can be a much more satisfying and demanding experience, but the man who has been up Great Gable or Helvellyn fifty times in summer along the popular paths can hardly be commended for his daring, although his devotion would be in no doubt.

But many years ago, before the mass invasion of the fells, our friendly little Lakeland mountains must have presented at least a minor challenge. They were then comparatively trackless and indifferently mapped, transport was non-existent so that considerable distances were nearly always involved, while equipment was of the most elementary description. And I believe that challenges of a sort can still be found in the fells today, even in summertime—if you avoid the well-worn tracks and seek out other ways up.

It seems to me that rock climbing has progressed as a sport to a vastly greater degree than fell walking. The earliest climbers sought out the easiest ways up difficult crags—gullies and chimneys and obvious lines of weakness—and gradually developed their technique, until today climbers are tackling the hardest ways up even overhanging cliffs. But fell walkers, by and large, still stick to routes which were well-worn fifty years ago—mostly the easiest ways up the mountains. Some of them discover a special challenge by trying to cover as many mountains as possible, but, despite all the great improvements in footwear and equipment generally, the easy availability of transport, the wonderful maps and guides and the difficulty of getting lost in reasonable weather, very few mountain walkers seem to go out of their way to probe the inner recesses of the fells or work out routes more interesting or demanding than the cairned highways. Indeed, it could be said that a man who has been up nearly all the Lakeland fells, but only by the well-marked tracks, may not really know his mountains and might be surprised—or even lost—if taken half a mile away from the paths he knows so well. Here, then, I suggest—after more than forty years of climbing and walking in the Lakeland hills—is the challenge; get to know your mountains better, even intimately, by discovering new ways to the top and eschewing, as far as possible, the paths.

Many interesting alternatives are available. You can, for instance, walk on a strict compass course, ignoring all paths and treating the walk as an exercise in navigation. Scafell Pike, nor' nor' west from Cockley Beck, might be an interesting one to start with, and you can easily work out a dozen more from the map. And then, at the end of the season, you might do worse than steer a compass course right across the Lake District—say from east to west—a challenging expedition if you pick a good line. Indeed, if you get down to your fell-walking in the first place at home with a good map you can plan all sorts of unusual expeditions which will give something of a challenge to your outings. I recall a friend who wanted to get the Pennine Way out of his system but had not the time to devote to the whole walk. So he did it piecemeal—in the evenings after work and at weekends—doing a great deal of motoring, but gradually adding several miles each week. And then the following year, when he found he had the time, he did the whole thing again, in the opposite direction, as a single walk, in nine days.

Another way to make your Lakeland fell-walking rather more challenging is just to take the most difficult route you can find to a chosen summit, viewing the problem from the valley rather than from the map. This is a favourite device of my own when I am not climbing, and should be adopted only by competent scramblers, preferably people with some climbing experience. The possibilities are almost endless, and may be varied to suit one's ability. There is, for instance, a challenging route to Pillar Rock from the Liza, using rock nearly all the way, but this is really an expedition for climbers, and should not be tackled alone. But nearly every Lake District mountain runs to rock on at least one side, and you can select routes, far away from the tracks, which can be anything from modest scrambles to moderately challenging ascents.

All walkers know the well-known ridges—Striding Edge, Swirral Edge, Sharp Edge and the rest—but even more interesting routes can be found if you take the trouble to seek them out. The Scafell Pike area, for example, abounds with possibilities, and other mountains worthy of exploration away from the tracks include Crinkle Crags, Hart Crag, Fairfield, Nethermost Pike, Red Screes, Blencathra, Wetherlam, Base Brown and many more. There is even a good scramble up Coniston Old Man which avoids tracks and quarries, and it is possible to work out an interesting route up Harter Fell, starting from the Duddon.

In time the adventurous walker will learn that places are often much easier than they look, but he will also acquire judgment, which is the most important thing in mountaineering, of which fell-walking forms a small part. The north-west ridge of Catstycam, for instance, looks quite tricky, but is really a very easy walk, while the craggy steps of Greenhow End, which can look challenging, provide an interesting way up Fairfield. There is also

Stickle Tarn

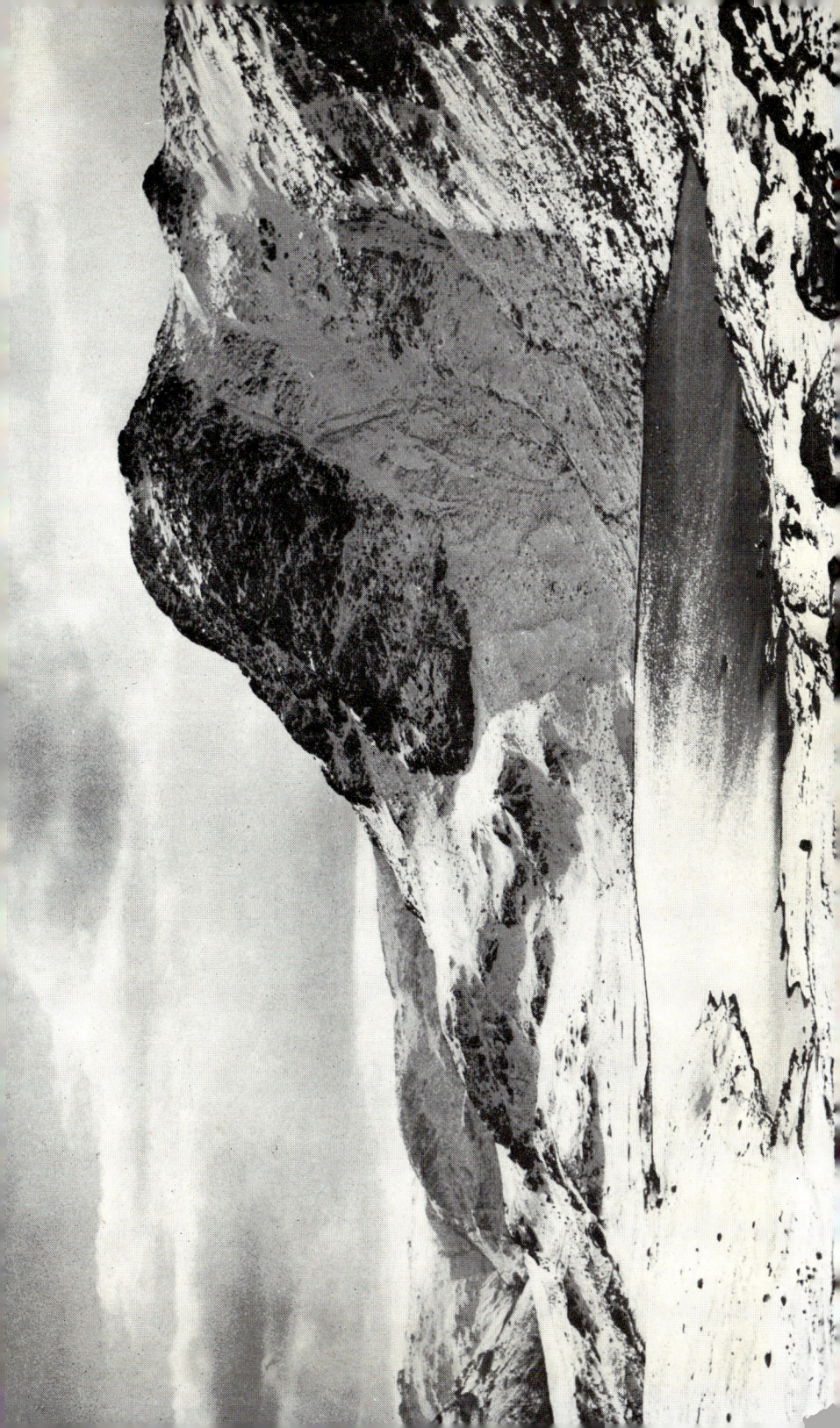

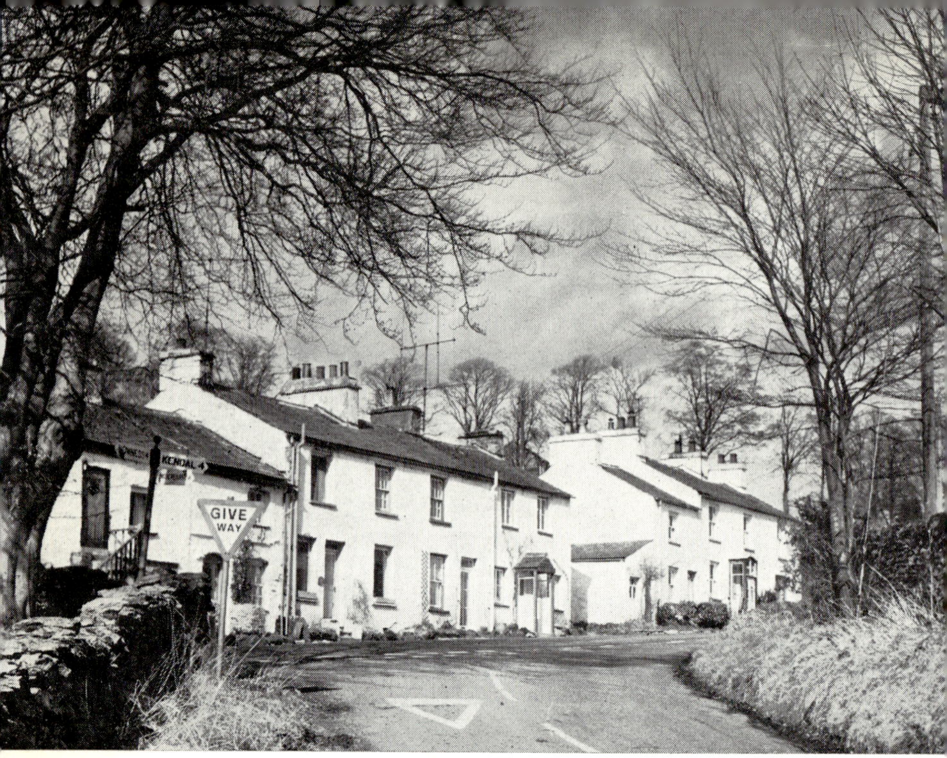
KENDAL 4
GIVE
WAY

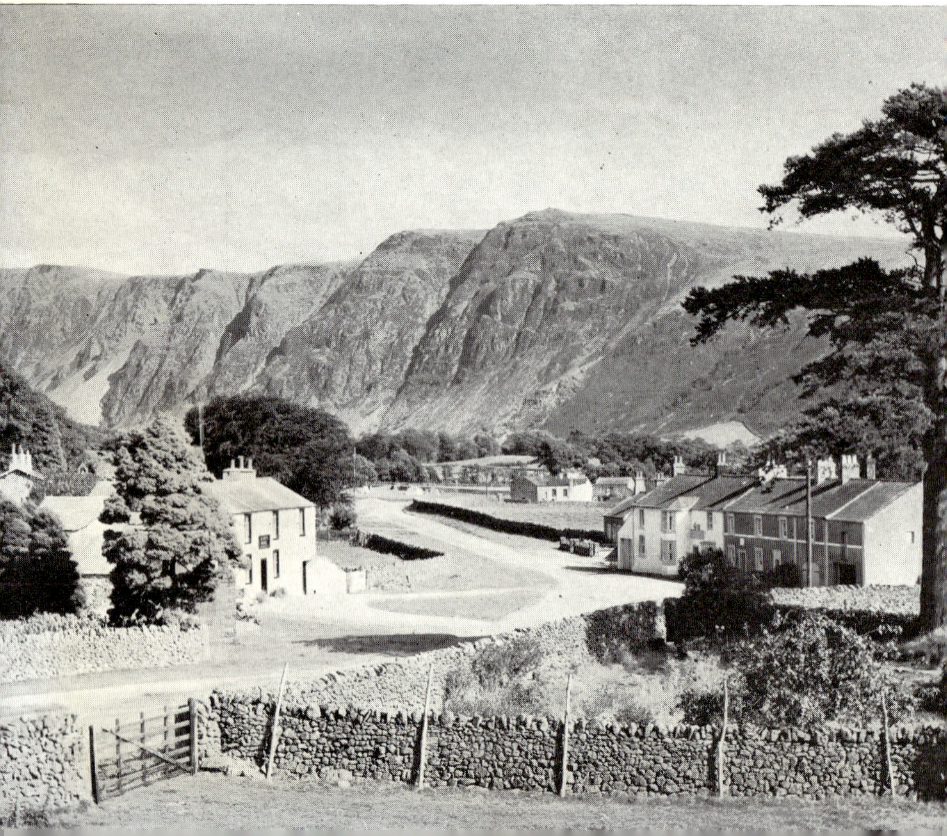

a rewarding rocky route across the side of Hart Crag above Deepdale, another up Red Screes from the top of Kirkstone, a route up Harrison Stickle by way of the ravine of Dungeon Ghyll and many possibilities at the head of Eskdale.

Again, you will find many people on Wetherlam most weekends, but I have always had the east ridge to myself—easy rock all the way if you pick the best route, but nothing anywhere to tax a competent walker. Ideally, this way up Wetherlam—or perhaps better still the descent—should be combined with the negotiation of Tilberthwaite Gill, provided you have the necessary experience. Two of us once came down this way, making a climb of it—down the waterfalls, over the pools, across the walls and in and out of the caves, carefully avoiding the ladders and bridges which in those days made a sort of staging up the ravine. We had a lot of fun and we got very wet indeed, but I suppose this is really an expedition—especially when there is a lot of water in the ravine— for experienced climbers.

But this brings me to another interesting method of ascending, or descending, a Lakeland mountain—beck scrambling. One of the most rewarding ways of going fishing in these parts is to fish the fell becks for trout, and it is an equally good plan to go up the mountains this way. You can either pick your becks from the map or select them on the ground, and the scrambling can vary from simple leaping across boulders to quite tricky climbs through waterfalls. Almost always the beck scenery is delightful, and you seem to make height easily, almost without effort, so interesting is the work. Every few minutes you turn a corner or top a pitch to see new scenery ahead, and the noise of the water and the thrill of finding the right route combine to make the ascent most fascinating—especially on a warm day. Sometimes a beck will start in the dale as a lazy river, become a necklace of tumbling waterfalls higher up and finish under the summit crags as a tiny spring trickling out of the boulders.

To follow these becks from the valley to their source can be a piece of pure exploration, for few people will have been there before, so that the beck scrambler can face a new challenge in his familiar hills and have a much more interesting day than the walker committed to well-worn tracks. So forget the tracks and the guidebooks—at least in summertime—try to seek out the

D

Crook
Strands, Wasdale

'backs' of the mountains, and make a point of exploring all the little valleys and combes and gills that give the fells their character. I've been exploring these places all my life and can still find something new.

SOME BYWAYS

Although the cloud shadows still chase gloriously across the hills while the ravens circle lonely crags and the old whitewashed farmsteads nestle easily in the hollows, Wordsworth's Lakeland is slowly changing. Rapidly, for example, the main highways through England's first national park are becoming either speed tracks or crowded processional thoroughfares, depending on the season, and in the more popular corners much of the quietude is disappearing. But the seeker after unspoiled natural beauty can still find it, provided he knows where to look. Ideally, he should be on foot, striding through the upland bracken and heather, where, even on sunny Bank Holidays, he can enjoy, in well-chosen places, superb scenery in peace and solitude. But if, lacking time, energy or youth, he must make his search by car he need not be despondent, for many of the lesser roads, including some of the passes across the fells, will take him through magnificent scenery and away from the holiday hordes. He can still park not far below the clouds, listen to the larks singing or the waterfalls splashing down the crags, and watch the buzzards soaring.

On the right day—a sunny August Sunday may be a bad choice—the road over Kirkstone Pass, topped by the third highest inn in England, can be a rewarding drive with its dramatic views into Patterdale on one side and the pastoral length of Windermere on the other. And on the western side of Lakeland there is the airy, unfenced road over Birker Moor from Dunnerdale to Eskdale with the unfolding panorama of the highest land in England. Or the Bootle Fell road over the 'back' of Black Combe, with views across the Irish Sea, Herdwicks nuzzling the bracken, curlews rising from the heather and an occasional reminder, in the old stones, of lost civilisations of long ago.

One of the finest expeditions, however, for the motorist seeking unmatched scenery, a chance of solitude and the thrill of a peep into 2,000 years of history is the drive from Little Langdale to Eskdale over the twin passes of Wrynose and Hardknott. As this is the toughest bit of well-surfaced motor road in the North of England, with Hardknott perhaps the most formidable piece of tilted highway in the country, he should be a confident driver, but you can get over in a well-laden, eight-horsepowered car if you take it carefully. There are half a dozen hairpins on each side of Hardknott with a gradient of one in four in places, but if you take the corners as wide as possible, keep the revs at a nice speed in low gear and avoid wheel spin, it is perfectly straightforward. I go over about twenty times a year in a smallish car—often at night in bad weather—and have never had any difficulty. Before the war when the surface sometimes resembled a boulder-strewn river bed it was a different matter. But Hardknott is more demanding than the highest motorable roads in the Highlands.

The number of gates annoyingly across the route from Ambleside to Eskdale has now been reduced from five to two, but the old man was still sitting last summer on his bench at Fell Foot, by the foot of Wrynose, carefully closing the gate after each car went through and picking up his honest copper now and again by reopening it. Near this quaint old house, with the arms of the seventeenth-century le Flemings still over the door, it is believed the Viking settlers met on a little knoll for their annual parliament; and over the passes on their way to the port of Ravenglass went the smugglers with their loads of rich merchandise, salmon poached from the Duddon and locally brewed whisky. And the feet of their ponies as they went trotting through the dark were bound in straw, the easier to escape the notice of the excisemen.

Perhaps the drive is best tackled from the Little Langdale side, with the easier pass coming first and the tremendous view of the long length of Eskdale, flanked by the Scafells, suddenly leaping into view as the car dips down over the shoulder of Harter Fell. But if you go this way, stop near the top of Wrynose for the backward view down to the lakes, woods and meadows around Ambleside—one of the principal rewards of the run in the reverse direction, especially when the evening sun lights up the floor of the dale and glints on distant meres. Near the summit of Wrynose in the Three Shires Stone, where, by disposing your body in awkward arrangements, you can claim to be standing in Cumberland, Westmorland and Lancashire at one and the same moment; and the siting of these county boundaries has ensured an assorted treatment of road surfaces, varying from tarmacadam to concrete. Down into Lancashire slides the road, with the infant Duddon on your right and the boulder-strewn slopes of Grey Friar towering above leftwards, while the Herdwicks wander across the unfenced highway and the ravens quarter the lonely reaches of Moasdale and away to the crags of Bowfell.

The ribbon of road climbing ahead of you to the skyline looks more like mountaineering than motoring, but by engaging low gear at the first steep hairpin and keeping there you will reach the summit of Hardknott in a few minutes and be able to peep out over a different world. Eskdale, with perhaps a sparkle of sea in the distance, is suddenly revealed—a long, green trough, spattered with woodlands and farmsteads and threaded by the winding Esk, and straight ahead is the line of the Scafells, brooding over the wildest dale head in England. And half-way down the zigzags, on a shoulder of fell, is perched the Roman fort of Hardknott, where the legionaries watched the pass and practised a civilisation undreamed of by the local tribesmen. You can see their bath house and the parade ground, the granaries and the commandant's house, wonder at the skill of their masons in the superbly fashioned walls, or look out where the Emperor Agricola once stood.

The 'Buttermere Round' of the four-in-hands may not be so adventurous as the way over the passes to the sea, and for part of the way may even be crowded, but it passes through scenery unsurpassed for colour and variety. First the run along the shore of Derwentwater, through the wooded glories of beautiful Borrowdale—with silver birches standing by limpid pools and beds of shingle—and the high fells peeping over the trees, and on to the hamlet of Seatoller, with the wood smoke rising straight through the larches. And then up and over the steep side of Honister Pass with backward views to the Helvellyn range and beyond, until suddenly you top the rise and look down into the perfect valley of Buttermere. This is the nearest thing in England to the Pass of Glencoe, the same savage drop with a mountain wall and dark crags on either side and, winding between great boulders, the beck leaping down the rocks. On the left is the shattered precipice of Honister Crag, where, for generations men, tunnelling in crazy galleries or hanging in ropes, have hacked the green slate—the best, they say, in England. And down past the Scots firs and the first lake-washed meadows is Buttermere—a valley 'made by heaven for summer evenings; green floor and purple heights, with the sound of waters under the sunset . . . and the greyness of the dew upon the grass'. You leave the pastoral piece of Buttermere and climb high into the fells to the gap of Newlands Hause, whence a long run round many zigzag bends and under the shoulder of Causey Pike brings you down to the mountain hamlet of Stair, and so through lanes of blackthorn and hazel to Keswick.

A rarely travelled Lakeland road nowadays is that into Mardale, flooded years ago to help Manchester's water needs. For 5 miles the road hugs the southern shore, providing superb views of the length of the High Street fells, where the Romans had their mountain highway, and it ends abruptly in the wild, craggy country beneath the passes of Nan Bield and Gatescarth. A new hotel replaces the old 'Dun Bull', now drowned, where the carousings at the annual shepherds' meet used to last three days, but you can look into secluded valleys where the red deer still roam or watch the shaggy fell ponies grazing by the mountain tarns. Mardale is approached along lonely, winding lanes from Penrith or Shap, but if you want to explore the real red-deer sanctuary of Martindale, you must go back to Pooley Bridge and traverse the southern shore of Ullswater to Howtown, on the other side of the High Street range. Steep hairpins bends protect the entrance to the sanctuary, and when you reach the dale head well beyond the ancient yews in the tiny churchyard you should seek permission if you want to wander into the fells to photograph the deer.

From all these byways—and there are many more—are magnificent views of the hills, so different from the familiar picture-postcard scenes, but perhaps the most splendid and all-embracing view of all for the unadventurous motorist is that from the terrace road that contours the lower slopes of Skiddaw through the hamlets of Applethwaite and Millbeck. Bassenthwaite Lake and Derwentwater, with the meadows in between, are at your feet, and beyond lies the lovely length of Borrowdale and a maze of sister valleys with a splendid upthrust of hills and wooded crags, and, as backcloth, the notched line of the Buttermere Fells and the ramparts of Great End and Scafell Pike. See this view lit by the morning sun and it will take your breath away; see it carved into relief by the long shadows of sunset, the hills rimmed with gold, and you will remember it for a lifetime.

THE LITTLE MOUNTAIN

On one of the few really wet days in the lovely high summer of 1969 two of us went over a little-sung mountain that seems to fail in only one respect—its height. To some people Haystacks, which does not achieve 2,000 feet, is not a mountain at all, but to the more appreciative it has much more interest and variety than many of the higher fells, and is perhaps the most exciting mini-mountain in the country. It has crags, gullies, waterfalls, some of the most perfect tarns in the district—including one on the summit—surprises round every corner and close-up views of the big mountains that make the heart of the fell country seem surprisingly compact. From where else, for instance, can the climber see at a glance the cliffs of Pillar Rock, Scafell Crag, Gable Crag and Boat Howe? There is nothing straightforward about Haystacks—people even argue about its name and height—and the tracks around the sprinkle of summits wander through the heather and the bilberry and around rock outcrops, tarns and reedy marshes in a delightfully haphazard way. Many years ago, before the tracks were trodden out, the knobbly top in mist, with the steep crags falling into Warnscale nearly 1,000 feet below, was an easy place in which to get lost; but this day, in spite of the rain, the way seemed clear enough. From the surrounding fells Haystacks often looks a dark, forbidding place, for the sunless crags face north and the heather and peat give it a sombre colour, but on the mountain, even in rain, there is a feeling of warmth and intimacy. And on a sunny day, with the tarns sparkling like jewels and the larks singing, the top of Haystacks becomes a fairyland and the line of lakes, far below, a string of pearls.

4

The Peace of the Dales

UNDISCOVERED PLACES

One evening about four years ago I was in a part of the Lake District where I had never been before—a little gap in the hills north of Skiddaw called Trusmadoor. Not only had I never been there before but I had never even heard of the place, which, after a lifetime of walking and climbing in the district was rather remarkable. There's nothing really exceptional about Trusmadoor —apart from its lovely name. Just a little nick in the undulating skyline of the Uldale fells, between the rather less-happily named Great Cockup and Meal Fell—a place known to shepherds and sheep and, years ago, to the miners, but perhaps not to many others. There's heather and bracken and bilberry and sweet-smelling thyme, grouse under foot and larks overhead, Scotland across the Solway away to the north and the great bulk of Skiddaw to the south. A wonderful place in the evening from which to watch the setting sun, the only sign of man being the Sandale television mast. The hamlet of Orthwaite, nearly 3 miles to the west, is the nearest habitation, and southwards, nearly 4 miles across the shoulder of Great Calva, is one of the loneliest houses in England—Skiddaw House. Here, for nearly half a century, with only his dogs for company, lived Pearson Dalton, for five days a week looking after the sheep that roam the hills. And near Orthwaite lies Over Water, Lakeland's most northerly and probably least-known sheet of water.

And yet all these places are inside the Lake District National Park. The locals know them, of course, but the vast majority of

Town End and Town Head, Troutbeck
(Overleaf) *Long House, Dunnerdale. Boot, Eskdale.*
Packhorse bridge, Deepdale. Head of Deepdale.

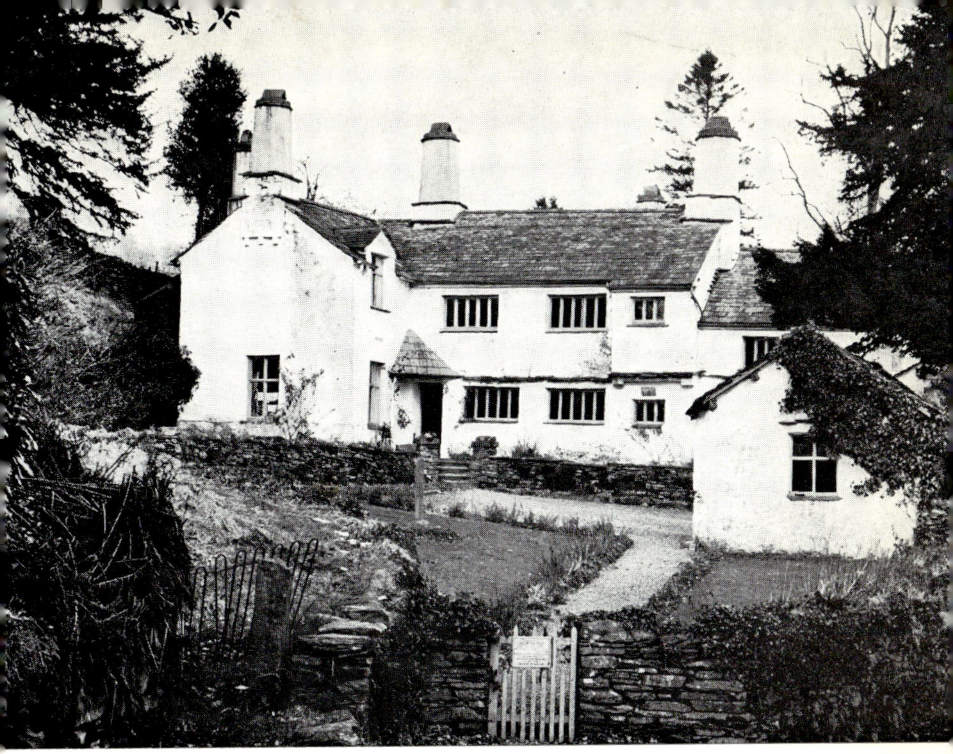

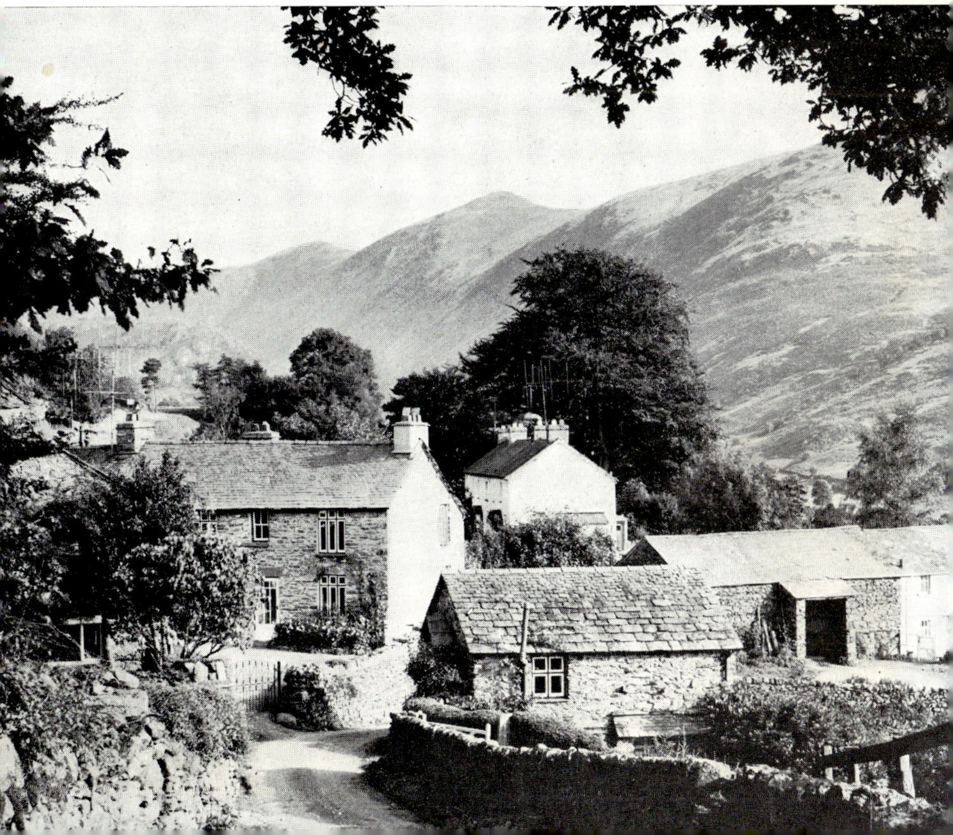

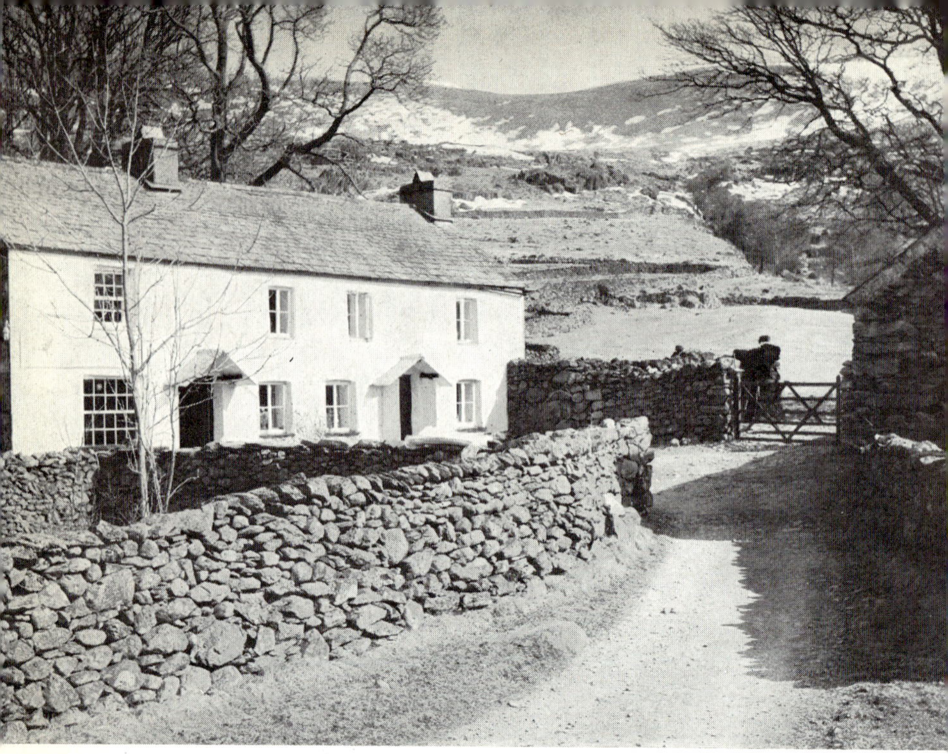

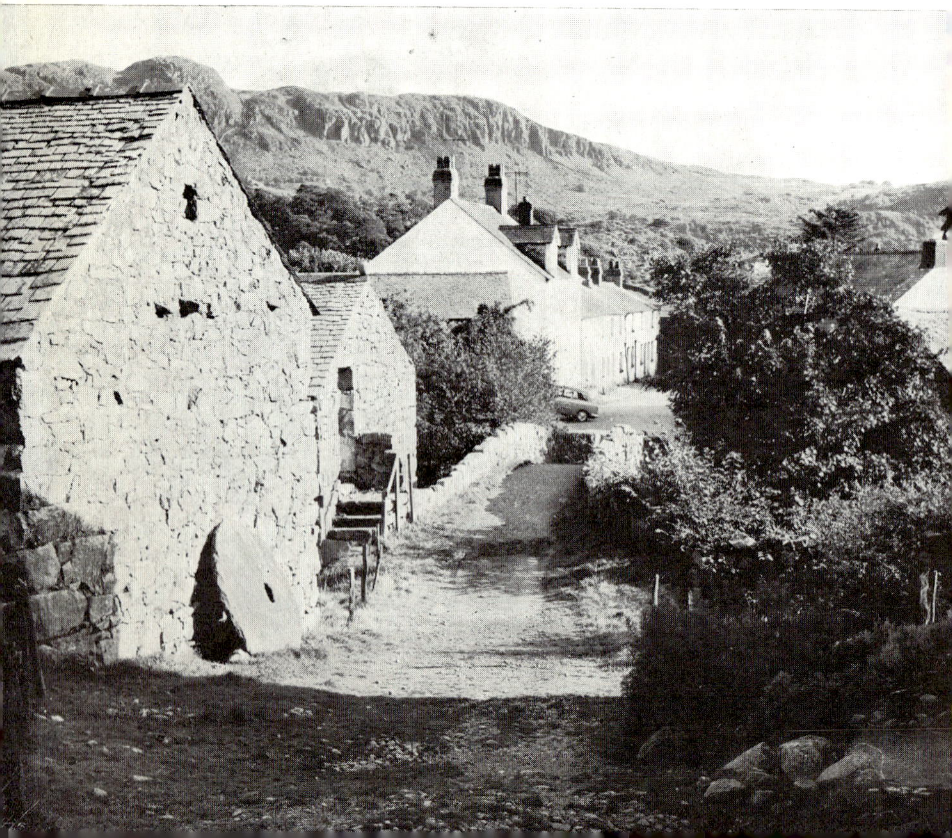

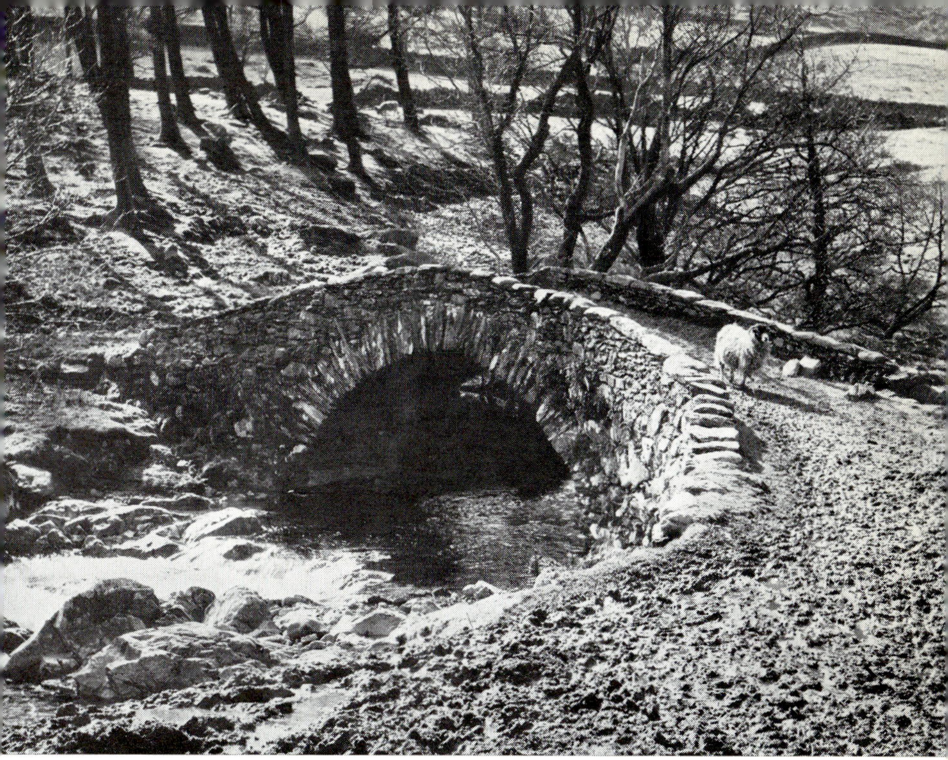

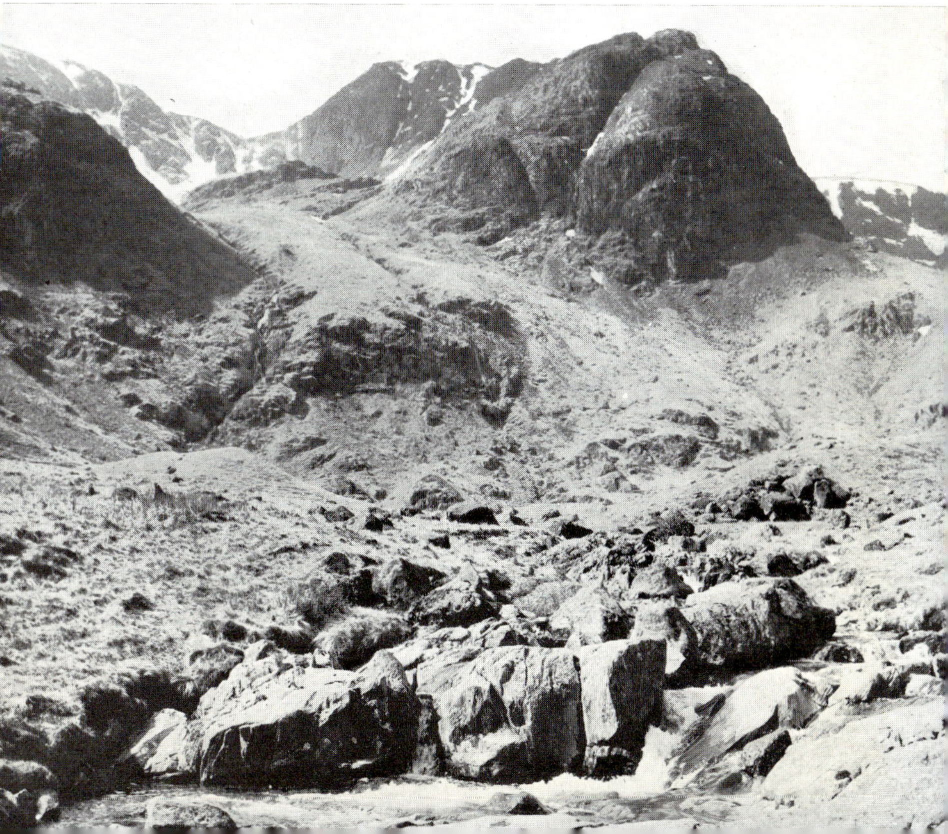

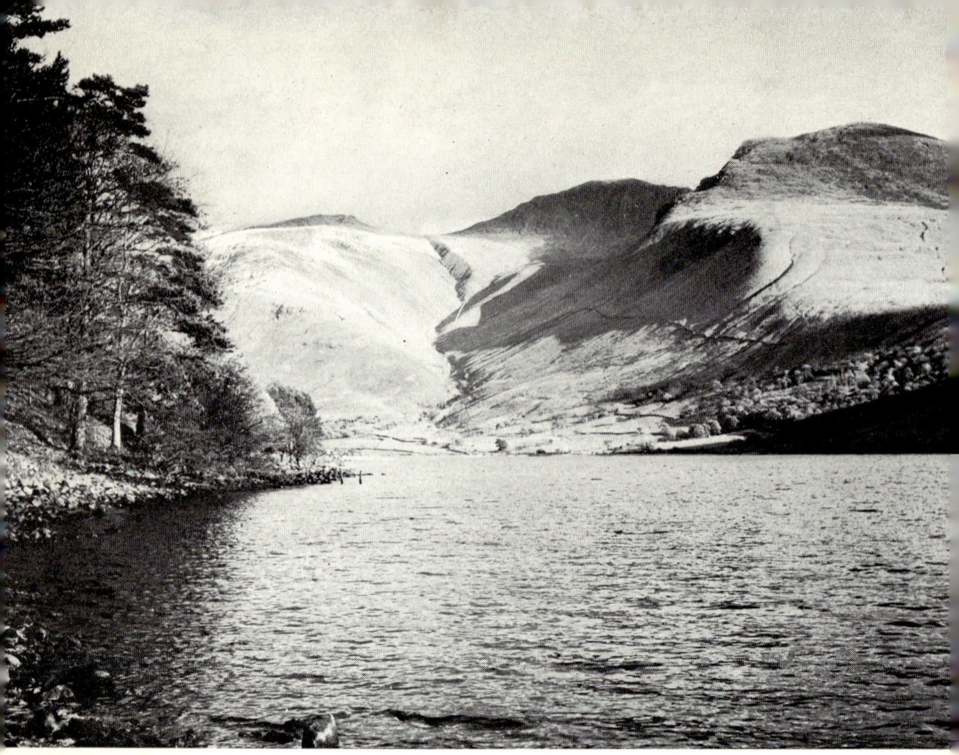

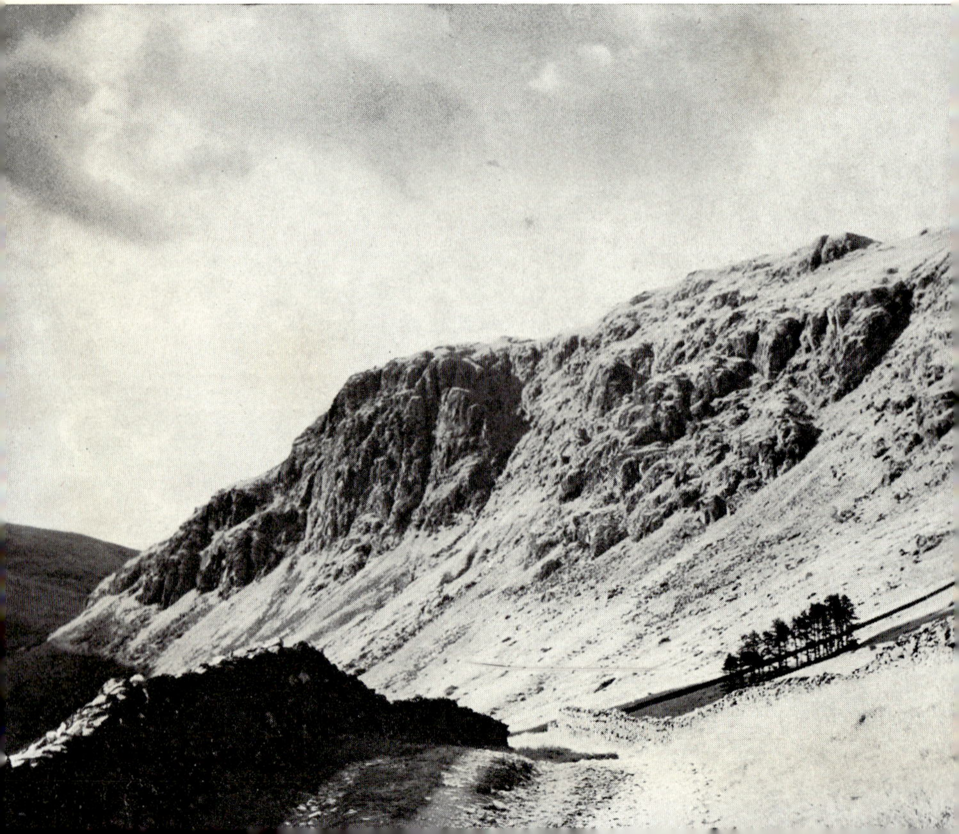

visitors haven't 'discovered' them yet, and for the time being these lonely places enjoy the quiet and seclusion that perhaps Langdale and Borrowdale once could claim. In the coming years I think this seclusion will tend to disappear as the popular haunts become more congested and the discerning visitor seeks quieter places, but I don't think they'll be ruined. There's not enough excitement in these out-of-the-way corners for the hordes, but there'll always be something for the connoisseur. Trusmadoor is unlikely to become as popular as Windy Gap on Gable; and the splendid Dash Falls near the great combe of Dead Crags just over the hill will never, fortunately, be another Aira Force.

The northern fells abound in these 'undiscovered' places, many of them well known to me, despite my ignorance of Trusmadoor, and there are many equally lonely and, in some cases, even more rewarding corners all over the Lake District, and especially around its perimeter. For example, everybody knows the main Coniston-to-Broughton road, but how many people have walked into the Coniston fells by way of the lovely Appletree Worth Beck? We used to go this way from Broughton Mills as youngsters, and it's still as quiet as it was in those days. The old road over Bootle Fell has now been discovered by motorists, but the winding byways and tracks over the Woodland fells, the home of ancient civilisations thousands of years ago, are still little used. This was charcoal-burning country, and even today the smell of woodsmoke takes me back to these parts where we often wandered as young-sters. A favourite bathing spot, I remember, was Beacon Tarn. Do many people, I wonder, bathe there today?

Thousands of people go over Styhead every year, compared with the handful or so who make their way up the far pleasanter route on the Wasdale side along the banks of the Lingmell Beck. There are thousands, too, who know Styhead Tarn and Sprinkling Tarn but have never been to Low Tarn, under Wasdale's Red Pike, Scoat Tarn under Steeple and the glorious little valleys of Nether Beck and Over Beck. Indeed, Seatallan, not far away, must be one of the least visited mountains in Lakeland. Many of these western fells are surprisingly neglected—the Starling Dodd range, overlooking Ennerdale, for instance, or the Loweswater fells, and even Whiteside and Wandope, within 2 or 3 miles of Buttermere village. And, farther west still, the hilly country

Scafell Pike and Scafell
Buckbarrow Crag, Longsleddale

around Ennerdale and Lamplugh—the nearest hills to industrial West Cumberland, a short bicycle ride away from the streets—is almost unknown to visitors. But it is magnificent moorland country within sight of the sea—the foothills to the roof of England.

In the southern Lake District there is some magnificent wooded country between Windermere and Coniston Water, not only the popular Hawkshead area but also around the Rusland valley, Satterthwaite, Oxen Park and Graythwaite—most of it outside the regular tourist zone. Farther east there is the still unspoiled Winster valley, one of the most pleasantly pastoral areas in Lakeland, the Lyth valley and all the lovely limestone country west of the Kent. Even in central Lakeland you often have the popular Mickleden valley in Langdale crowded with tourists while the neighbouring, even finer, valley of Oxendale may be deserted. Or Far Easdale packed with people and the valley of the Wyth Burn quite empty. And while hundreds are walking up Grisedale, there will be very few in Dovedale and Deepdale and even fewer up Pasture Beck or by Angletarn Pikes. Not many people get into upper Kentmere or Longsleddale or Woundale or even Scandale, the nearest valley to Ambleside, while the splendid valleys to the west of Haweswater—Riggindale, Rampsgill, Bannerdale and the valley of the Measand Beck—must be unknown territory to many visitors. Swindale is rarely visited, nor are most of the quiet valleys around the Shap road, including the eastern Wasdale and Borrowdale, and Bannisdale, only 6 miles from Kendal. Indeed, I've never seen anybody in Bannisdale, nor in Wet Sleddale, before they flooded it, and you can walk right over the rising moorland of Potter Fell on a summer bank holiday and not see a soul.

For all these reasons I take heart that Lakeland is very far from being finished—even in the height of summer—but you must know where to go. Of course, the really private places you keep to yourself, and I don't think I've given any of mine away. I make you a gift of Trusmadoor, since it was new to me, and I would suggest many really worthwhile corners to the east of the National Park, which are almost as splendid as many places inside it.

WORDSWORTH'S DUDDON

Wordsworth, they say, wrote thirty-four sonnets about the Duddon, believing it to be the loveliest river in Lakeland and therefore, perhaps, in England. Nowadays many people dismiss Wordsworth as old-fashioned and rather fuddyduddy, but his opinions on scenery should not be ignored. But, Wordsworth apart, anybody who knows Lakeland really well could hardly fail to place Dunnerdale among the half-dozen most beautiful and least-spoiled valleys, and some will put it among the three finest. The Duddon must have been one of the first Lakeland rivers where I went adventuring as a child. For as long as I can remember Dunnerdale has always meant shadowed pools on a hot summer's day, the spring glory of the birches and the daffodils, the autumn scent of woodsmoke at dusk in the tiny hamlets, a quiet churchyard, the chatter of the river among the rocks, a flat valley floor and the fells standing up high all round.

But mostly, I think, Dunnerdale means trees and water—the birches and the rowans with the grey rocks peeping through and the river never very far away. For the river means more to Dunnerdale than many of the becks mean to other Lakeland valleys. Dunnerdale has no lake, but for nearly 15 miles the Duddon enriches the valley with magic and laughter. All the way from its source near the Three Shire Stones it dances merrily down to the sea through some of the most intimate, varied and colourful scenery in England. And if you see the estuary sparkling in the morning sunlight from, say, the road over Gawthwaite Moor you will never sigh for bigger, more exciting rivers.

I think we went on our very first motor drives to the Duddon —sometimes to pick the daffodils, but more often to picnic somewhere near Seathwaite, where the rocks, pools and waterfalls provided a small boy with all the adventure he needed. No doubt other families went that way, but I can't remember seeing any, although nowadays every square 10 feet of space along the roadside into which a car may be manoeuvred has its picnic party any fine Sunday afternoon. And down on the coast at Silecroft, where once only the locals went to splash in the breakers, the motorists now go on sunny Sundays in their hundreds.

But Dunnerdale is still largely unspoiled, not being so easy of access as, say, Borrowdale or Langdale. Barrow draws its water from Seathwaite Tarn, but the casual visitor does not notice this, and although the Forestry Commission have been busy for years towards the head of the dale, they have by no means spoiled the valley and in places have even given it an added beauty. For this is the sort of twisted, knobbly valley that can take conifers far more graciously than a long, straight strath like Ennerdale.

Sixty years ago W. G. Collingwood wrote that the dale was much the same as when Wordsworth wrote his sonnets, and there has been little change this century. The road is better surfaced than it used to be, but, mercifully, it is still too narrow in its upper reaches for coaches and too twisting and humpbacked for speed. The old inn at Seathwaite is still without chromium plate and ornate cocktail bar, and, as like as not, you will take your drink in a stone-flagged parlour with notices about ram sales and wrestling competitions pinned to the walls and perhaps hunting trophies hanging from the old beams. Before you reach Cockley Beck you will have gates to open, although not so many as there used to be, and along the whole length of the valley I don't think you'll see an advertisement or a knick-knack shop or even a café. But you could get tea, no doubt, in one of the charming little cottages with roses growing over the porch and forget-me-nots in the borders.

For those who must be doing something on their holiday Dunnerdale is hardly the answer, and so the valley is spared the menace of mass tourism. Although a crag near the Wallowbarrow Gorge was 'discovered' a few years ago, there is little other rock-climbing to speak of, nothing for the sailors, rowers and water-skiers, no shops, no easy through-route for the over-cautious motorist, no public spectacles and nothing for the wet day. Nothing, in fact, but perfect scenery, a score of quiet walks through the woods and airy routes to the high fells, the low farmsteads nestling into the hills, a cluster of sleepy hamlets, the back of the Coniston fells on one side and the new woodlands of Harter Fell on the other. Bowfell and the Crinkles straight ahead and the Duddon leaping and splashing down from the mountains to the sea.

Weasels, they say, jump across the stepping stones, and wild goats used to graze around the gorge. Below Birks Bridge where the river is forced through a canyon between the rocks there is the uncanny shape of a human leg fashioned out of the rock by the force of the waters. Near Ulpha is Lady's Dub, where, long years ago, the lady of the manor is said to have disappeared into a chasm among the rocks while being pursued by a wolf. And on the surrounding heights above the valley there are old cairns and the remains of long-forgotten settlements, and, 2 miles west of Duddon Bridge, a circle of huge stones—mysterious and still unexplained.

The Duddon is the boundary between Cumberland and Lancashire, between the Skiddaw slate—the oldest of the rocks, which goes to make Black Combe—and the volcanic rock of which the Coniston fells and the central mountains were made. And the difference is quite distinctive—different mountain shapes, different vegetation, different scenery; Black Combe, bare, smooth and barren and, on the opposite side of the valley, the precipices of Dow Crag.

Dunnerdale produced its storybook character—Wonderful Walker, curate for over sixty years, and doctor, teacher and lawyer to the valley, all on £50 a year. He made home-brewed beer which he sold to his congregation on Sunday afternoons, and when he died left £2,000. You can read about Wonderful Walker in the guidebooks, for this is Seathwaite's only claim to fame— but this will not get you very far. Better to explore the valley on foot, following perhaps the course of the river from the sea to its source, which means deserting the road for much of its length.

First the road rises through rich woodlands, past the old bobbin mills at Ulpha and then on through a quiet pastoral section to the gorge and Wallowbarrow Crag. From here to Birks Bridge is perhaps the most perfect section of the dale, wild rock and woodland scenery, the red and green of the rowan berries and the birches, and the tumult of the beck. And then the level floor of the dale to the head of the valley, and the farmhouse of Cockley Beck where the river swings east to the top of the pass. You can see the whole length of the dale from the tops of the Coniston fells— a valley twisting between the rocks and the woods, with hardly a farmhouse and, from this distance, no traffic and no people. What a tragedy it will be if this lovely dale is ever 'opened up' into a through-route race-track with every facility laid on for the holidaymaker. When this happens the real Dunnerdale will be no more.

THE HUB OF LAKELAND

The twin, sharply scooped valleys of Easdale, dropping steeply eastwards in green shelves and craggy steps from the great central plateau of High Raise, always seem to have about them a strange air of exclusiveness. It is not so much the fact that some of the most delightfully situated houses in Lakeland are grouped about the entrance to the sanctuary but more the inescapable feeling that about half a mile beyond the bustle of Grasmere you enter a rather special place. Perhaps the notices have something to do with it, for few parts of the Lake District—save for reservoirs and forestry plantations—are so plastered with restrictions. You can't, for instance, park your car in the lane approaching the 'shrine', and for a mile or two you are strictly adjured to keep to paths, close gates and keep out of private property. I am not suggesting this is wrong, but merely that it is slightly irritating, however necessary it may be from the landowners' point of view. And it adds to the feeling which persists until you are well into the dale that this heavenly place is some sort of private parkland reserved for the connoisseur of natural beauty.

For Easdale, splendidly girt with fells and crags, cloaked with scattered woodland and threaded by leaping becks and waterfalls, is indeed a heavenly place, and the twin valleys provide the ideal walk on a winter afternoon. At most times of the year you can find quietude in the deep-cut dales, right in the centre of Lakeland, for although the area is popular enough, the valleys are so winding and secluded that crowds are soon lost or not noticed. I have always found something of an unchanging, almost primeval atmosphere about these lonely dales which you can see, probing westwards towards the setting sun, from the main highway through Lakeland. For, once past the intake fields, you can see how the ice has sculptured the corries and damned up the tarns. And 2 miles out from Grasmere you are looking at a tumbled landscape unchanged by time.

You wander up a quiet Grasmere lane, stroll past the lovely houses perched under the steeps of Helm Crag and, in a little over an hour, you can be standing on top of the very hub of the Lake District. High Raise is not an exciting summit in itself, but it is the centre of the National Park, and if I did not dislike indicators on mountain-tops I would say that here perhaps is one summit where such a thing would be almost appropriate. Draw a circle of perhaps 15 miles radius centred on High Raise and you enclose all the mountains in the Lake District that matter, and if you stand by the cairn you can see nearly all of them, crowded distantly all round the horizon. Here, surely, is the perfect upland promenade, as flat as a Derbyshire moorland, but encircled on all sides by unseen depths.

It was still and close one afternoon just before Christmas by the waterfall in Far Easdale Gill under the crags of Deer Bield, but on the top of High Raise the wind was bitter and the frozen turf and clumps of stag-horn moss covered in a white mantle of frost. High White Stones we used to call the mountain when I was a lad, but this is really the name of part of the summit plateau distinguished by its grey rocks. This day, however, the whole plateau was white with frost, all the pools frozen and each blade of grass a miracle of tinkling, feathered beauty.

The only person I saw all day, once beyond the last field gate, was encountered on the summit, he approaching from one direction and myself from the other. This was not particularly strange, but the fact that he was an old friend whom I hadn't seen for a year or two was perhaps interesting. Add to this the odd coincidence that he has the misfortune to be my 'double' and that we are both frequently taken for each other, and you must agree that the encounter was at least unusual. Indeed, the chances of his weekend expedition from London and mine from near Kendal culminating—from different approaches—at exactly the same point in the same moment are probably astronomical. Anyway, we both remarked upon it and later continued our separate ways, pondering meantime the often strange dispensations of providence.

I came down from the craggy top of Sergeant Man and down along Green Gangway, through the outcrops to find Codale Tarn lying dark and forbidding in the shadow of the mountain. Here is the perfect upland tarn, the scene of many a bathe on summer days. But it looked less friendly this time. You can see in this lonely corrie how aeons ago the ice must have piled up its scourings and blocked the outlet from the combe to form this perfect pool, which they say is good for both trout and perch.

Farther down the fellside slumbered Easdale Tarn itself, a smooth black mirror encircled by holly trees in a silence so complete you could have heard the insects talking. Years ago I had many a rough meal in the ruined hut near the edge of the tarn. I believe it was built last century as a shelter for ponies and their riders visiting the tarn, this being a favourite expedition of those days. Soon after the last war it became, for a short time, a mineral-water stand, run by an entertaining Irishman, but many years before that it was a place for afternoon teas, and I seem to remember a boat being kept on the tarn. But those days are long since past.

I hurried down the fellside this December day, through the black bogs below the waterfall—the route to Stythwaite Steps in Far Easdale is a far pleasanter walk—as dusk descended over the dale. The Christmas holly pickers had all gone home, the jackdaws had gone to sleep in the rocks by Kitty Crag and the first lights were yellowing the darkness 1,000 feet below 'The Lion and the Lamb'. There was a feeling of snow in the night air, and sure enough it came.

AN EXCITING VALLEY

When the queues are strung out along the approach to Striding Edge and the cars thickly clustered by Grisedale Beck you will find nobody—except perhaps a climber or two on Hutaple Crag —in the twin valleys of Deepdale and a great peace and quietude along its 3 miles of loneliness. For although Deepdale attracted its first handful of climbers more than twenty years ago, it has still not been 'discovered' by the multitudes and remains almost completely untouched by the hand of man. Its entrance lies athwart one of Lakeland's main highways, but the valley must look almost exactly the same as it did 1,000 years ago.

Few Lakeland guidebooks mention the valley. Deepdale is clearly indicated on the one-inch Ordnance Survey map—the second main valley on the left after the descent of Kirkstone Pass into Patterdale—but no signpost points up the dale, and most motorists hurrying to and from Ullswater probably hardly even give the valley a glance. From the old stone bridge at the entrance to the dale a rough road leads past an occasional cottage and farm for a few hundred yards up the valley, and then peters out. Thereafter the map shows not even the tiniest track, but there is one at least as far as the glacial moraines half-way up the dale, and within the last few years a few scratchings up to the crags have been added. But nothing more, apart from the sheep trods, which, like all sheep trods, lead nowhere.

Deepdale is a place to be enjoyed by the connoisseur of wild, unspoiled scenery. It holds no lake or tarn and cannot even boast a waterfall of note, but when much of the rest of Lakeland is overrun by tourist traffic, littered with sandwich wrappings, choked with petrol fumes and noisy with transistorised dance music, Deepdale is clean, lonely and quiet. Towards the head of the valley is a cliff called Ern Nest Crag—the crag of the young eagle—and it is likely that this was one of the last Lakeland valleys where the eagle nested before he was driven out of the district by human beings and hunger. Today the raven nests in the crags and buzzards frequently come into the dale. I once sat in the grass near the moraines left by the ice, and throughout much of a lazy summer afternoon watched four buzzards slowly soaring high above the valley. They gained height like eagles in great leisurely sweeps, and I watched them until the tiny specks merged into the glare and my neck was getting painful. So, for a change, I studied the antics of the young lambs gambolling down the beck, while the ewes quartered the greensward for succulent herbs. There were trout in the shingly beck, I remember, and the turf was flecked with tiny flowers, and there was no sound at all except for an occasional distant slither of scree and the trickling of the beck over the stones.

Once you have left the entrance to the dale there are few trees in Deepdale and the meadows are soon behind you. It is a deeply cut dale, as its name implies, and as you stroll farther towards its head you have the impression you are penetrating into a sanctuary. Gradually, the mountain walls on either side steepen, the valley narrows and then, after about 2 miles, the floor of the dale itself

E

begins to climb until you emerge, with some little effort, into the upper reaches of the valley, right underneath the crags. And this is where you will discover the real glory of Deepdale—twin hanging valleys, buttressed by some of the boldest rock walls in Lakeland, untracked and probably deserted, and dramatically rimmed by the southern outliers of the Helvellyn range. On the right sort of day, with the cloud shadows racing over Deepdale Hause, St. Sunday Crag in sunlight and the northern crags of Fairfield looking dark and grim, but etched here and there by lines of flaming gold, there is no finer scene of wild mountain beauty in the district.

This is the best side of Fairfield. To the south and west he presents merely bulk, height and gently curving grass slopes, but to the north and east—the Deepdale side—the mountain is all crag and scree, great gullies and towering pinnacles, a sheer rock wall dropping down into remote hanging valleys. You can peep down into upper Deepdale from the summit of Fairfield or, better still, from Cofa Pike, and if you have come up the long, easy ridge from Ambleside the scene is a complete transformation. Nothing but the gentlest of grassy slopes one moment, and the next, yawning precipices just below your feet. And sometimes the evening view of these Deepdale crags from the Helvellyn range is really impressive, particularly when the gullies are packed with snow and the late sun is catching the crags.

The two coves or hanging valleys of Deepdale—upper storeys above the level valley floor—are Link Cove beneath Hart Crag and Sleet Cove underneath the summit of Fairfield. They are separated by a spur sometimes known as The Step, which strides out some distance across the valley and terminates in the crags of Greenhow End. Grouped around these coves are the crags, the biggest being Hutaple Crag in Sleet Cove and Scrubby Crag just below the Hart Crag–Fairfield summit ridge in Link Cove. You can identify Scrubby by its vertical cracks and chimneys, and Hutaple by Curving Gully, a 500-foot scimitar-shaped slash down the western side of the cliff. All these cracks, chimneys and gullies and many of the steep rock faces in between have been climbed, mostly during the past fifteen years, but although there are now dozens of climbing routes here, the area has not really achieved popularity. For the cliffs are still vegetatious and the rocks greasy and unpleasant in bad weather. Most of the climbs are in either the severe or very severe class, and the crags, especially Hutaple, have something of a mountaineering flavour about them and often a considerable feeling of exposure. The rock is also inclined to be treacherous in places. I happened to be involved in some of the climbing exploration in this area and remember very vividly an occasion when a huge block of rock, weighing perhaps a ton, swayed outwards when I reached up for a hold. It was rather a tense moment hanging on and holding the baby, so to speak, until my companions were able to come up and relieve the situation, and the hunk of rock could be safely dropped down to the screes. This was on an early ascent of Migraine—it certainly gave me a headache—and it is now a little harder than when first climbed.

It seems remarkable that we used to walk along the Fairfield ridge and round this valley head before the war and never realised there was such magnificent climbing on these crags. We spotted the crags, certainly, and knew the curving gully well by sight, but assumed that if there was any climbing there it must have been discovered long before. (We used to think the same thing about Eel Crags in Newlands until somebody did something about it.) In Deepdale it was Alf Gregory, later of Everest, who decided that the crags might be worth looking at. He had been exploring a new crag in Dovedale and then, in 1948, moved over the ridge into Deepdale and found he had discovered a new climbing ground. In the main he contented himself with climbing the more obvious routes and left the development of the area to two Preston climbers, J. C. Duckworth and G. Batty, and others, who went straight on to the major crags of Hutaple and Scrubby, without knowing of any previous exploration. Some extremely hard routes have since been put up on these steep, exposed crags by very able young climbers, but it is still unusual to find them populated, even in summertime.

Above and between the crags are scree shoots and gullies— Black Tippet and Flinty Graves are two of the names—and it was down one of these places and over the edge of a cliff that two girls fell to their deaths, probably during a snowstorm, several years ago. And for a long time their bodies lay undiscovered in the snow. But I would not say this dale-head has an atmosphere of tragedy, although the climbs do not always seem quite the light-hearted adventures you may enjoy elsewhere. Up on these wild precipices where there is hardly a scratch to indicate that people have been there before, one feels a little remote, and in bad weather it is easy to wish you were safe in the combe instead of stuck high up on greasy holds. I think it was on one of these steep climbs that I knocked in my first piton as a belay at a time when if you carried pitons at all—which very few did—you hid them away and kept quiet about it.

Down in the combe there is a sheepfold, and here you can while away a long summer's afternoon by the side of the beck, watching the birds, studying the flowers or the insects, or just watching the walkers working round the ridge of Fairfield, Cofa Pike, Deepdale Hause and St. Sunday Crag. I must have been there a score of times during the past few years, but only once can I remember meeting another party, although there may have been a few more climbers recently. On our last visit, instead of frightening ourselves on the crags, we spent part of the day lying in the sunshine by the waterfalls in Deepdale Beck. Almost the only trees in Deepdale, once you have passed the meadows, are the rowans near the beck, and this day the red berries were hanging in great clusters over the water. You could hardly imagine a lovelier place. Below us the beck meandered in gentle curves round the moraines, and above and around us splashed into delightful rock pools, the spray glinting in the sunlight. Between the rowans dripping ferns hung over the beck, and here and there great cushions of purple heather clung precariously to the rock walls. Far above soared the great crags, and a wisp of white cloud was caught on the summit of Cofa Pike. The only sound was the tumult of the falls and the only living things the sheep on the distant fellside.

Later from the top of the mountain wall we looked down into the sanctuary and watched the evening sunlight catching the edge of the crags so that they seemed to be rimmed with gold. The shadows were creeping across the combe when we trotted down the fellside towards Patterdale, and in a short time we were weaving through the traffic over Kirkstone.

Perhaps Deepdale will always be neglected because, for many people, there's just nothing there—nothing except some of the best climbing and walking in the National Park, solitude and quietude, waterfalls, birds and flowers, superb views and the feeling, once you are really inside the sanctuary, that you have found a very special place. Deepdale was just like this before anybody discovered the Lake District, and I believe that, no matter what lies ahead for the National Park, it will be much the same in ten or twenty years time.

THE DALE THEY SAVED

Although its entrance lies only about 4 miles from Kendal and no more than a stone's throw from the main A6 highway, the lonely valley of Longsleddale remains much as it was fifty years ago or, for all I know, 100 years ago or more. While the people of, say, Little Langdale have to endure the summer turmoil of constant traffic, Longsleddale folk can get on with their farming undisturbed, just as their fathers and grandfathers did before them. The reason, of course, is that there is no through road, while what tarmacadam there is remains mercifully narrow. Some years ago there was a proposal to link the valley with the neighbouring dale of Kentmere by a road of sorts over the shoulder of Green Quarter Fell, but, fortunately—and before the hullaballoo began—the project fell through. Had the road been built, the weekend motorist would have been presented with a brand-new circular tour, and two valleys would have been ruined—or changed for ever, depending upon how you view these things.

But between the wars the peace of Longsleddale was shattered for a time by industrial traffic, earth-moving machinery and pick-and-shovel gangs. This was when they brought the Haweswater tunnel through the fells and into the valley at Stockdale, and this is the way Manchester's water goes—underneath Gatescarth Pass and the Mosedale track, out near the whetstone 'mine', where they used to dig out slabs of gritstone for sharpening the harvest scythes, and down the valley to Garnett Bridge. A few years ago there was the fear that the bulldozers would return to Longsleddale and that a second tunnel would be built to take the extra water Manchester wanted to pump from Ullswater into Haweswater. But the Minister, while allowing Manchester to take water from

Ullswater, threw out the Longsleddale tunnel, and the valley could breathe again.

Longsleddale is one of the 'natural' valleys of Lakeland, unexploited—except for the hidden tunnel and the old quarries—unspoiled and even unpreserved. Its beauty is comparable with that of some of the more famous dales, but few people except perhaps discriminating Westmorland folk go there. The valley has no inn, no shop, no policeman, no bus shelter, no car park, no advertisement signs and no ice-cream stand—just a long narrow valley with several well-cultivated farms and a dale head as striking as those in the western dales. The track winds up to the pass between the crags of Goat Scar and Buckbarrow, with the hidden waterfalls and pools of the Sprint in between. After you pass the fine packhorse bridge at Sadgill you are in a wild countryside equally reminiscent of a Scottish glen or a corner of Afghanistan. Mountain birds live in the crags and foxes go to earth there, while more than once I have surprised a red deer working his way south from Riggindale. The pass is disappointing when it falls away into Mosedale, but before then it has all the quality of, say, upper Eskdale or the Coniston fells.

Few of the guidebooks mention Longsleddale, although the valley is said to be the Long Whindale of Mrs. Humphrey Ward's novel *Robert Elsmore*. Garnett Bridge, at the entrance to the dale, was once a busy little mill village—woollen mills, a corn mill and a bobbin mill—and the coppice fellers also used to sort out their bark there. At one time the old cobbler was a famous tanner of cow hides as well as a well-known fisherman and shot. It is still a picturesque hamlet, and still completely unspoiled, although the main road is only a quarter of a mile away. There used to be a youth hostel in the valley, and at one time the Fishwicks at Sadgill catered for the walkers coming over the fells, serving tremendous meals, but those days are now over, although I've no doubt accommodation can still be found in the dale, if required. A bishop once had his country retreat in the valley, but there has been no rash of building in recent years, and I read somewhere that not one house was built in Longsleddale in fifty years. The quarries at the head of the dale are no longer worked, and I once spent the night in the old quarry sheds. More than once I've gone on ski from Sadgill to the head of Gatescarth and on to the top

THATTO HEATH
BRANCH LIBRARY

of Harter Fell and then skied all the way back—a fine expedition. We've also enjoyed many excellent climbing days on the steep front of Buckbarrow and once or twice put up new routes, but the crag has never become really popular, which is not a bad thing.

The wild head of the dale is excellent fox-hunting country, and there are several borrans known to the hunters in the rocks below Goat Scar and Buckbarrow. Once when I was up there I ran into a fox shoot, with the farmers spread out at intervals right up to Harter Fell.

A few years ago some friends asked me to suggest a part of Lakeland they could visit on August Monday and yet avoid the crowds, and I sent them into Longsleddale. They left their car at Sadgill and went for a bathe in the pool below the waterfalls near the head of the dale, afterwards walking round Buckbarrow to the top of Tarn Crag and down to the valley again. And from leaving their car to their return they saw nobody all day. These are the sort of places we must cherish in Lakeland, for there are not so many of them today as there used to be. Last century M. J. B. Baddeley, writing of Longsleddale, observed: 'Farmsteads dot the valley throughout. The church occupies a prominent position half-way up it, and altogether, it is difficult to picture a scene in which peace, contentment and beauty are more happily combined.' Fortunately, this is still the case today, and many lovers of the real Lakeland hope that it will always be so.

ABOVE THE FLOOD

There's much to be said for visiting the lonely Mardale fells nowadays, for fairly soon the area may be indistinguishable from the rest of Lakeland, with traffic and parking problems along the narrow, twisting road and perhaps even queues for teas in the rather austere-looking hotel that replaces the drowned Dun Bull.

For the past thirty years—since Haweswater was doubled in size and converted into the biggest reservoir in England to cope with Manchester's water needs—Mardale has been a forgotten valley. People don't come to see a dead lake and a lifeless dale—especially on the less popular eastern fringe of Lakeland. But the completion of the motorway through Westmorland and the promise of increased public access to the lake when Manchester's water-treatment plant near Kendal is finished will change all this.

With the opening of the motorway tens of thousands of people who had never been near the Lake District before discovered they were only half a dozen miles away from one of the lakes—and the rush began. And when the restrictions on access are lifted Mardale and Haweswater will jump back into the guidebooks and the travel brochures again. For Haweswater and Ullswater are the nearest lakes to any motorway, with the former particularly accessible from near the new Shap interchange. Soon, therefore, we can expect greatly increased car-parking facilities in Mardale, probably camping and caravan sites, rowing, bathing and fishing in the reservoir, picnicking, perhaps new catering and accommodation and even new footpaths. It will be Mardale's second metamorphosis in forty years—first the flood and the end of 1,000 years of husbandry and pastoral pursuits, and then the tourist invasion from London and the Midlands. I wonder whether they will be resurrecting another King of Mardale? The last male in the direct line after a dynasty lasting for nearly 700 years died before the flood, but man's ingenuity in these days of gimmickry knows no end.

For those who treasure the loneliness of the hills and the quietude of an ancient dale, Mardale, therefore, has much to offer before the 'invasion'. The valley is still a lovely place—if you stand with your back to the dam—and especially around the mountain-encircled head of the dale. The heights of Harter Fell, High Street and Kidsty Pike look down on quiet waters; red deer and fell ponies roam the lonely green trough of Riggindale; the hedges and the woods along the lake shore are filled with birdsong; and the old dales road is as silent as the country lanes of our youth.

Preferably, you should go there when the reservoir is full, although there can be compensations, if the water is low, in the revelations of strange sights at the southern end of the lake. The long, dry summer of 1969 and the increasing demands for Lakeland water from distant places had drawn down the lake level to show a wide, ugly, white verge around the shore, but bits of old Mardale also appeared. One day, for instance, you could see the old walls, roads and field fences peeping above the mud, and even the remains of some of the farmsteads. Sheep were trying to graze on sodden mosses normally below lake level, where their forbears cropped the sweet grass before the last war; and two new islands had popped up since my previous visit. And from Rough Crag you could almost, in imagination, look down again on Mardale Green and cast your mind back to days when Haweswater was just another lake with people living around it.

According to Jonathan Otley, writing in 1830: 'The farm houses are sheltered by trees, the houses mostly walled without mortar, and the lake is well stocked with fish of various kinds, but chiefly reserved for the table of Lowther Castle . . . it is a sweet, retired spot.' But today Lord Lonsdale has to get his fish from somewhere else, and all the houses are gone. Another description of Mardale, written only about fifty years ago, read: 'One of the loveliest spots in Lakeland with one of the most beautiful of all the lakes. Not so wild as Wastwater, nor quite so beautiful as Derwentwater, but partaking of the delights of both. There is an air of peace and repose which is very attractive, and it is free from the hordes of tourists that are such a drawback to Derwentwater.'

But Mardale is still a very beautiful valley, for you cannot ruin a dale by doubling the size of its lake. Changed, it undoubtedly is, and the old atmosphere of a homely dale has gone, for the church and the inn and the farms have long since disappeared. But if you forget the notices and look across the lake when it is full you will see a valley of great character and charm, with scattered woodlands, fine becks and waterfalls, and an encircling ring of craggy mountains—their best sides—with some of the most perfect tarns in Lakeland nestling below the tops. There are no car-parks, except the one at the end of the road, no caravan or camping sites, no shops, filling stations or advertisements, and no traffic. Even the hotel that Manchester built by Guerness Wood to replace the old 'Dun Bull' has mellowed during the past thirty years. And the red deer still wander up Riggindale on to the heights, and Harter Fell, High Street, Kidsty Pike and the lovely Measand Beck are just the same as when I was a boy.

At one time Mardale was a busy, thriving valley with many farms, lead mines in Benty Hollows and Guerness Wood, and a considerable trade with the villages between Kendal and Penrith carried by pack-horses over Gatescarth Pass. An account of life in the dale more than 150 years ago refers to the large chimneys inside the houses, where joints of meat were suspended to dry for winter use and the householders used to gather for comfort. Under the smokey dome sat the women knitting or spinning wool or flax, the men carding the wool, the schoolboy doing his Latin, and the ancients telling tales of border strife or old legends of the dale. The men wore clothes of native fleece, home-spun and woven by the village weaver, while the women's garments were made from finer native wool, dyed to the weaver's fancy and made by an artisan at the owner's fireside.

The farm furniture would include a long oak table, with a bench on each side, at which the whole family, including servants, ate together. Chairs of heavy wainscot work with high arms were in use as well as three-footed stools. As light for the winter evenings candles were made of peeled rushes and dipped in the hot fat of fried bacon. The usual food consisted of leavened bread, made of a kind of black oats, boiled animal food, the produce of the dairy and a limited supply of vegetables.

The old oaken cupboards, carved with the owner's name and various scrolls and devices that used to stand opposite the open fire on the hearths, were still in use at the old 'Dun Bull' before it was swept away in the rising waters. Seventy years ago there were still eight farms in the dale. Many things disappeared with the flood, one of them the shepherds' meet that had been held at the 'Dun Bull' for nearly 100 years. Before that the meet was held on the top of High Street, with horse-racing and the usual sports of those days, which necessitated the carrying of barrels of beer to above the 2,500-feet contour. In Joe Bowman's day the meet at the 'Dun Bull' went on for two or three days, visitors sleeping out in the barns after the day's hunting and the long nights of revelry. Today, of course, all this is forgotten, although there's still a meet at Bampton near the foot of the dale.

But you escape from depression at Mardale by taking to the heights, and this is the real joy of this neglected area in crowded days. Nearly every time I go into this part of Lakeland I stumble on sights not often seen in more popular places. You often see herds of red deer in Riggindale, for instance, and once I surprised a little group of them on a rocky ridge of High Street. One moment they stood frozen into immobility on the summit like statues and as surprised as I was myself; the next, they were half-way down the rocks into the corrie.

And one day, mounting straight out of Riggindale on to the craggy top of Kidsty Pike, I disturbed three fine fell ponies, standing on the very summit—a magnificent picture if I'd had my camera ready. These heights, with their springy turf and long, smooth ridges, make easy walking country, and you can rattle off seven or eight tops in a day without much effort.

One afternoon, with sun slanting down the Nan Bield, the crags of Harter Fell in black shadow and the tarn twinkling as if it was high summer, you could almost forget the ugly shoreline of the lake and the dead hand over the valley. There were twenty-four cars in the car-park—the most I could ever remember—and it was full, but the occupants had scattered over many square miles of countryside, and the hills were silent.

They say that 150 years ago the redoubtable Mrs. Dean with her touring theatrical company came over the Nan Bield to play at Mardale and Bampton. Down the rocky track came the ponies laden with actors and actresses, boxes and baggage, grease-paint and props. Kendal had been hit by cholera, but the show must go on, and Mardale seemed the best place. And perhaps Mardale, the loneliest dale, may come to life again some day.

SUMMER ON GABLE

Autumn had been slowly creeping up to the fells, and the last day of the best summer for years would soon be only a memory. Perhaps it came one day when I was wandering alone over Gable and the Borrowdale fells—a day of sultry heat and hazy blue distances, of lazy farm dogs sleeping in the shade, and smoke from the cottage chimneys spiralling slowly above the birches. Down by Stockley Bridge a proud father photographed his children splashing in the Derwent, and higher up the fellside a paraffin stove, tended by two youngsters, was roaring away merrily on a shelf of rock by the beck—so still was the morning. Only one tent by the quiet waters of Styhead Tarn, nobody by the stretcher box, but two or three specks of red and blue above Piers Gill on their way to the Pike. Far below, the great bowl of Wasdale slept in the haze and, in the distance, the length of Wastwater shimmered in the sunlight and the plains merged into the sea. Perhaps half a dozen people were on the well-scratched trail to Gable top, and the sight which, on a day of worsening weather, could have been alarming, became, on this lovely day, slightly comic. All were in low shoes and making poor progress in fits and starts on the sliding scree while one stout, middle-aged matron, in bright red mackintosh, had abandoned the ascent half-way and was being helped down—vowing loudly never to return—on the end of a belt. But the summit was deserted, and there was nobody to share with me the sight of the dark green carpet curving down Ennerdale, and the ridges of the Buttermere fells melting into the skies. And later, in the sun-kissed saucer of Gillercombe, on a couch of saxifrage beside the dancing beck, only the ravens and the sad-faced Herdwicks for company.

5

Days in the Hills

SOME JANUARY DAYS

The visitors come to Lakeland in the crowded and often wet months of July and August, but some of the best days can be in January, when we generally have the fells more or less to ourselves. Glancing through my diary, I am reminded of three of those January days—just short, simple days in the hills, but particularly rewarding at the time because the rest of the country seemed to be enduring the usual dreary winter of rain, fog or slush. One of these days, I recall, was a lovely mixture of rising morning mists and afternoon sunshine, with hardly a breath of wind, superb skyscapes and between the gold-flushed clouds, wonderful distant views. A slightly colder nip in the air and some snow on the hills would have brought complete perfection. Everywhere seemed strangely quiet and peaceful, and the only noises the little friendly ones like the distant barking of dogs or the murmur of a waterfall in the next valley, and once, on the top of Helm Crag, the sad cry of the curlew. The fell country seemed deep in its winter sleep.

A coachload of heavy-booted walkers was tumbled out into the morning sunshine in the middle of Grasmere, and I watched them crowd the lane into Easdale and set off, with well-laden rucksacks, towards Greenup Edge. They had come from a distant town for fresh air and exercise and must have been delighted at their good fortune at striking such a wonderful day. They knew where they were going and did not need to consult maps. I never saw them again, and throughout a fairly long walk over the tops the only other people I saw all day were one man near the top of Helm Crag and two people sitting by the cairn on Sergeant Man. Yet these were the central hills of Lakeland on one of the most wonderful days for months.

Helm Crag—'The Lion and the Lamb'—may be the best-known little hill in Lakeland but there were only two of us enjoying the magnificent view from the summit that Sunday morning. The mists were still hanging in the meadows, but above them the hill soared steeply towards blue skies. A cotton-wool haze lay over the waters of Windermere and the woodlands spiked through the greyness, but the fellsides sparkled in the sunlight, and here and there a tarn or a mountain pool flashed silvery as a mirror. Perched on the head of 'The Lion', I could see and hear the cars going over Dunmail Raise, 500 feet below—little toy cars in blue, yellow or grey, they seemed—and the pleasant sounds of pails rattling in a dairy or farm dogs at play came winging up the fellside on this stillest of winter mornings.

On the way up the fell I had disturbed the jackdaws in the little crag where the holly trees grow, and for half an hour I listened to a curlew mournfully circling the summit, with his liquid call, without spotting him. For some time I prowled about among the magnificent chaos of tumbled rocks that litters the curious trough just below the summit, for I believe that somewhere in these shattered remains of what must once have been a fine precipice is a huge inner cave worthy of exploration. I know of several caves in these rocks where a party could spend a comfortable night, but have never found the biggest one of all, where, I believe, you could hide, if not an army, at least a company. But I had no torch and my dog kept disappearing into awkward places and constantly needing rescue, so I left it for another day.

The familiar walk over Gibson Knott and Calf Crag, with high fells all around and the glories of Easdale on your left, must be one of the pleasantest little walks for a Lakeland half-day, but soon we were down at the stile on the track that leads over the Edge and down into Borrowdale—a lonely stile which for many years has been all that remains of the county boundary fence. We went up to High Raise by way of Mere Beck and Deep Slack, passing on our left the fine little tarn that, like many others in this area, has no name. During the day I passed three or four nameless pools besides the trio of Easdale, Codale and Stickle tarns. As we approached the 2,500-feet contour the soft ground gradually hardened, until on the top we were treading on ice and frost, and it was time to put something a little warmer over my shirt sleeves. High Raise—the summit itself is known as High White Stones— is sometimes described as marking the very centre of the mountains of Lakeland. In shape it is a dull mountain, but what a splendid viewpoint.

Perhaps the best approach for catching the sudden emergence of the view was ours that Sunday—a long slog over featureless ground, rather than the approach from, say, Greenup Edge or the Langdale Pikes, One moment you are toiling across some of the least rewarding slopes in the district, the next the ground drops below your feet and you are looking out across the best of Lakeland. Almost all the hills of Lakeland, at all points of the compass, may be seen from High Raise, but perhaps the view to the west, across the depths of the Langstrath valley, is the best. That day the whole line of the highest land in England from the Scafells to Skiddaw seemed strung across the horizon, sharp against the westering sun, and topped here and there by banks of white cloud. The sunlight and shadows and the golden flush across the clouds gave the scene its splendour—that and the swoop of the valley down from our feet so that we could see much of the high land from its very base. Especially dramatic in the view was the steep bulk of Gable as seen 'sideways on'—a huge wedge high in the sky, matched a little farther to the north by the black precipice of Honister Crag with Pillar in between. I could see a corner of Derwentwater, a strip of Bassenthwaite and the little pool on Rosthwaite Fell we know as Tarn at Leaves, but the Solway Firth and the Irish Sea were hidden by banks of cloud. And turning round, there were the Coniston Fells and Bowfell, the long line of the Helvellyn range and the Dodds, and, away in the distance, towards the east and the south, the Northern Pennines and the hills of the West Riding.

Survey columns on the tops of our mountains are not particularly beautiful objects, but the one on High Raise seemed to fit well enough into the view that day. The browns, oranges and greys of the stone contrasted well with the frosted ground at its base and the soaring backcloth of the fells, and I was disappointed

I had no colour film with me to record the view with the sunlit column, perhaps, in the foreground.

From High Raise it was a short journey across the plateau to the prominent cairn of Sergeant Man and a sudden change of view, with the precipice of Pavey Ark and the crags of Harrison Stickle rising dark and sinister against the background of the Coniston Fells. Soon we turned back for Grasmere along the Blea Rigg ridge, picking our way round little hillocks and past tiny tarns until we could drop down by way of Blindtarn Gill into Easdale. Whenever I go this way I think of the tragedy of many years ago when a man and his wife perished in a snowstorm on these fells, leaving behind their six young children in the cottage at the foot of the beck. The place has always had a tragic atmosphere, and the quagmire of Blindtarn Moss and the rough fellside above has often seemed to me a difficult place for inexperienced people, perhaps overcome by darkness or exhaustion. I think the well-known tragedy happened in Wordsworth's time, and the heroine was the eldest child, a girl of 11 years. She looked after her younger brothers and sisters for two days before setting off to Langdale to raise the alarm, and during this time kept up the spirits of the youngsters and did all the work, including feeding the baby, milking the cow, winding up the clock and keeping the fire in. Later the orphans were taken into the homes of several Grasmere families and cared for, largely due to the efforts of Dorothy Wordsworth.

The first lights were appearing in Grasmere as I crossed the beck and walked up through the woods and back to the car. It had been another very simple day in the hills, over very familiar ground, but I had seen magnificent unspoiled scenery that would help me to survive 'dark days of urban depression', as Sedgewick once put it. During the whole day, there and back from Grasmere, the only evidence of the hand of man I had seen were the ruined fence on the county boundary, the survey column on High Raise and an occasional cairn.

The other two days—a wonderful January weekend, in fact— were good examples of the frequent inaccuracy of the B.B.C. weather forecasts—so far as the Lakeland hills are concerned. The Saturday forecast was the better of the two, with bright periods probable but also fog, while on the Sunday we were to

Crummock Water, with Solway beyond

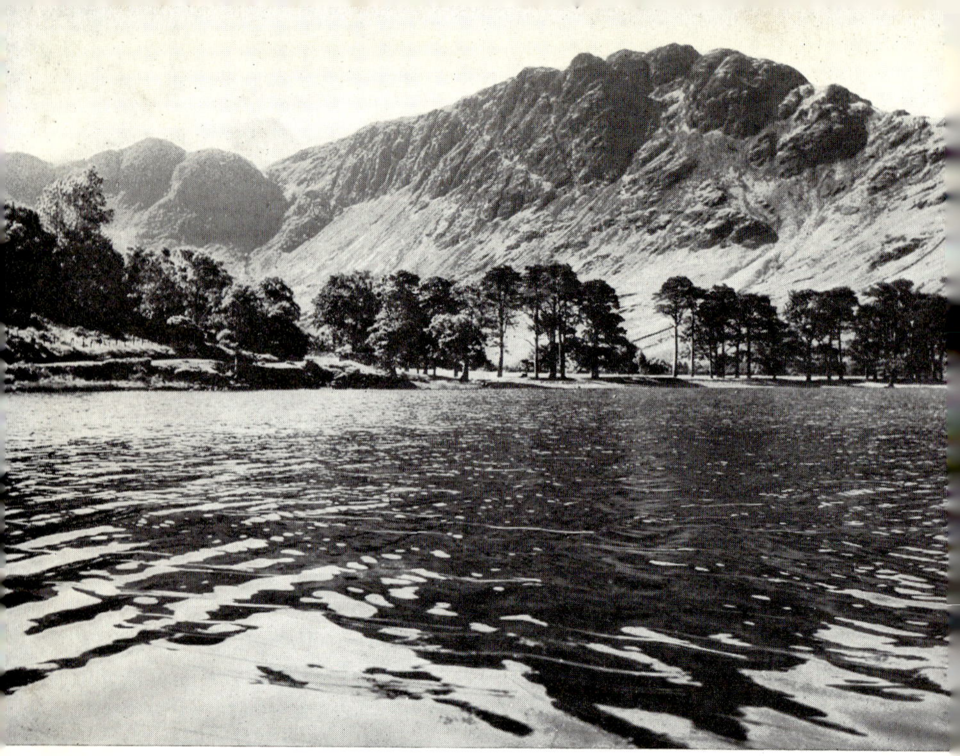

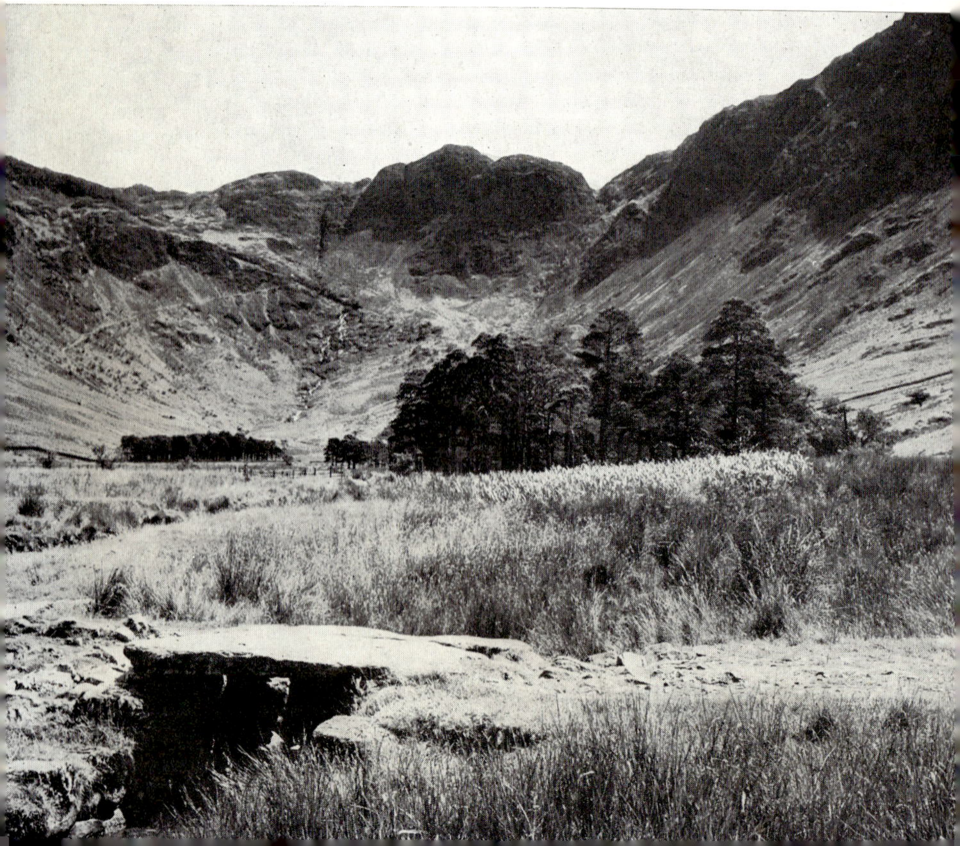

expect cloud and rain. In the event, the sun shone down on the Lakeland hills out of an almost cloudless sky throughout both days, and there was hardly a breath of wind. True, there was mist hanging about in some of the valleys, but this served only to enhance the splendour of the snow-laden hills, soaring out of the vapours towards the sky. And all the mountains were gripped with frost, so iron-clawed and complete that all the little sounds were silenced. Indeed, if you kept away from the crowds on the hills that weekend—and there were crowds in places—they must have been the quietest places in England. The becks were stilled, the birds absent or silent, and no grass on the snowbound tops through which the breeze might sigh. Not even a slither of scree. Just a silent, white world. I was fortunate to be out on the hills on both days—each time in the Helvellyn area. For most of the Saturday I was on my own, although occasionally with one companion; on the following day I had scores of jolly folk for company. Each day had its own charms.

It was on the drive over the high road between Ings and Troutbeck on the Saturday morning that we first realised the day was going to be an exceptional one. There is no better roadside view of the Lakeland fells seen from the south than that from the summit of this road below High Borrans. Half the mountains in Lakeland lie stretched out along the horizon, with the lake in the foreground and the wooded country west of Ambleside in the middle distance, and, if the hills are snow covered and the day sunny and clear, as on that Saturday, the effect is quite magical. On such rare occasions the mountains look as if they have been carved out of marble—just blue shadows and glistening white slopes soaring up into the heavens.

Patterdale looked a study in orange and brown as we topped Kirkstone, and Brotherswater was lightly skimmed in places with ice. But the next day it was frozen right across and the bays of Ullswater were frozen, too. As we mounted higher, Lakeland slowly unfolded itself and we could see farther and farther across the ridges to the east. In the foreground the pointed peak of Catstye Cam probed the sky and sent its steep sunlit, snow slopes down into the dark valley of Keppel Cove, and higher up we came upon the Helvellyn ridges plastered in ice, sweeping round their hanging valleys and tilting down into Patterdale. We could

F

Buttermere and Haystacks
Warnscale Bottom, Buttermere

see the 'fog' which the B.B.C. had mentioned. The three reaches of Ullswater lay hidden in a shimmering of mist, and beyond, Penrith and the Eden valley seemed to be swallowed up in miles of cotton-wool. And behind the floating mists the long wall of the Northern Pennines stretched along the eastern horizon—Cross Fell with its familiar collar of deeper snow below the summit, the radar station just discernible on the top of Great Dun Fell and the dark, saucer-shaped gap of High Cup Nick, all snowbound and shining in the winter sunshine.

But it was not until we reached the whale-backed summit of the range that we could enjoy the whole panorama of winter Lakeland. All the mountains were equally recognisable, the pointed triangle of Bowfell, the characteristic hump of Great Gable, the jagged line of the Scafells, the familiar shapes of the Coniston Fells and, round to the north the grand shape of Blencathra. No Lake District mountain looks better in the snow than Blencathra—the photographers' delight. It is the sharp ridges sweeping down towards Threlkeld that make the picture. In summertime these inoffensive ridges blend into the background of the mountain and are not particularly striking, but under snow they seem to become knife-sharp and aggressive, an invitation to the mountaineer. And, at the same time, the mountain seems to double its stature, so that from some places along the Penrith-to-Keswick road on a bright day in winter it can almost look like a jagged Alpine peak.

Gradually, as the hours went by, the sunlit Northern Pennines, sailing above the sea of mist and the rich warm colours of the lower slopes, seemed to retreat farther and farther away, while the western peaks of Lakeland changed from glistening snow mountains into dark rather forbidding silhouettes. But it was still too early for the magic of the sunset. We sat on the summits in our shirt sleeves, drinking our coffee and soup, and resting before pointing our skis down the frozen slopes; and marvelled— particularly on the Saturday—that here, 3,000 feet above sea-level, there was still not a breath of wind.

On the Sunday the sunlit fells in that corner of Lakeland were alive with folk. From the top of Stybarrow Dodd we could see what looked like a score of people on the distant summit of Helvellyn—tiny, black matchsticks outlined against the sun; and later, with skiers, climbers, walkers and sightseers mingling on the frozen snow, Sticks Pass became almost crowded.

And as the afternoon turned into evening and the shadows lengthened across the rock-hard snow, we watched, all of us, the pageantry of the sunset. By now the western hills had turned blue–black, and the sky was blazing in orange and gold. Gradually the great ball of the sun dipped down behind the Borrowdale and Buttermere fells until, quite suddenly, the sunlight disappeared from the snow at our feet and the freezing cold of evening crept down over the mountains.

The first star shone brightly down in the south-east and somebody suggested it might be the American satellite. But soon it was followed by other stars, and they were winking all around us out of a black, cloudless sky as we slowly skied down the icy fingers of snow to the valley. And later we came stumbling down the track into Patterdale in the darkness, laden with our equipment and slipping on the icy patches, guided by the lights in the cottage windows, after two of the most wonderful days that winter Lakeland can provide.

HIGH SUMMER

High summer seemed to come to the Lakeland fells one year on a sleepy Sunday in May—a sultry sort of day, far too hazy for good colour photography, with flat lighting everywhere, and no wind to send the cloud galleons sailing across the sky. Yet the snow still lay in deep drifts on the highest land in England, and there was even a patch of it on the northern side of Green Gable. On the summit of Great Gable the little wooden crosses and imitation poppies, faded and weather-worn, were still stuck around the war memorial after six months of exposure to one of our longest winters.

Nobody else was on the summit and nobody on Gable Crag on the north side of the mountain, which was just catching the westering sun as I left. Pillar Rock, a disappointing mountain feature until you come quite close or, better still, get to grips with its superb walls and cracks, merely merged into the fellside, Low Man, High Man and then the drop into Jordan Gap, seen in profile, hardly looking the finest lump of rock in England. The massed conifers in Ennerdale appeared like a dark carpet spread across a dead valley, but even from 3 miles away on a dullish day Robinson's Cairn stood out boldly. What a wonderfully sited memorial to a man of the mountains.

For a time I passed along Moses' Sledgate, that cunning track through the fells about which we know so little. Who was Moses, the smuggler? Did he transport his whisky, brewed in some secret still among the crags, along this lonely track through Lakeland to the coast, or was it wadd, stolen perhaps from the plumbago mines in Borrowdale? Or was he just a quarryman, doing some fairly inoffensive trade in slates? In his book, *Thorston Hall*, O. S. Macdonell has a character called Moses Rigg who takes a man wanted for murder along his own private 'trod'. 'I took him by a gate that no folks ken of, save my sel'',' said Moses in the book. 'It's by Gable, an't 'Sty, an' to Hause o' t' Esk, an' Lingcove, an' so t' Duddon. We got to Ulverston that night.' And every climber knows Moses' Finger, the lump of rock near the top of Gavel Neese, where begins the traverse across Great Gable to the climbs on the Napes. Some people think Moses had his hideout in the smugglers' 'hut' on Gable Crag, but I doubt whether dalesmen could have reached the place 200 years ago. And there were no clues there that Sunday—just a yard or two of tumbledown wall perched half-way up the crags and the rusty remains of a sardine tin.

On the side of Green Gable a voluntary warden of the National Park was looking for some of his charges on a fell-walking course, but I'd seen no coloured anoraks. On Brandreth three people with a map had no idea how to get back to Rosthwaite, although they had left there a few hours before. On Fleetwith Pike three farmers were out with their dogs—a most unusual sight, for they were not 'looking' sheep but merely enjoying a walk in the afternoon sunshine. On the side of Kirk Fell my dog lay with his nose pointing along the ground, trying to hypnotise a fat Hardwick standing on a rock ridge a few yards away, and I managed to get the two of them in one picture, with the flat fields of Wasdale below. Like most of his kind Sambo did not like sharp screes, and after the long, hot slither from the top of Gable to Beck Head he was glad to slide into a pool and soak his tired limbs.

On Brandreth I noticed one of the commonest sights of the Lakeland fells—long lengths of derelict iron fences, just the uprights and the straggling wires. There seems no chance that they will ever go, for there must be thousands of them scattered over the district, and the job of removal is just too big to tackle. But, ugly though they may be, these bits of disused fencing have their uses at times—particularly as direction aids during thick snow or mist. One wire fence I have in mind indicates the line of a rock climb—Grey Knotts Face on Gillercombe. The climb follows with remarkable exactitude the line of the wire fence, which may be seen from below at both the top and bottom of the crag.

The fells were full of sheep that Sunday, but I saw no lambs until I came down to the pass. Sambo was interested in one little fellow, only a day or two old, but I would not let him near. The ewe, too, was even more anxious that he should not approach too close. Normally this sheep, or any other, would have been prepared to run when it saw my dog, but as a new mother she realised she now had responsibilities and discovered a new courage. With a snort and a toss of the head she actually advanced towards Sambo as if to do battle for her lamb, bleating a few yards away, but then thought better of it and just glared.

Down on the top of Honister it had been a busy day—with a constant stream of traffic over the pass and the quarries filled with cars. The new youth hostel near the summit seemed nearly completed and looked as if it would fit well enough into the scarred landscape. I went up the remains of the old track towards the workings on Honister Crag and looked across the head of the valley to a favourite climb, Honister Wall, which from this angle looked completely vertical. There was a flicker of blue and brown high up in a corner, and I knew that a climber was working his way up the climb, but I was too far away to see any more. I wished I had a pair of field glasses with me, for I thought I heard the sounds of a piton hammer, which seemed odd on this particular route.

I drove part of the way down the old road from the top of Honister and thought back on those days when the pass was still rough and the traffic very intermittent. But Hause Gill, which runs down the side of the pass, is still a lovely beck and Seatoller a picturesque mountain hamlet. Borrowdale was filled with evening sunshine, and Troutdale looked a perfect haven of peace, which is more than can sometimes be said for it during some August weekends. It seemed impossible that such a perfect valley as Borrowdale could so often be the scene of hooliganism, noise and deliberate destruction, but this is unfortunately the case, and just about that time the dalesfolk were demanding a resident policeman.

THE ROOF OF ENGLAND

On a warm June day in Borrowdale a few years ago you could still see where the floods had come down from the mountains ten months earlier—one of the most concentrated storms of the century, but time, aided in places by man, had already covered up much of the damage, and some day soon only those who know where to look will be aware of the changed landscape. The steep runnels of new scree, gouged out of the Seathwaite side of Glaramara, for instance, had looked startlingly white the previous autumn, but were now weathering well and slowly being re-carpeted by the bracken and the ling. And the great boulders that were swept down Grains Gill or sent hurtling down the fellside had now settled down in their new sites, perhaps a mile or two away from where they had been resting for hundreds of years.

Stockley Bridge across the infant Derwent, which had survived at least 200 years of storms, had been half washed away by the floods of the previous August, but had now been carefully rebuilt, and the work of channelling the beck away from the hamlet had almost been completed. Thousands of tons of boulders had been coaxed into banks behind wire mesh, trees planted to mellow the changed contours, walls rebuilt, fences repaired, fields ploughed and farmhouses redecorated, so that visitors, knowing nothing of the previous year's disasters, might go away without realising that the wettest corner of England had been transformed. It is still the wettest place in the country, according to the rainfall figures, but the good folk of Seathwaite and Borrowdale can now sleep easier in their beds, knowing that a catastrophe of the magnitude of 1966 should in future pass them by.

Two of us walked through the valley on perhaps the hottest

day in 1967. The beck that ten months earlier had been a swirling torrent 10 feet deep had almost disappeared; the tar was melting on the roads; the farm lads, brown as Arabs, were working in the hayfields, stripped to the waist; and the pool by Grange bridge was far too shallow to risk a dive. In Grains Gill it was exactly like an oven. There was not a breath of wind, and the heat seemed to come off the rocks like sound from a gong. Tiny insects whirred in the dry grass, the huge bulk of Great End straight ahead shimmered in the haze, and the perspiration poured into our eyes and dropped off the ends of our noses. Trudging up through the gorge with rucksack straps biting into bare shoulders, and thoughts of a bathe in Sprinkling Tarn at the end of the day uppermost in our thoughts, it was difficult to realise that this little corner of tilted land had staged eight of the ten wettest days in the country during the past 100 years, and, seventy years ago, the wettest Lake District day in history, with more than 8 inches of rain within twenty-four hours. But, down in the gill, the rowans hung over shadowed pools where the water was still deliciously cold, waterfalls cascaded down the rocks, and moss and bilberry plants dripped with moisture. The sheep nosed their tiny lambs out of our path and coaxed them up the steep sides of the ravine.

We were on a lazy day and all for taking straight lines and avoiding wearisome diversions. The straight line from Seathwaite to Scafell Pike goes up Great End, so this was the way we went. Straight lines—as the raven flies, if you liked—make good mountain exercises, and a favourite straight line of mine is up Moasdale across Lingcove Beck and up Little Narrowcove ('Lile "Arra" ') to the Pike. You can make this ruler-straight, but our Great End route has a slight bend and might not suit perfectionists. Leaving the Esk Hause track, we struck straight up the crag by one of the central gullies. Great End faces north-east, and its crag hardly ever gets the sun, so that we thought this would be as cool a place as any on such a scorching day. But we had forgotten how high is the sun's zenith in June and were discouraged to notice that its rays were just lighting up the rock face. However, once we were well inside our gully, we were in the shade, and presently came upon snow. Just a few feet of it every now and then—sugary stuff that swished down the gully when kicked and would hardly take a step, but polished and slightly frozen on top. It made a pleasant change from the rocks in the gill, which had been hot to the touch. We climbed slowly and carefully, for these gullies that can be such a joy, when ice-filled, to the winter mountaineer are incredibly loose and unsatisfactory in the summertime and probably best avoided. And they are, of course, rock climbs, although very easy ones, and are not for walkers. But it was wonderful to be in the shade, between dark, damp walls, and everything either cold or wet instead of hot and dusty. Coming out at the top into the sunshine was like coming up out of the London Underground with its cool air into the glare of the city streets.

There were a dozen schoolboys from the south of England near the cairn, but they'd no idea where they were or how to get down or even which way they had come; I hoped their master did. They thought Great Gable was Scafell Pike and could not tell us the name of the valley from which they had ascended nor even its direction, although we guessed it had been Borrowdale. Their footwear and equipment left something to be desired. Of course, they were unlikely to come to any harm on this glorious day, but we wondered whether their approach would be just as casual if they revisited the hills some time—perhaps on a day when conditions on the tops turned out to be completely different from those in the valleys. This is how many accidents happen—people not taking sufficient trouble to find out what it's all about and learning the rules beforehand.

We continued in the hot sunshine over Broad Crag and Ill Crag to the Pike and then came down to the Corridor Route and so to Styhead. These coves underneath the summit ridge of the Scafells, on both sides, together form perhaps the best mountain country in England, and yet untracked ways can still be found into their inner recesses, for most people keep to the main paths. The tremendous gashes of Piers Gill, Greta Gill and Skew Gill were filled with evening sunlight, hiding their morning menace, as we came down the mountain, and Gable filled the foreground. A look through the glasses revealed half a dozen people on the summit, but we couldn't spot any climbers on either the Napes or Kern Knotts.

Down by Styhead Tarn there were family picnics and children splashing in the water, and it seemed rather too crowded for our bathe—and much too filled with reed and weed. The pool near

Sourmilk Gill was too shallow and the water by Grange bridge nothing like so deep as usual, so we went on to Derwentwater and finished the day with a quiet swim in one of the little bays. Pleasantly warm water, the islands riding like yachts at anchor on the glass-smooth surface, and sunlit Skiddaw smiling down made a perfect picture. And hours later the sun went down behind the Borrowdale birches and a long, lazy Lakeland day of high summer crept quietly to its close.

ROCKS AND POOLS

A rocky pool in the Derwent just above Seathwaite Farm—cold, clear and invigorating—brought me back to life after a walk over the highest land in England on one of the hottest and heaviest days of 1969. There was thunder in the air and low clouds over Great End, and the farmer, relieved at having got in his hay at last, forecasted rain—quite correctly, as it turned out—before nightfall.

I find it easier to cope with hot, humid weather in the hills than in the towns—despite the much greater exertion. Stripped to the waist, it doesn't really matter how much you perspire, and a quick bathe at the end of the day can make you feel like a giant refreshed. If you pick your spot there's no need for a costume, and a towel is quite unnecessary. With practice, these quick bathes, with only boots and trousers to discard, can be something of a fine art and completed in a couple of minutes. Ideally, the pool should be fairly deep but need not be more than a yard or two wide. Nearly every beck has several—sometimes in the most unlikely places—and you can get the job over and done with while less determined people are still thinking about it. I once achieved a bathe in a tiny pool in the Lingmell Beck while a party was getting over the stile at the foot of Brown Tongue, and I'm quite sure that none of the people on the track to Stockley Bridge this evening knew there was a naked man in the river only a few yards from the path.

Of course, these are emergency bathes perpetrated merely for cooling-off purposes, and not to be confused with proper bathes in the mountain tarns and larger pools, which may require a certain amount of reconnaisance—for diving possibilities, for instance—and can be enjoyed for as long as you feel like it. Rather surprisingly, there was nobody in Styhead Tarn that day —I passed it twice—for the smooth rocks at the south-eastern corner make a useful diving platform.

I don't usually time myself over the hills, but I did this time— one hour to the top of Styhead (average), another hour to the Lingmell col (rather slow, I thought), a third hour to the top of Scafell by way of Lord's Rake and the West Wall Traverse (including a stop for lunch in Hollow Stones), and a fourth hour to the top of Scafell Pike by way of Broad Stand and Mickledore (very slow indeed). I gave up stop-watching after that, since I was thinking about my bathe and trying to decide whether to have it in Styhead Tarn or Taylorgill Force and then walk down sedately, so as not to perspire, or whether to trot down, leaving the bathe to the last possible moment before the car. In the end I decided on the latter expedient, which meant that I went into the water in the right state for such a dip, with the perspiration running into my eyes. This way, the shock of immersion really blows away the lethargy and brings you back to life.

There were one or two slightly strange encounters during the day. The first was with a youth, most unsuitably dressed in a long, floppy raincoat and wearing gumboots. He was also wearing ordinary town clothes underneath, and carrying a thick stick about 6 feet long. Stripped to the waist but used to the exertion, I was perspiring freely up the Corridor Route towards the Ling-mell col, but this youth, wearing all these heavy clothes, passed me as if he was after some record. Obviously, he had never been on the mountain before, for he asked me the way, and he didn't even know its name. Perhaps he had never been on any mountain before, for neither his clothing nor his progress were sensible, but he dashed on, coat-tails trailing behind him and his gumboots skidding on the rocks, and I wondered how he came to be on Scafell Pike on the hottest day of the year. Certainly I admired his enterprise, his energy and his obvious fitness, while wishing he had sought some advice about the subject before he left the valley. Had the expected rain come on sooner than it did, he could have been in trouble in those gumboots. These are the sort of young people who so often come to grief in the hills.

Another encounter was when I was coming down Broad Stand and found two youths scrambling about in the upper reaches of Mickledore Chimney. They were trying to get down to Mickledore and, finding themselves at the top of the steep drop above the screes, were casting about to find an alternative route. They had unsuitable footgear and admitted, when I questioned them, they had no experience of rock-climbing. They were merely looking for an easy way down to Mickledore. I thought it unwise to take them with me down Broad Stand, since I had no rope with me and no idea of their ability, so I directed them back to the summit and told them how get down by way of Foxes Tarn.

Thousands of people down the years have found themselves in much the same situation as these youngsters, since the obstacle of Broad Stand (or Mickledore Chimney) is the only example in the Lake District, or indeed in England, of a route between two adjacent mountain tops which cannot be tackled—or easily by-passed—by the ordinary walker. Both these routes are rock-climbs —although, admittedly, very easy ones—and need the necessary experience. But the ordinary walker, unfamiliar with Scafell and wishing to get to Scafell Pike, will naturally—even after consulting his map—go off in this direction. I am very much against signs or any other direction markings in the fells, but I have often thought that some sort of indication, perhaps carved on a rock, near the summit of Scafell, showing the walkers' way off, would be helpful in very many cases.

Through the heat haze and cloud you could just make out the shape of Wastwater, 3,000 feet below, and the blue outline of the hills around Eskdale, from the top of Scafell that day. Over on the Pike I could see the tiny pool of Broadcrag Tarn, the highest tarn in England. There were several parties on the Pike, and the quickest way down seemed to be by way of the Broad Crag col and down to the Corridor Route, which proved to be deserted. Nobody, either, except the sheep, in Taylorgill Force, but, later, the road to Keswick was choked with cars.

SCAFELL IN JULY

Some of the July days in Lakeland in 1967, with cloudless, blue skies, warm sunshine from dawn to dusk, brilliantly clear views and just enough breeze to keep the flies away, were as perfect as any I can remember. Even after the sun had dipped behind the blue hills in the evening, the western sky remained a blaze of gold for hours, and at midnight there was still enough light to see across the valley. On one of these perfect days I went up Scafell from Wasdale Head; that is to say, from the finest valley head in England I went up to the most magnificent ring of crags in the country. It was a day for superlatives, and perhaps the only jarring note was the incredible inefficiency of some of the drivers encountered on Hardknott on both outward and inward journeys. Drivers in the wrong gear who stalled, just ahead of you, on the steepest corners or refused to give way to ascending traffic. The condition of both Hardknott and Wrynose passes is deteriorating somewhat, and this, I hope, will have the effect of keeping the worst of these drivers away. A good surface is an invitation to the most inexperienced people to go joy-riding over these passes, with sometimes disastrous results. Indeed, it is remarkable there are so few really serious accidents on this route, for I hardly ever go over without seeing quite appalling driving. Far better when the passes had only rough surfaces and there were half a dozen gates across the road. Then you only went over if you had to do so, and the joy-riders weren't interested.

But once into Eskdale on the way out this July day the views were so lovely you forgot your irritation, and I turned right at Santon Bridge into paradise. First through the woods, with the sunlight flooding through the branches and lighting up the shadow-dappled road, and then, near Wasdale Hall, the sudden view of the Screes looming far above the lake and the smooth beauty of Wastwater itself. Wastwater, the deepest lake in England, often looks dark and gloomy and, frequently, storm-tossed, cold and forbidding, but this day it looked as friendly as a Swiss lake—unrippled, blue and inviting. Indeed, I don't think I've ever seen it so smooth or so blue, and the tremendous rampart of the Screes looked double its height with the reflection.

Farther on, two sun-burned youths, stripped to the waist and wearing hay-making hats, were standing on rocks in the water fishing, and they were still there when I returned, several hours later. I hope they had caught something. The new screes left by the big rockfall a year or two earlier still showed light grey against the weathered rock, and it will probably be years before the scar disappears. Similarly, the rock avalanche that fell down the slopes of Grey Friar into Wrynose Bottom during the big storm in August 1966 still leaves its mark, and although the roadway has been repaired, the fellside will show where the torrents came down for a long time yet.

I went up the fellside from Brackenclose, the climbing hut built in 1937, which is one of the best examples of concealment ever achieved in the Lake District. From almost every side it is completely hidden by trees, and thousands of people pass within a short distance of it every year without even noticing it. The sun was blazing down as I worked my way up Brown Tongue towards Hollow Stones, but the views opening up ahead are so magnificent on this approach that you forget the toil. First, the huge mass of Black Crag straight ahead, and then, as you gain height, you see the dark precipice of Scafell Crag, the soaring slabs of the Pinnacle Face and, facing the shadowed cliffs across the combe, the sunlit rocks of Pikes Crag. There is no finer circle of crag than this in England, and on a sunny day no greater contrast in mountain architecture.

At this time of day the great cliff of Scafell Crag is cold and sunless and, when viewed from Hollow Stones, looks even more vertical than it really is. While Pikes Crag, full in the sunlight, always looks friendly. This July day, from the familiar boulder in Hollow Stones where one has lunched on so many occasions in the past forty years, you could see every chimney and crack on Pikes Crag and easily pick out the Horse and Man Rock on the serrated summit ridge. There were two parties on Scafell Crag—one climbing Botterill's Slab, the smooth wall that sweeps up leftwards from Rake's Progress, and the other tackling the vertical Flake Crack on Central Buttress, once the hardest rock-climb in Britain and, even today, one of the most exhilarating routes in the country.

Lying on my back against the boulder and shielding my eyes

from the sun, I watched the leader trying, for half an hour at least, to lead the Flake direct, that is to say, without assistance from his second at the chockstone, just below the overhanging finish. But he never managed it, and it was another member of the party who finally led on to the crest of the Flake, pulling up on the magnificent holds that top the almost holdless wall. Mine was a grandstand view of one of the most spectacular climbs in the country, but thereafter my route to the top was by way of the humble Lord's Rake and West Wall Traverse, which threads its way through most impressive rock scenery. I went on to the Pinnacle by way of the easy scrambling route from Jordan Gap, but, although I know the crag pretty well, I decided that, being alone, this should be the limit of my climbing.

On the top I remembered a day about forty years earlier when two of us camped out on the summit of Scafell, and soon after dawn we saw England, Scotland, Ireland and Wales—the last (the Glyders) by walking perhaps 100 yards across the boulders. This afternoon the views were superb but not that good. The Isle of Man, above and behind the cooling towers at Calder Hall, was very clear indeed, but Ireland was hidden in the haze.

To complete the traverse of the mountain I came down Broad Stand, which I must have been up and down a few dozen times, even in ice and snow. The same party was still on Central Buttress —the original leader still on the Flake, which he must have been studying for about two hours—but the sun was beginning to work its way round on to the crag, and they would have sunlight and warm rock for the last pitches.

This was perhaps the best part of a very lovely day. The sun was now moving into the west, throwing long shadows across the floor of the combe. The first rays were gilding the Scafell crags, but the light was now striking Pikes Crag sideways on, so that the buttresses between the cracks and chimneys were thrown up in bold relief.

The larks were singing as I ran down Brown Tongue, a pair of ravens slowly circling Lingmell and unseen aircraft making vapour patterns across the blue zenith. Down in the Lingmell Beck the little waterfalls splashed into perfect pools, each one ringed with grey rock, while rowan, birch and holly hung over the waters, offering delicious shade. The smoke rose straight from the camp-fires in the valley, the lake shone like silver in the evening sun and the picnickers were brewing tea by the shore. Somewhere near Wasdale Hall I looked back at the hills, already turning that unforgettable shade of blue that one can remember with affection at the other side of the world. Just another simple day in the hills, a day without achievement of note, but packed full of pictures of mountain Lakeland in all its summer glory.

PEACE ON PILLAR

The day before the long, hot summer of 1968 came to an end I went to Pillar Rock to get away from the Lakeland crowds—a wonderful transition from noise and scurry to remote loneliness and quiet serenity. On the way I passed the crowds at Waterhead Bay, the picnickers around the ice-cream man at White Moss Common, the great splash of colour of the camp site at Causeway Foot and the bustling streets of Keswick, and pictured what it would be like on top of the Rock.

There might, I thought, be a pleasant breeze on top as a change from the hot, sultry morning, and there would certainly be the exhilaration of the great rock buttresses plunging vertically downwards beneath one's feet to the river far, far below, and the long view down Ennerdale, past the conifers, the lake and the farmlands to the sea. Remote as a church steeple, but ample space on the tiny summit to stretch out to sleep or smoke or just to look out over half of Lakeland from one of its most delightful eyries. Since I first went up Pillar Rock about forty years ago it has nearly always been like this on top—quiet, deserted, or nearly so, warm, sunny and restful—and it was like it again this time.

There were the usual frightened drivers on Honister, stalling just ahead, and more family parties picnicking by the side of the pass than I had ever seen before. But the Gatesgarth Beck on the other side was almost dry and the sound of splashing waters strangely stilled. From the Richardsons' farm, which looks the same now as it did in the 1920s, I could see the clouds stealing over High Stile, but the sun was still glinting on the rough, slabby rocks of Grey Crag and touching, here and there, the track winding over Scarth Gap into Ennerdale. It was warm work scrambling over the pass—I met perhaps six other people—and I was glad to get down the other side and on to the ride through the conifers and down to the Liza. Here, in the dark tunnel between the thick forest of spruce, it was delightfully cool and the carpet of fir needles a pleasant change from the sliding banks of dusty scree.

The trouble with this walk from Buttermere to the Rock is that, having reached the top of Scarth Gap, you have to lose most of your height gained and start again from the Liza with 1,200 feet of steep fellside to ascend before you reach the foot of the crag. It was hot and sultry this August day, and waterless after leaving the Liza, but there were compensations. The heather, for one thing—great purple banks of it right up the fellside—and, equally plentiful, the bilberries, ripe and succulent, providing refreshing handfuls whenever required. And, perhaps even more encouraging to the tired walker, the sight, high up and straight ahead, of the tremendous precipices of the Rock—the tallest cliff in England and looking from this angle like two great cathedrals piled on top of one another.

I went up the Rock by the Old West Route, which is believed to be the way taken by the first man to reach the top more than 140 years ago. It is a simple way for climbers, but it is not, of course, a walker's route. There were six people on the summit— two old friends I had not seen for years, and four young 'tigers'. These were the only people on the Rock all day, so far as I could see the only people on that side of the mountain, and the first people I had seen since the top of Scarth Gap. So much for the popularity of Lakeland during an August heat-wave—packed thousands in the villages and on the lake shores, but almost nobody on the tops or around the fell tarns.

The view, as usual, was superb—nothing below our feet until the massed conifers 2,000 feet below, the silver thread of the Liza winding down to the lake and the westering sun glowing on the Ennerdale fells until they shone like gold. Sometimes I have fancied I could hear the waters of the Liza from the top of the Rock, but there was no sound whatever this day, not even a distant slither of scree made by an adventurous sheep in the corrie or the sighing of the wind in the crags. It was warm, windless and sunny

Fishing in Ullswater
Ullswater

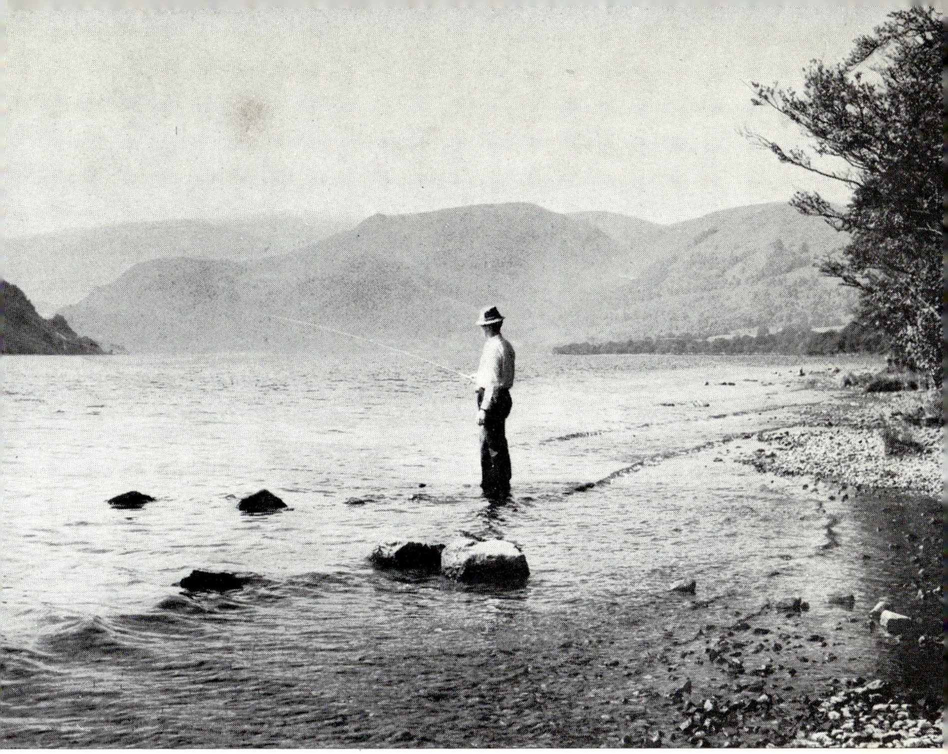

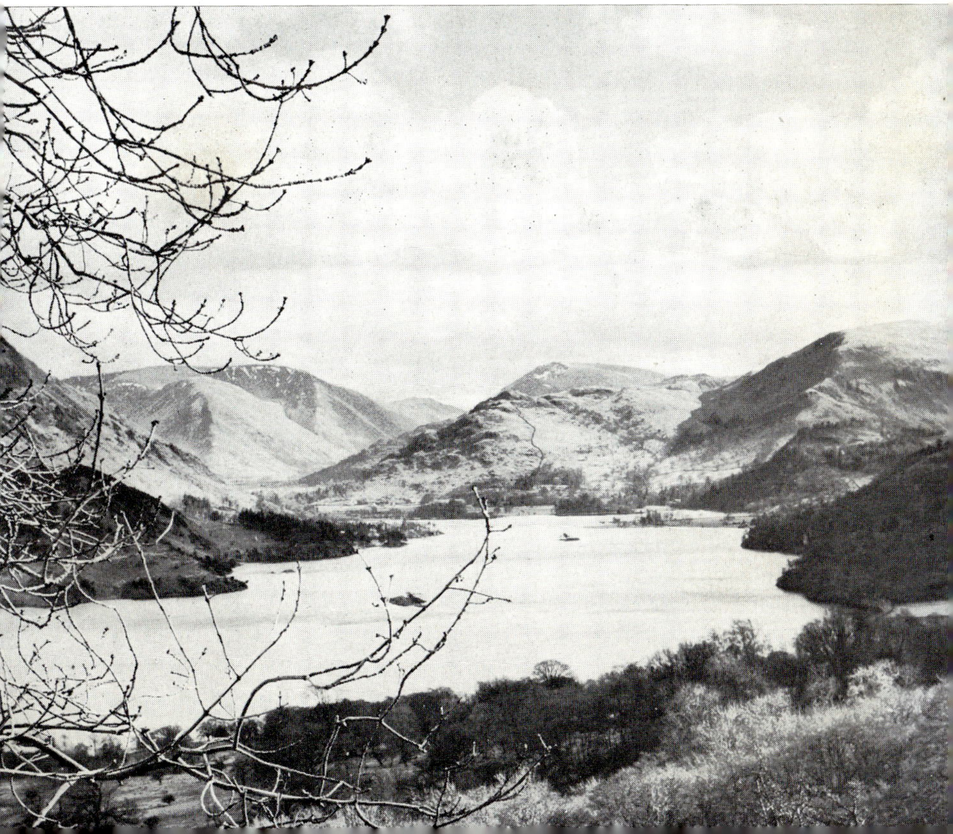

and completely devoid of midges which, on calm August days, sometimes plague the climber on the Rock.

Perhaps half an hour later it was time to go—the others to do another climb, myself to get off the Rock and over to Buttermere. My descent route was Central Jordan, the climbers' quick way off the Rock by sliding down a vertical crack, and I was soon trotting down the fellside with only one thought in mind—where on earth to have a bathe. There was nothing on the Buttermere side, apart from the lake, which would probably be thronged with motorists, making a dip without a costume rather tricky. So I plumped for a pool in the Liza, where the only disadvantage would be that half the walk would still be ahead and the refreshing effects of the bathe nullified by the time I reached the car.

I could hardly have chosen a more perfect place—deep, cool waters full in the evening sun, white rocks, clean shingle and nobody about. Greatly refreshed, the climb through the conifers and up and over the dusty fellside went easily, and there was time to enjoy the delights of a perfect summer's evening in the hills. Straight ahead from the mounting track up the screes rose the slightly less familiar 'back' sides of Great Gable and Kirk Fell—blue, evening shapes with the crags of Boat Howe and the north face of Gable just catching the sun, so that every crack and slab seemed revealed. Below, and threaded by the Liza, the vast carpet of conifers spread right up the dale, and above, white billowing clouds sailing slowly across the heaven. The dark carpet is not so offensive as it used to be years ago. You don't see the straight lines of the planting so much now, and the fringes of the forest seem to be merging more gradually into the fellside. But no other Lakeland dale has been so changed by the hand of man as this one.

And so I came down to Buttermere, the valley according to Collingwood 'made by heaven for summer evenings . . . green floor and purple heights with the sound of the water under the sunset'. The High Stile range was now a dark wall, but across the floor of the dale the fells glowed in the sunshine, which danced on the waters of the lake and gilded the old stone barns. The little cluster of trees at the head of the lake and the lovely sweep of white shingle looked exactly the same as when I first saw them as a boy—one of the most perfect pictures in the whole of the Lake District.

G

Ennerdale Water

Everything about the head of the dale looked neat and tidy as it always does. The contrasting shapes of the newly cut, bright green fields made a pleasant pattern, the campers' tents were pitched tidily along the side of the wall, and not higgledy piggledy across the meadow, and the sheep and cattle made long shadows along the turf. There was a busy tinkling of pails at the dairy by the farm, and small, brown calves, quite unafraid, came forward to be nuzzled. A perfect evening scene that I hope will continue in Buttermere for ever—although I have the strongest doubts. And then back home over Newlands, through the crowded streets of Keswick and over the Raise, past the water skiers on Windermere, and along country lanes for a meal and a proper bath.

TWO TARNS

Among the 500 mountain tarns in the Lake District—this number if you count every pool large and deep enough for a comfortable bathe—are two Angle Tarns, one under the northern crags of Bowfell, the other, 12 miles to the north-east, above the farmhouses of Patterdale. Few pairs of mountain pools have less in common. The Bowfell tarn is higher, deeper, more often visited, and much smaller than the other, while its waters are colder, often dark and sunless, and sometimes, under certain conditions of weather and lighting, almost frightening. But the Patterdale Angle Tarn, although less well known, has always seemed to me a particularly welcoming place, no matter what the weather —a straggly shaped pool with islands, headlands and little reedy bays dotted with water flowers and an indented shore-line patterned with miniature crags and grassy hummocks. Bowfell's tarn is a mountain pool, dramatically sited and fed by springs that seep out of the screes, but the Angle Tarn that lies within sight of the Roman way over High Street is a jewel of the lower fells left behind after the ice had scooped out the moraines in which it lies. Here is a place for whiling away a sunny afternoon or a haunt for adventurous children to act out their fantasies. If you sat long and still enough at the right time of day you might well see fell ponies and red deer or, if you were really quiet, perhaps a fox slinking round the outcrops in search of food or his bield on some distant crag. And always the sheep cropping the lush turf and the ravens quartering the sky.

6

Some Characters

PROFESSOR OF ADVENTURE

Had he lived, Millican Dalton, Professor of Adventure, would have been 100 years old in 1967. As it was he died, a long way from his beloved hills, at the age of 80, but many people still remember with affection a most lovable character who seemed to have found the secret of a really happy life.

Borrowdale always reminds me of Millican Dalton, and when I was there last I remembered days when I used to bump into him at the post office laying in his groceries—a devil-may-care figure in home-made clothes, Tyrolean hat with jaunty pheasant's feather, deeply tanned face and little pirate's beard. He would have his bicycle with him, and this would be so laden with stores, tents, ropes and other possessions as to be unrideable by anybody less agile than Millican.

His summer residence is still there on Castle Crag—a cave in the rocks where he lived for months at a time every year and entertained his guests. Although a redoubtable camper until the end of his long life, Millican did not believe in roughing it if he could make himself comfortable, and I have slept in many worse places than his cave. He had his own fireplace with a seat adjoining, a bed of dried leaves (supplemented with down quilts if required), a little pool of fresh water and gadgets of every description for suspending tins and other requirements. He was a first-class cook —although a vegetarian—and you could always tell when he was in residence by the plume of blue smoke rising among the trees high up above the Borrowdale road. Above the entrance to his

THATTO HEATH
BRANCH LIBRARY

cave, letters, neatly cut in the rock, warned the visitor: 'Don't waste words, jump to conclusions,' but when you got to know Millican Dalton he was quite prepared to open out, and would happily argue for hours about any subject under the sun.

Millican Dalton lived for adventure and the open-air and found what he wanted in the hills, on the rocks, in the woods and on the lakes and tarns around Borrowdale. One day he would be taking some novice climbers up the Napes Needle, the next day exploring the Doves' Nest caves underneath Glaramara or shooting the rapids in the Derwent on a home-made raft, sailing on Derwentwater or scrambling up Lodore in spate, right through the waterfalls. He seemed to enjoy it all, no matter what the weather, and right up to his seventies remained a boy at heart.

I met Millican Dalton several times between the wars, but before our first meeting I knew what he looked like, for you would see his photograph in some of the Keswick shops, perhaps advertising climbing boots or other equipment. 'Millican Dalton, Professor of Adventure,' it said on the photograph, and he certainly looked the part. And later I discovered he rather liked his title.

He was born in Cumberland, not far from Alston, and in his early years worked in a London office. But this must have been a frustrating life for somebody like Millican Dalton, and soon he threw up a commercial career and settled down—if you could call it that—to become a sort of professional camper and mountain guide. I'm not sure whether he was the first Lakeland climbing guide, for Gaspard, a guide from the Dauphiné, was based at Wasdale Head for many years before the First World War; but he was certainly the most unusual one we have ever had and one of the kindliest. I never climbed with him myself, but I have heard from some of those who did that a day out with him was always good fun. He never asked for a fee, but simply a little towards camping expenses, for his needs were only frugal and money didn't mean much to him. Life to him meant getting out into the hills or woods with congenial companions. He had no real ambition, but he was modest, considerate to others, incapable of doing a mean trick and universally liked and respected, despite his rather eccentric appearance and outlook on life.

He was not a lazy layabout, afraid of work, but an intelligent man who had thought things out for himself and decided on his way of life. And for fifty years he trod out his lone pathway to the stars, doing good in his own way, giving a great deal of pleasure to many and not caring one rap what the rest of the world thought. You could say he got out of the rat race before it began, but he never wavered from the views he formed as a young man, and he lived his philosophy to the end—a happy man at peace with the world.

He started off, I believe, by making tents and rucksacks, and developed his camping and climbing activities later. Sometimes he would take small parties to the Alps or perhaps camping in Austria, giving instruction in glacier work and snowcraft. But he was only really at home in the Lake District, and must have had a better knowledge of the woods and crags around Borrowdale than anybody before or since.

He never became one of the great climbers, but he was a very safe leader, and I don't think he ever had a fall. His knowledge of the woodland flowers, the trees, the different types of rock and the curious features of the district, was immense, and he particularly delighted in his expeditions to Doves' Nest Caves, where, with flickering candles stuck on to bits of tin, he conducted parties up and down the subterranean climbs. At one time he was the secretary to the Holiday Fellowship at Newlands. When he was living during the winter months in the south of England Millican went in for tree climbing in Epping Forest, conducting parties up the giant beeches and enjoying himself almost as much as if he was swarming up the Cumberland crags.

It was quite impossible to imagine him leading a normal city life down south. He would look incongruous in a city street, but in and around Borrowdale he fitted into the scenery—a real Robinson Crusoe of the dales. I don't remember him wearing stockings, and he left the edges of his jackets and trousers un-hemmed, like a North American trapper, but he kept himself spruce and clean and had the manners of a gentleman.

The Lake District has produced many hermits and other queer folk down the years, but Millican Dalton was no hermit trying to get away from the world, but a realist trying to come to grips with it in his own way. He loved company and was never happier than with a crowd of open-air folk, especially young people. He lived as he did to be close to nature and because he had no time for modern life's restrictions and regulations. I believe he had a tiny income and, with his tent making and his guiding, managed to eke out enough to live on. The important thing is that Millican Dalton had the courage to live the sort of life he believed in.

He gave the impression that he was an extremely happy man, and he gave happiness to many people, I don't know whether he had any relatives, but I feel that his final tragedy was that he should die in the south, far from the fells and probably alone. Only a few months before his death he had been planning his expeditions for the coming summer, but these were not to be, and he never came back to his cave in the mountains.

Castle Crag remains a sort of memorial to this friendly, lovable man who never made an enemy. There's never been anybody in the Lake District quite like Millican Dalton, Professor of Adventure and Gentleman of the Hills.

WHO WAS MOSES?

Every walker and climber who goes into the Lakeland hills knows Moses' Trod, the well-defined track that runs up the side of Great Gable out of Wasdale Head, continues across the head of Ennerdale, contours around Green Gable and Brandreth, and finally loses itself somewhere near the Honister drum-house. For perhaps a century or more people have wondered what the track was for, when it was first used, and who Moses might have been, but nobody has ever been quite sure of all the facts.

Moses' Trod is a mountain-track of tradition, but its antiquity is uncertain, while Moses, about whom I have written earlier, remains a legendary figure. Some people say he was a smuggler who brought his contraband from the port of Ravenglass to Wasdale Head and hauled it up Gavel Neese on a wooden sledge—perhaps by pony—and across the mountains, following the contours, to the quarries at Honister. But why he should take such an arduous route and why choose such a hideout, is not explained.

The Moses of legend is a whisky-distiller, and they say that somewhere in the hills he had his still. It is even suggested that this might have been the ruined stone hut which can be found near the top of Central Gully on Gable Crag, but this seems an unlikely story. True, the origin of the hut, 'discovered' by the pioneer climber, John Wilson Robinson, about eighty years ago, has never been satisfactorily explained, but it is well off the track, and can be reached only by a rock-scramble unlikely to be tackled by a dalesman more than 100 years ago—and a heavily leaden dalesman at that. No shepherd would ever build a hut in a place like this—even if he could get there—so it might well have been a hideout or even a lookout, for it commands a tremendous view. One suggestion is that the hut might have been a refuge for the Derwentwater Radcliffe family during the 1715 rebellion, but this seems a little far-fetched.

A slightly more probable story is that Moses was not a whisky distiller and smuggler, but a stealer of wadd from the old plumbago mine in Borrowdale. This was the most important mine of its kind in Europe—the quality of the graphite was world-famous —and the precious wadd fetched very high prices. A great deal of smuggling went on, particularly at night, when the lanterns of the thieves could be seen moving over the tips, and an Act of Parliament was passed for protection of the valuable mineral which was used for munitions, among other things. The men were stripped and searched on leaving the mine and there were armed guards on duty, but the stuff was regularly stolen, and there are many old tales of exciting battles in the hills.

So that Moses might well have been one of the smugglers taking the wadd from the mine, up Honister and then along his track to Beck Head and down the steep, but handy, descent of Gavel Neese to Wasdale Head, where he might have met his contacts and handed over his sacks. They say that a pony-load of the stuff was worth £800, even in those days. This would be an incomparably easier trail for a laden man or pony than the ascent of Gavel Neese, which most people find quite steep enough even without a load.

Sometimes the trod is called Moses' Sledgate, but it is unlikely that Moses used a quarryman's sledge for his long haul, for the track is too narrow and bumpy. Almost certainly he would be on foot, leading his pony, if he had one. If he used a pony, where did he keep it when he was busy in his hut on Gable Crag—if he used the hut?

It is possible that the term 'sledgate', which is quite often used even today, originates from a mishearing of the word 'slategate', for Wasdale folk say that an old slate-track came down the side of Gable and that this is how the first slates were brought to Wasdale Head. It seems strange that Wasdale, which apparently has no slate of its own, had to import the material from over the mountains, rather than from the coast, which would have been an easier journey. Before slate came to Wasdale they say the buildings were roofed with split stones brought out of Mosedale. There is ample evidence to point to Moses' Trod having been originally a slate-track, for there could be no other clear reason for such a route, carefully contouring the hills, except for the steep descent of Gavel Neese. You can, for instance, still pick up small fragments of slate along the Trod, even on Gavel Neese and other parts where there is no natural slate.

Almost certainly, therefore, Moses came along this old track with his slate (or perhaps, occasionally, his wadd) and old Will Ritson of the Wastwater Hotel, for one, used to say he brought whisky. He claimed that Moses was an old man when he (Ritson) was a lad, but Ritson was a noted story-teller and might well have invented the tale.

Moses, he said, made his whisky at the Honister quarries out of the bog-water he found up there, for it was said that bog-water made the best whisky. Ritson said that Moses brought the whisky along the Trod on the back of a pony and used to hide it among the piles of stones in the fields at Wasdale Head. Now and again he would be caught and his 'worm' (still) impounded, but later the magistrate would give it back to him—because he made such good whisky.

Other evidence suggests that Moses was already a legend in Ritson's day and probably lived in the eighteenth century or earlier. The Buttermere Slate Company have stated that in the mid-eighteenth century slate was carried by packhorses and donkeys from the Honister quarries to Drigg by way of Wasdale, but that a century later it was taken down the screes to the Honister coach-road on sledges

That knowledgeable Lakeland authority, the late Rev. H. H.

Symonds, was among those who discounted the theory that Moses was a smuggler or that the ruins on Gable Crag had ever been a distillery or whisky store. Mr. Symonds believed that most of the smugglers used Styhead, and he could not credit that these bold men would have needed to place a still in such a precarious spot on the 2,500-feet contour when there was distilling enough going on in the valleys.

But another Lakeland authority, the late Mr. George D. Abraham of Keswick, the pioneer climber and photographer who died in 1965 at the age of ninety-three, firmly believed Mr. Symonds to be wrong. In 1953 Mr. Abraham was the president of the Keswick Mountaineering Club and walked up to the Dubbs Quarry hut at the back of Fleetwith Pike to declare it open as the club's new hut. Shortly afterwards he told me he was quite sure that Moses—he called him Moses Rigg—was a whisky distiller and smuggler, and that he had a still on that wild ledge on Gable Crag. Sixty years earlier, he said, the 'hut' on the crag had a roof and was stone flagged. Furthermore, there were signs in those days, said Mr. Abraham, that a still had been there, and it was fairly common talk in the dales that this was the place where Moses brewed his stuff. In fact, Mr. Abraham knew one Dan Tyson, a relative of the Tyson who once kept the inn at Wasdale Head, and Dan, he said, had worked with Moses.

According to Mr. Abraham, Moses was also a quarryman (to add respectability to his other more lucrative occupation), and he lived at Dubbs Quarry. Tracks from his 'sledgate' went down to Seatoller and also by way of Warnscale Bottom to Buttermere. Somewhere deep in the side of Dubbs Quarry there is said to be a long shaft, and here, it is believed, Moses had another store, for in those days it was not advisable to have all your eggs in one basket.

So we still do not really know who Moses was, or what exactly he did, and his famous Trod and also Moses' Finger, the pillar of rock near the top of Gavel Neese, will probably always remain matters of legend. Another possible memorial is Smuggler's Chimney, a rather strenuous cleft in Gable Crag quite close to Central Gully. This chimney was first climbed about sixty years ago and was presumably given its name to commemorate the legendary Moses.

Although we will probably never know the facts about Moses and his Trod, I prefer to keep my romantic impression of this ancient route through the hills—even though it may be eyewash. I must have been along the Trod dozens of times, and I have often tried to picture a little, old quarryman brewing his whisky up in the rocks near Dubbs Quarry and taking the stuff along his track at dead of night, with one ear cocked for the excisemen, hidden, perhaps, behind a shoulder of crag. Over the shoulder of Brandreth he would go, across the head of Ennerdale and underneath Gable Crag, to his lookout point at the top of Beck Head, and then helter-skelter down the side of Gable to the Wasdale fields to cache his bottles. Or perhaps he had wadd, stolen from the Seathwaite mine and carried laboriously up to his hideout at Dubbs Quarry, or even on Gable Crag. I hope he made a good living out of it, whatever he did, for quarrymen lived a terribly hard life in those days. And I'm sure that bog-whisky brewed from the moss at the back of Fleetwith Pike would be the real McCoy.

A LAKELAND SPORTSMAN

If John Wilson had been alive today he would probably be the president of Ambleside Sports. He would also be a big man at Grasmere sports and Rydal sheepdog trials, perhaps the Master of the Coniston foxhounds and almost certainly either the Commodore of the Royal Windermere Yacht Club or a former Commodore. His name would never be out of the newspapers, and his photograph would often adorn the glossy magazines, so that to the outside world he would appear to be the very embodiment of the Lake District.

But John Wilson died more than 100 years ago, and you never hear about him today, although one old writer insisted he was 'greater, more interesting, and more lovable as a human being' than Wordsworth, Ruskin, Coleridge or Southey, and deserved to be just as long remembered for his books. Will Ritson, the famous landlord of the Wastwater Hotel, knew him well, and there could be people still alive who can remember Ritson—he died in 1890—but that is the nearest we can get to John Wilson. Even his house, 'Elleray', on the slopes of Orrest Head above Windermere, was pulled down so long ago that nobody alive will remember it. Professor John Wilson they called him—he became Professor of Moral Philosophy at Edinburgh University, acquiring the quali- fications after securing the job—and he wrote under the pseudo- nym, 'Christopher North'.

But mostly he was a man who loved life hugely and threw himself, heart and soul, into every sporting activity in the Lake District. Something like a more realistic version of the famous 'Lordy' Lonsdale, with only a hundredth part of the nobleman's fortune, but perhaps more human kindness and real love for his fellow men.

And yet John Wilson was not Lakeland-born, but was a Scots- man from Paisley, who fell in love with the district when he was an undergraduate at Oxford. He inherited £40,000 from his father, bought and enlarged a farmhouse at Orrest Head, built up the estate and used it as his base for nearly fifty years until his death in 1854. Very soon he became a leading figure in the Lake- land countryside, and his exploits quickly became the talk of the district. Tall, broad-shouldered, sunburned and energetic, he was for ever striding over the hills, hunting, fishing, riding his pony, wrestling, boxing, cock-fighting, dancing and drinking hard in the little inns.

Once, with two friends and all armed with spears, they chased a bull across the fells by moonlight, another time he was upsetting a boat on Wastwater for the fun of it, or wrestling and jumping with Will Ritson. But he loved small, defenceless creatures, and it is recorded that a sparrow that took refuge in his study was fed and cared for, and lived in the house, on and off, for more than ten years.

He was a great fisherman, a mighty hunter and always ready to take on bullies, rowdies or professional pugilists at the fairs. But he was also sought out as an after-dinner conversationalist and was a popular figure at hunt balls and county dances. He drank hard, as was the custom of the day, but was never quarrelsome, only using his strength and skill in the defence of the underdog— a sort of Lakeland Robin Hood.

He died before the foundation of the Royal Windermere Yacht Club in 1860, but he had his own fleet of yachts on the lake long before then. Indeed, he had so many sailing boats on the lake that he was known as 'The Lord High Admiral of Windermere', and he probably started the regattas that were such a feature of the district for many years. And it was Professor Wilson who presided at the annual wrestling competitions that used to be held at the old Ferry Inn on the Lancashire shore of the lake, and were really the forerunners of Grasmere sports.

Nobody knows when Cumberland and Westmorland wrestling began, but it must be 500 years old, and could be much older. Perhaps the Vikings introduced it. But John Wilson kept it alive in the early nineteenth century, and it was he who founded a wrestling academy at Ambleside, giving a championship belt and encouraging the local gentry to support the game. So that although wrestling at Ambleside has only taken on a new lease of life within the last quarter of a century, the tradition of the local sports really goes back for more than 100 years.

Wilson was a great one for practical jokes, often feigning disaster to scare his friends or telling stories of such enormity that they even outstripped those of his friend Will Ritson, who prided himself on being 'the biggest liar in England'. But he would watch all night by a sick servant's bedside or tend with his own hands a wounded dog.

The professor knew how to entertain, and on one occasion Sir Walter Scott stayed at Elleray and was fêted there on his fifty-fourth birthday. There was a glittering company of guests, including Canning, Wordsworth and the local gentry, and the professor laid on one of the most magnificent regattas that had ever been seen on Windermere, with at least fifty boats and barges in splendid procession. 'The bards of the Lakes,' stated an old account, 'led the cheers that hailed Scott and Canning; and music and sunshine, flags, streamers and gay dresses, the merry hum of voices, and the rapid splashing of innumerable oars, made up a dazzling mixture of sensations as the flotilla wound its way among the richly foliaged islands and along bays and promontories peopled with enthusiastic spectators.' You don't get goings-on like that in Lakeland nowadays.

But this materialist who never owned fewer than fifty fighting cocks was an extremely sensitive writer and a poet of some distinction. His companions, besides the sporting dalesfolk, were the Lake Poets—Hartley Coleridge, de Quincey, Wordsworth and the rest—and the literary giants of the age often travelled to Westmorland to stay for a while in his lovely house with its remarkable views across the lake. John Wilson had won the Newdigate Prize while at Oxford, and many of his poems were well received, but nobody reads them now.

One of Wilson's greatest attributes was his determination and fortitude. His happy life at 'Elleray' came to a sudden end—although he retained the house as a retreat—after he had been defrauded of much of his fortune, but he accepted the blow with stoicism and moved back to Edinburgh. Here he worked hard on the newly started *Blackwood's Magazine*, quickly carving out a new career in trenchant, hard-hitting journalism. The magazine soon became the country's leading intellectual publication, often arousing the fiercest controversies, and 'Christopher North', as he called himself, perpetrated some of his best and most bitter writing during this busy, tumultuous period. His professorship, much criticised because of his lack of theoretical knowledge, came later, but he studied his new subject and mastered it, and also took the advice of Sir Walter Scott to 'forswear sack, purge and live cleanly like a gentleman'.

Professor Wilson made no great mark in the world of philosophy, but he won the affection of thousands of students and helped to shape the lives of many public men. So that when he died they said that one of Nature's gentlemen had passed on. There are no memorials in Lakeland that I know of to John Wilson, and as a poet and writer he is forgotten, but much of our Lakeland heritage owes a great deal to this muscular Christian who loved to live life to the full. He must have been a staunch comrade, a lovable personality and a great man—the patron saint, perhaps, of Lakeland sport.

THE KESWICK ADMIRAL

Just about the time the first tourists were 'discovering' the Lake District there came to live in Keswick a remarkable man called Peter Crosthwaite, who styled himself 'Admiral of the Keswick Regatta, Keeper of the Museum, Guide, Pilot, Geographer, and

Hydrographer to the Nobility and Gentry'. In his own day Crosthwaite perhaps did as much for Keswick and the Lake District as the Abrahams were to do more than 100 years later, but for many generations now the 'Admiral' has been no more than a name in the local history books. The Abrahams have left behind them many hundreds of beautiful photographs, several books and their name on a number of rock climbs, but Peter Crosthwaite seems to be almost forgotten.

A few years ago, however, some of Crosthwaite's old maps of the principal lakes were reproduced, and a geography lecturer, Mr. William Rollinson, was able to give us some interesting notes on what was really the first accurate survey of the largest stretches of water in England. I have compared Peter Crosthwaite's maps—first published in the 1780s, and all but one of them to the scale of 3 inches to the mile—with the modern maps of the Ordnance Survey, and they are remarkably accurate. And when compared with earlier maps—and especially my earliest Lakeland map by Robert Morden in 1680—it can be seen at once that this Cumberland farmer's son must have been an extraordinary man.

Morden and most of the other map-makers who came before and after him merely roughed in the lakes as elongated ink-spots and guessed wildly at the mountains, but Crosthwaite obviously surveyed them with mathematical precision. You could use them today and not be far wrong. Crosthwaite didn't bother himself very much with roads and tracks, being more interested in the configuration of the lakes and rivers, but he did give his public something you don't get on maps today—the names of the 'gentry' owning the larger and more impressive houses, and the best 'viewpoints' in the area.

The 'Admiral' was curiously humble before his gentry—although charging them a shilling to go into his museum, as against sixpence for the 'country people'—and very keen on the 'stations' from which the tourists might view the scenery. On nearly all his maps he listed not only his own viewpoints but also those of Thomas West, who had earlier published the first guide-book to the Lakes. It was West who first encouraged the genteel tourists of the day to go about the district with one of his guides in one hand and a plano-convex mirror in the other. To look at the scenery they turned their back on the view, and studied it, as a reduced image sometimes gilded by coloured filters, from over their shoulder. A less rewarding way of enjoying the scenery can scarcely be imagined. At all events, the 'Admiral' must have made a lot of money out of boosting tourism—he sold thousands of maps at 1*s*. 6*d*. each or 9*s*. the set—and his museum flourished for more than sixty years.

Peter Crosthwaite's career was certainly unusual. He was born of farming stock at Dale Head in the Cumberland parish of Crosthwaite in 1735, served his apprenticeship as a weaver, and then turned to seafaring, serving with the East India Company. In his mid-twenties he became the master of a gunboat used by the company to protect their trading vessels from marauding Malay pirates, and it was in these distant waters that he must have learned the arts of navigation and surveying. He married a Keswick girl on his return to England, became a customs-officer in Northumberland, returned to Cumberland to settle at Naddle Beck, near Keswick, and then moved into the town square, where he opened his museum.

Earlier, in Northumberland, he had shown himself a man of imagination and mettle by inventing all sorts of curious things, from a portable bathing-machine and an improved Aeolian harp to 'a machine for saving people from fires in large towns'. It was not surprising, therefore, that when Joseph Pocklington, the owner of one of the islands on Derwentwater and a great Lakeland eccentric, thought up his scheme for a Keswick regatta with mock 'sea battles' on the lake, he chose Peter Crosthwaite as his 'Admiral'.

These Keswick regattas must have been rowdy occasions, with the hills 'echoing to an amazing variety of sounds' from the cannon and muskets, but these sort of noises were nothing new in Lakeland, for cannons were regularly discharged across Ullswater for the benefit of the tourists. According to William Gilpin, who had been searching for the picturesque in Lakeland even before West, 'the variety of awful sounds . . . have a wonderful effect on the mind, as if the very foundations of every rock on the lake were giving way, and the whole scene from some strange convulsion were falling into general ruin'. How fortunate we are that these childish pranks have long since been abandoned as

Steeple and Scoat Fell
Ennerdale Water and Anglers Crag

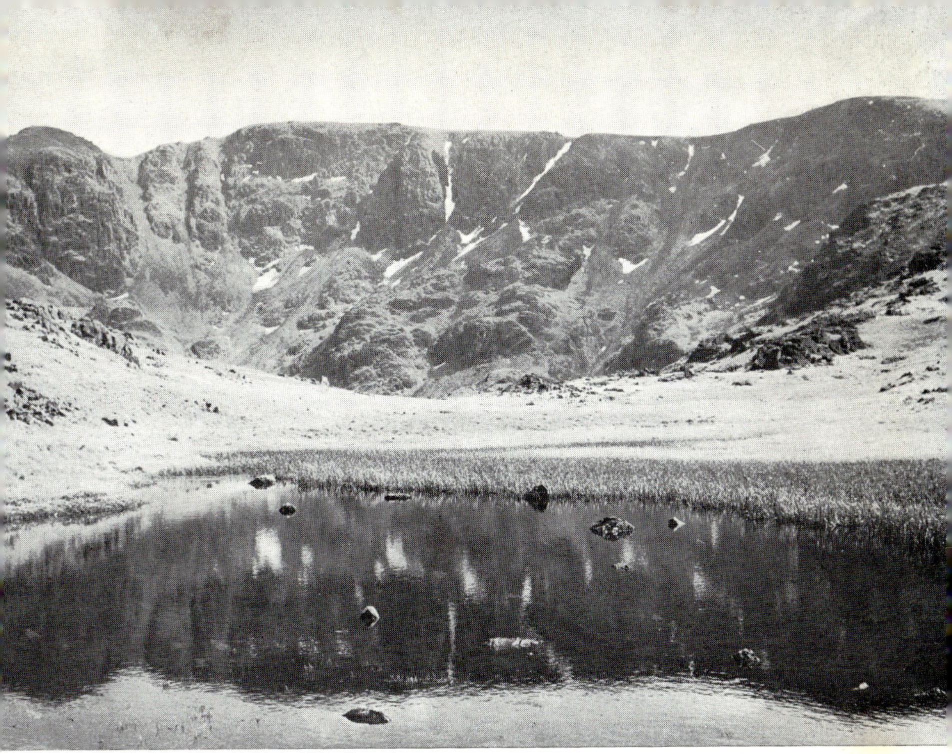

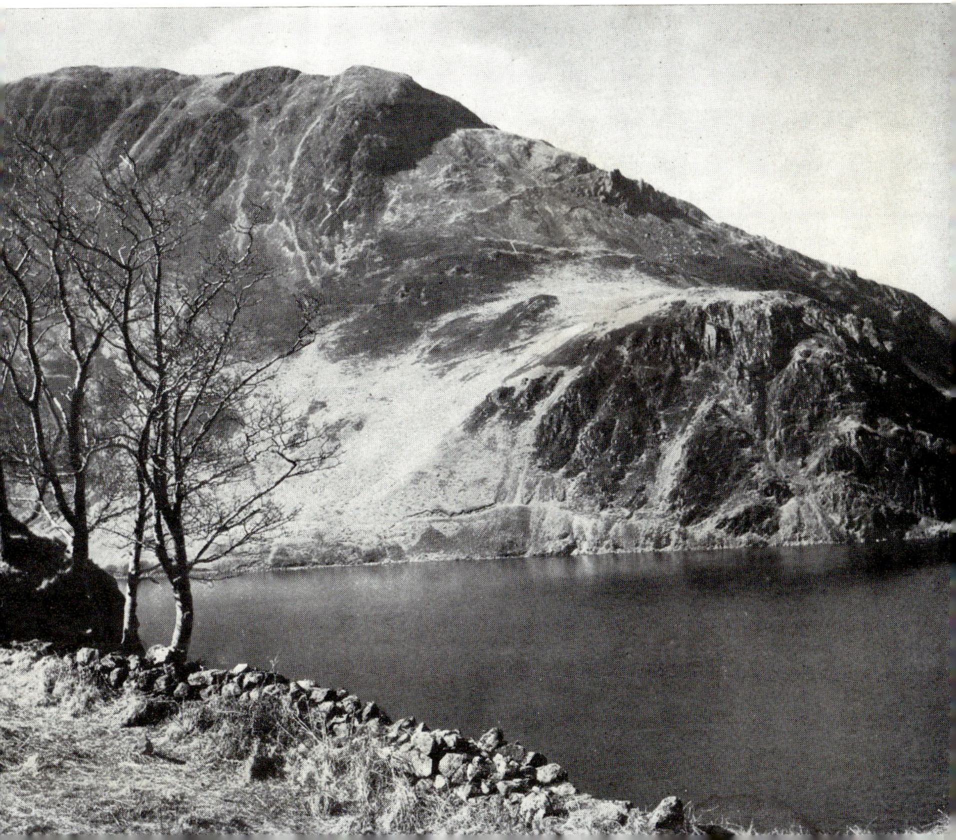

tourist attractions, although the noise of the traffic going over Kirkstone on a holiday weekend can be nearly as bad.

Crosthwaite embarked on his survey of the major lakes in order further to encourage 'the Nobility and the Gentry' to visit the Lake District, after having first lit the flame with his Keswick regattas. His other main project was his museum, which, apart from the usual attractions of minerals, coins, ornaments, musical stones and the rest, also contained Crosthwaite himself banging drums to the accompaniment of a barrel organ. The insistence upon noise at this early stage in the development of the Lake District as a tourist attraction—sea-battles and cannon-fire on the lakes and even a din in the museums—seems curious, but Crosthwaite doubtless knew his public.

He also bitterly resented opposition, so that when a second museum was opened in Keswick he brought out a handbill accusing his rival of 'low cunning' and 'mischievous falsehoods'. He also attacked James Clark, who did a second survey of the lakes, calling his book a 'shameful imposition upon the public' which would grievously harm the tourist business. But despite these irritations, Crosthwaite continued to do his best to open up the Lake District to the tourist, constructing, at his own expense, a pathway to the summit of Latrigg, surveying a route for a projected canal from Cumberland to Keswick and even pushing forward a plan to lower the level of Derwentwater by one foot so that 136 acres of land could be brought into cultivation. He claimed that in this last project he had the support of Wordsworth and Coleridge, but this seems unlikely. His maps, now available to a twentieth-century public, will no doubt become his monument.

Crosthwaite's poems, which grace several of the maps, may be dismissed as rather flowery rubbish, but the little drawings, surrounding the lake shores, are most interesting and probably— apart from his rather exaggerated mountain studies—as accurate as the maps. Most of them show the houses of the gentry he seemed so anxious to please, and by studying them we can peep backwards into the Lakeland of nearly 200 years ago.

Peter Crosthwaite, Admiral of the Keswick Regatta, deserves a place in our local history, and the old sea-dog would have been delighted to know that the descendants of his early tourists were still buying his maps in the 1970s.

H

Seat Sandal from Grasmere
Kentmere

A FAMOUS OFFCOMER

Robert Southey, who lived for forty years at Keswick in a house above the Greta and was the Poet Laureate of England before his friend Wordsworth, loved winter in Lakeland. 'The very snow,' he wrote to a friend, 'which you would perhaps think must monotonise the mountains, give new varieties; it brings out their recesses and designates all their inequalities, impresses a better feeling of their height and reflects such tints of saffron, or fawn or rose colour to the evening sun.' And again: 'The lakeside had such ten thousand charms; a fleece of snow or of the hoar frost lies on the fallen trees or large stones; the grass-points that just peer above the water, are powdered with diamonds; the ice on the margin with chains of crystal, and such veins and wavy lines of beauty as mock all art.' It was in winter when he did most of his work—'for we are as much out of the way of all society as if we were cruising at sea. From November to June not a soul do we see—except, perhaps Wordsworth, once or twice during the time.'

Although everybody has heard of Wordsworth, and the Americans descend in hundreds every year on the places associated with his life in Lakeland, not many people bother very much with Southey nowadays, or indeed with the rest of the 'Lake Poets'. There is a marble effigy near the altar in Crosthwaite Church, Keswick, where Southey worshipped for many years, and here and there in a few Lakeland homes or hotels a picture of the man, but little else. Not many Lakeland lovers could tell you what he looked like, and his memory is mostly kept alive in school-books and perhaps in a few anthologies by his extravagant 'How does the water come down at Lodore?' and his ballad 'After Blenheim'. And yet Southey was perhaps the most learned and bookish of all the Poet Laureates, worked harder than most of them and conquered difficulties that would have crushed and disheartened other men. While his descriptions of the Lakeland of 150 years ago are wonderfully expressive.

Southey was the brother-in law of Samuel Taylor Coleridge, who wrote 'The Ancient Mariner' but left Lakeland after ten years, on and off, at Greta Hall, Keswick, and spent the rest of his life in London opium haunts, dying there in 1843—the same year as Southey. It was Coleridge who persuaded the Southeys to share his Keswick home in 1803, and Southey stayed in the same house for forty years, looking after Coleridge's family as well as his own.

I once spent an evening in Greta Hall. It was then, and possibly still is, the junior girls' boarding house of Keswick School, but, unlike Wordsworth's Dove Cottage, is not open to the public. Coleridge, who moved in shortly after it was built in 1800, loved the house, but once he had started taking opium to allay the pains of gout, spent little time in Cumberland and eventually had his life and his genius ruined by the habit. He called his opium his Kendal Black Drops, probably because he first bought them in that town as a quack medicine, and it is one of the tragedies of the literary history of England that so brilliant a man should have fallen so completely under the spell of the drug. The Wordsworths and other literary people in Lakeland tried to help him, and he once started a weekly paper in the district, but it failed after twenty-seven issues. And even in his last years he was cheated by scoundrelly publishers. But Southey lived on at Greta Hall, bearing his sadnesses—the loss of children or their leaving home, the decline of his wife and his own later ill-health—with fortitude, writing hard, and playing his part in the life of the district.

He was a tall, long-legged man, with a fine head of hair—dark and curly in his youth—prominent nose and well-marked features with large brown eyes. Much of his day he spent among his fine library of books, but he took regular exercise, stepping out along the walks around Skiddaw in clogs with a book under his arm. He is said to have especially enjoyed the Applethwaite road under Skiddaw, the Brundholme woods circuit of Latrigg, the walk to Watendlath, the way to Walla Crag and Falcon Crag, and the road up Newlands. Of the scene looking across Derwentwater to the mountains on a still day, Southey wrote: 'As I stood on the shore, heaven and the clouds seemed lying underneath me; I was looking down into the sky and the whole range of mountains, having one line of summits under my feet and another above me, seemed to be suspended between the firmaments. Shut your eyes and dream of a scene so unnatural and so beautiful.'

Sometimes the poet wandered far into Lakeland. Once he went by way of Matterdale into Patterdale and then to Angle Tarn,

Haweswater and down to Brotherswater. The next day he was up
Helvellyn and Dollywaggon and down to Grasmere, and on the
third day into Langdale and home by Stake Pass—expeditions
that few people thought of tackling 150 years ago.

He also joined in the social activities of Keswick—once organis-
ing a subscription ball—and tackled such jobs as thinning the
trees in front of his windows, so that he could see more of the
lake, or bridging the Greta with stepping-stones. 'We lead as
pleasant a life as heart of man could wish,' he once wrote, but he
worked hard at his books and papers, keeping two families going,
carrying on an enormous correspondence and befriending struggling poets and other unknowns.

He seems to have planned his days carefully, fretting on his
short journeyings away to get home, and enjoying both the
comforts of his family circle and the claims of his social world.
His exercise was taken to keep himself fit, for he was not a country-
man in the same sense as was Wordsworth and spent long hours
among his books, whereas Wordsworth preferred to compose his
poetry out of doors.

Southey was probably Keswick's most famous 'offcomer', for
forty years residence in Lakeland—even in those days—did not
qualify one to be a local. He had been born in Bristol, where his
father was an unsuccessful linen draper, and later lived with an
aunt in Bath. After attendance at an academy run by a broken-
down tradesmen he worked hard at his books—Spenser, Sidney,
Pope's Homer, his Latin and his Greek—and later went to
Westminster School, from which he was expelled for criticising a
flogging prefect in the school magazine. Eventually he went to
Balliol, where he made many influential friends, although all he
learned at Oxford, he used to say, was some swimming and boating.
He wrote his epic poem, 'Joan of Arc', when he was only 18,
refused to take Holy Orders, tried to learn medicine, but found he
didn't like it, fell in love, lived in Portugal for a time and returned
to study law.

But he was as little interested in the law as in medicine, and,
instead, wrote his second great poem 'Madoc'. For a time he lived
among the literary men of the age in London and elsewhere,
sometimes from hand to mouth, until the invitation from Coleridge to come to Keswick, where his real life began. He never

recovered from the loss of his first wife, although he married again, and his later years were clouded by a brain disease. Then he caught a fever, and the end came in March 1843.

Wordsworth and a son-in-law were the only strangers present in Crosthwaite Churchyard at the funeral held on a cloudy day— but one which was brightened, it is said, by a ray of sunshine that touched the grave. You can see Wordsworth's epitaph on the marble effigy. Southey's *Life of Nelson* is still read by those who appreciate stylish writing, although many of his other works are now forgotten.

But the Lodore Hotel, next to the famous fall, perhaps owes quite a lot to this quiet man who loved the beauties of nature. In his 'The Cataract of Lodore' the Poet Laureate needed fifty-one lines—without a single full stop—and 122 separate descriptions to tell us exactly how the water came down. It is a masterpiece of observation, imagination and ingenuity:

> . . . and flapping and rapping and clapping and slapping,
> And curling and whirling and purling and twirling,
> And thumping and plumping and bumping and jumping,
> And dashing and flashing and splashing and clashing . . .
> All at once and all o'er with a mighty uproar,
> And this way the water comes down at Lodore.

You will not often see Lodore like this, but when you do, remember this sad, sensitive man who loved the Lakeland hills 150 years ago, and was able to describe them with such accuracy and affection.

THE LONELY SHEPHERD

For forty-seven years a Lakeland shepherd, Pearson Dalton, lived alone with his dogs, his goats and his cat in the loneliest house in England, 1,600 feet up in the fells at the back of Skiddaw. His job was to look after more than 1,000 sheep roaming the eastern and northern slopes of Skiddaw, and his home, for nearly half a century, was Skiddaw House, a former shooting box belonging to Lord Leconfield, which is nearly 4, very rough, mountain miles from the nearest habitation.

During all these years Pearson, a stoutly independent dalesman who never married, looked after himself in his primitive quarters, with only his animals and his little battery radio set for company —often cut off in winter by gales, blizzards and deep snowdrifts, with a winding mountain track his only link with the outside world.

But towards the end of 1969 his employer, fearing that if the old shepherd were to become ill or die he could be without help for days, decided compulsorily to retire him, and one November day Pearson reluctantly locked the door of Skiddaw House for the last time and left his lonely home for good. For the last time, too, he made his way over the trackless fells to his sister's home at Fellside, near Caldbeck—a mountain journey of 7 or 8 miles he knew more intimately than any other man. Every Saturday for forty-seven years he had made the same journey to spend his weekend in the comparative civilisation of a lonely fellside hamlet, and every Monday morning he walked back over the fells to Skiddaw House and his workaday week. But now he was to spend his retirement at his sister's home—a retirement pleasantly sprinkled with a bit of foxhunting and trips to Keswick. He did not know whether he would ever see Skiddaw House again.

A friend of mine, Mr. E. H. Kirby, a retired bank manager living in Keswick and an inveterate mountain walker, called to see Pearson Dalton as he was packing up his few possessions for his journey into retirement. On the way up the mountain track Mr. Kirby met Mr. Billy Porter, the young farmer from Mirkholme, near Bassenthwaite village, who was bringing down Pearson's furniture and bedding in his jeep. In a sack on the floor of the jeep was Pearson's cat, then 13 years old, on her way to spent her last days at Mirkholme, where his nannie goat—rumoured to be 22 years old—had already taken up residence. The billy goat and two kids had died fairly recently, so that Pearson was left with his five dogs, who were to walk back with him on the familiar trek over the fells.

Inside the house Pearson was 'tidying up' for the last time and chatted with Mr. Kirby about his lonely half-century up in the hills. He went to Skiddaw House in 1922 to look after the sheep on a month's trial, stayed for forty-seven years and saw no reason for retiring. At one time, he recalled, he used to do the journey to Fellside in two hours, but recently it had been taking him two and a half hours. One recent Monday—a terribly wild day—he had decided, unusually for him, that the conditions were bad enough for him to postpone his return until the Tuesday, but this did not happen very often. Mr. Kirby told me at the time that he understood Skiddaw House would be closed down, as the farmer at Mirkholme had taken over the flock of sheep. 'It will now be a ghost house,' he commented.

Skiddaw House, originally a shooting box, is really three cottages joined together. There was a bath and toilet and rather simple sleeping accommodation, and Pearson had installed some furniture. He had some rather tattered old books and his old radio set and a comfortable old sofa covered in sacking. Lighting was by an oil lamp, but he always kept a good coal fire. The goats were kept in a shed, but the dog and the cats slept indoors. At one time milk was brought regularly to the house, but for some time Pearson had been making do with tinned milk. There is a shelter belt of trees around Skiddaw House—the only trees for miles.

Pearson Dalton at the age of 75 in 1969 was still a fine-looking dalesman, tall, upright, with a healthy complexion and obviously, despite his age, a very fit man. In a sense he had been the twentieth-century hermit of Skiddaw, although he always retained his weekly association with the outside world.

The real 'Skiddaw hermit' was George Smith, a Scotsman, who died nearly 100 years ago. He lived in a sort of wickerwork 'nest' on a ledge of rock in the gill above Dancing Gate farm on Dodd at the western end of Skiddaw. Smith was an unusual man, with a cultured background, who went hatless and barefoot, wearing tattered clothes, a shaggy mane and a bristling beard. He earned a living by painting portraits in oils and water-colours, and I dare say there are still examples of his work scattered about the district, their origins perhaps unknown to their owners. His lonely life came to an end in a Scottish hospital after he had set out on foot to visit the land of his birth.

But Pearson Dalton, a real Lakeland dalesman, is unlikely to leave the district, and when I last heard of him in 1970 was enjoying his retirement. After cheerfully tackling the loneliest job in England for nearly half a century it seemed to me at the time that he had earned it.

THE FINSTHWAITE PRINCESS

Nearly 200 years ago there died in the little wooded hamlet of Finsthwaite, near the toe of Windermere, a mysterious young woman 'with wondrously fair hair'. And ever since then the local folk have been arguing about whether she was really the daughter of Bonnie Prince Charlie and, at one time, perhaps a claimant to the throne of England. Finsthwaite has its hilltop tower, a monument to naval victories in Nelson's day, but probably nothing very exciting had happened there until the 'Princess' arrived in 1745—just after the Prince passed through Kendal—and perhaps nothing much has happened there since.

The 'Princess'—a fair-haired and good-looking child—arrived with two servants and went to live in seclusion in Waterside House. She died in 1771 and was buried in the name of Clementine Johannes Sobieski Douglass. It was said she ordered that no tombstone or epitaph should be placed over her grave, and for more than a century her resting place was unmarked. I believe the present romantic story has only been in circulation for fifty or sixty years, and the uncharitable might suggest that it was put out to attract visitors to the area. Certainly it put Finsthwaite on the map and encouraged much scholarly research in many quarters. I am not qualified either to confirm the story or to tell Finsthwaite it has been hoaxed, for this would require endless research, but my inclination is to allow the legend to continue.

For, true or not, it is a good story, and there seems no harm in wondering how much truth there could be in it. The story is that the mysterious young woman was the illegitimate daughter of Bonnie Prince Charlie, by his mistress Clementina Walkinshaw. The two middle names are Polish, and Prince Charles' mother was Princess Sobieski of Poland. Prince Charles Edward is known to have used the name Douglass when he was travelling incognito.

The Finsthwaite 'Princess' is said in one old account to have been 24 when she died, but according to other records she had lived in the hamlet for twenty-six years and was an infant when she arrived. Prince Charles Edward and Clementina, his mistress, were both born in 1720, which could fit in with the theory that their daughter was an infant twenty-five years later. It was also being said, at the beginning of the present century, that the 'Princess' was the daughter of another mistress of Prince Charles—his cousin Princess de Talmond, who was born Jablonoffski—another Polish name. Princess Clementina Sobieski, the mother of Prince Charles Edward, was the daughter of the King of Poland and a godmother of Clementina Walkinshaw.

The Lancashire historian, Belle Halliwell of Preston, has claimed there is still no positive evidence to substantiate the story that the mysterious woman buried at Finsthwaite was indeed an illegitimate daughter of Bonnie Prince Charlie, and in support of this she produced, a few years ago, a further interesting point. Apparently, when Prince Charles Edward died in 1788 his daughter 'Charlotte' was with him. This daughter, said Mrs. Halliwell, was a former illegitimate daughter whose birth he had legalised. She was later created Duchess of Albany, and her mother, it was claimed, was Clementina Walkinshaw.

This would not have prevented another illegitimate daughter appearing in Finsthwaite, but, apparently, the Prince had declared he never had any other children. If this is true, the Finsthwaite 'Princess' was not his child. Realists argue that the Finsthwaite 'Princess' was nothing more than a delicate or weak-minded girl, boarded out in the country because she was an embarrassment to her parents. But the name, with all its associations, is not easy to explain away. When the 'Princess' was buried there was at first, as I have said, no tombstone, but later a headstone was put up bearing the words, 'Behold Thy King Cometh' and her name. And later still the late Canon C. G. Townley wrote on the subject in the Finsthwaite parish magazine, and the legend grew.

One interesting point, perhaps not generally known, is that the will of the former owner of Waterside Farm, Finsthwaite—on the Rusland Road from the Swan Hotel—was witnessed in 1770 by Clementina Douglass and James Douglass. But who was this James Douglass? All we do know is that the church sexton, tidying up the graves in the churchyard when the church was rebuilt, is said to have disturbed an adjoining grave 100 or more years ago. And as he dug he unearthed, so they say, a lock of pale gold hair.

This is all I know about the story—a story which dates back to the time of Culloden and could have finished in a sleepy corner of Lakeland. Some day, perhaps, an historian may unearth all the facts and probably blow all the romance away. But in the meantime, while not swallowing the story, I'll put it down as just another quaint mystery of the fell country.

A CHANGED VALLEY

*For 200 years beautiful Borrowdale, threaded by the
lovely Derwent and crowded with woodland and waterfalls, has been a paradise for the walker but—in spite of its
score of crags—the Cinderella of the Lake District valleys
for the rock climber until about thirty years ago. The
climbers who came to Borrowdale before the war were
mostly on their way to better things on the great cliffs of
Scafell, Pillar and Gable, and few bothered themselves
with the handful of climbs on the rather vegetatious, low-
lying crags they could see peeping through the trees alongside the road through the dale. There were then only
about thirty climbs in the valley, and although a few
were worthwhile routes, the others seemed hardly attractive
except for the occasional 'off day'. But within a generation
everything has changed, for Borrowdale now has more than
300 climbing routes of all standards, ranging from
beginners' practice climbs to challenging lines up overhanging rock, demanding the most up-to-date technique
and skill, and the valley has become one of the country's
major climbing centres. The man who did most of the
pioneering was the late Bentley Beetham, the remarkable
schoolmaster who also climbed on Everest and spent
fifteen of his later years working out nearly 100 routes in the
most unlikely places—sending down tons of loose rock,
vegetation and even sawn-off trees in the process. His
successors have been young men from Keswick and farther
afield, who, within recent years, have pushed exploration of
the steepest crags to somewhere approaching finality; and
the latest guide to the area recorded another 100 severe
climbs within the past ten years. And these pioneers have
not only made new routes but have developed a new climbing trend—the attraction of steep rock within easy reach of
the car rather than the lure of the mountains. Almost
another sport, but tremendously challenging.*

7

Gaps in the Hills

THE OLDEST HIGHWAY

They say the wild geese and swans on their way south from the frozen north first discovered the gap through the hills that has been known for something like 1,000 years as Dunmail Raise. Almost certainly this ancient road that used to wind up the fellside above Grasmere—nowadays it sweeps up—and drops steeply down into Cumberland on the other side is the oldest highway in the Lake District. But it is nothing like the quiet coach road I remember as a boy.

My earliest memory of Dunmail Raise is of being thrown over the handlebars of my bicycle on the Thirlmere side nearly fifty years ago. I can clearly remember the bumps and the gravelly surface, but no cars came along while I dusted myself down and tried to straighten out my front wheel, for Lakeland was a different place in those days. Picture postcards still advertised Dunmail Raise as quite a test for either walkers or motor cars, but today you can zoom over the summit in comfort and safety at 50 miles an hour or more—but see less of the scenery.

Since my first trip over the pass—on a youthful cycle marathon from Barrow to Keswick and back—I must have been over Dunmail hundreds of times, at all seasons and at all hours of the day and night, and despite the changes of recent years, I still have an affection for this historic highway. As I write (in early 1970) the sheep still crop the sweet fell grass on either side of the road and wander across the tarmac when you least expect them, but soon this hazard to sheep and motorists may be removed. In

Wordsworth's day the road climbed up from Grasmere 'in mazes serpentine', as he put it, and the sheep were never in any danger. But now that the climb has been widened and straightened out, so that the traffic may be unhindered, the sheep slaughter has become serious and the farmers are rightly unfuriated.

The obvious solution might have appeared, at first sight, to be the fencing of the highway, but the top part of the fell is common land—part of Lord Lonsdale's commons, leased to the National Trust—and commons are not normally fenced in the Lake District. Fencing, too, would take away the impression of open space and wildness that you still sense when you cross the moorland, but sheep are important, and a sensible solution had to be reached. One of the complications seemed to be that not only were the sheep at greater risk because of the encouragement of faster motoring but also because the new highway itself, with its handsome verges of short, sweet grass, was proving a welcome attraction to the animals. They were crossing the unfenced commons and then straying farther and farther down the pass, grazing on the succulent verges, within feet of the speeding traffic, as they went. Negotiations proved protracted and even vehement, but eventually an arrangement of cattle grids was being discussed—a course which had always seemed sensible, although, apparently, not as straightforward as might have been supposed, for financial reasons.

There are many lengths of unfenced moorland traversed by motor roads in and around the Lake District, but perhaps none so widely used by traffic as Dunmail Raise. The cattle grids on Orton Moor seem to serve their purpose, and although you still meet sheep on the tarmac there, they can usually be avoided without difficulty. The sheep go to sleep in the roadway on Wrynose and Hardknott, and you have to be careful driving over these passes at night, but nobody would suggest that this highway should be fenced.

By now, perhaps, on Dunmail the planned dual carriageway sweeps past King Domhnall's cairn on the summit,* and much of the romance has disappeared from this lonely gap in the hills. Only the sweep of Seat Sandal and Steel Fell still remains—this, and the sight on summer days, as you breast the top and look

* This project has now been shelved. August 1970.

down into Cumberland, of the sunlight on Skiddaw. But the old cairn that marks a battle of long, long ago will still be there. The Battle of Dunmail Raise is said to have taken place about 1,000 years ago. Domhnall, son of Owain, was the King of Cumbria, and legend has it that he chose the site, 'where river runs north or south with the storm', for his battle with King Edmund of England, following a meeting with a wizard in Gilsland Forest. The Saxons invaded from the south and joined battle on the pass with the Cumbrians, who at first drove them down the hill. But later they were attacked by treacherous allies of the English, who surrounded Dunmail and slew him as he called his warriors around him for their last stand.

But the knights of the Cumbrian king carried away his crown lest it should fall into the hands of the Saxons, fought a rearguard action up the rocky beck towards Grisedale Tarn, evaded their pursuers in the mists and cast the crown into the depths of the tarn—'until Dunmail come again to lead us'. And every year, they say, the warriors come back to the tarn, draw up the crown and carry it over Seat Sandal back to the pass where the king is still sleeping beneath the pile of stones. They knock with their spears on the cairn, but each time the king replies from his tomb, 'Not yet, my warriors, not yet.'

That, or one of the many versions of it, is the legend, but the truth is not nearly so romantic. The historians say there was indeed a battle on this spot in 945 or 946, when the King of Cumbria was defeated by Edmund of England, but Dunmail was taken prisoner and lived for another thirty years, dying at last in Rome, where he had gone on a pilgrimage. But the heap of stones on the summit has been there for centuries, and the story has been handed down through the long history of Cumbria. And when Manchester came to Thirlmere to build their dam they got their navvies to rebuild the old cairn, and it is still there, and now, presumably, will always remain—a little bit of history surrounded by tarmacadam and passed every day by hundreds of motorists who perhaps neither know or care.

'Nowt good,' they used to say in Westmorland, 'ever comes ower t'Raise', but down the centuries a great stream of travellers has passed this way—the monks, the miners, the wool merchants, pedlars and poets, all going about their business on foot, on horseback, by four-in-hand; and today the tourists drawing their caravans behind them. It was a turnpike road at one time, and you paid your toll at Town Head on the Grasmere side, while some of the coachmen's tales of the crossing have gone down into local history. Not many packhorse pones came this way—mostly they went over Wrynose and Hardknott—but for generations before the motor charabanc first rattled over the pass the highway was used by the carriers, the farmers' carts and the Royal Mail. And when the railways came there still remained this gap of 21 miles between Windermere and Keswick; and the road has become the most important highway through Lakeland, although today, in places, it degenerates at times to a speed track and elsewhere, at holiday time—before the widening—a slow choking funnel blocked with crawling vehicles.

In winter time, since it is steeply pitched, especially on the Westmorland side, the pass is sometimes blocked by snow or skidding vehicles, although not so often as the Shap fells road, and perhaps the new alignment will bring about an improvement here. Certainly we will get used to the new road in time, but many will still sigh for the more leisurely days when Dunmail Raise had about it an atmosphere of the past and visitors sent home postcards of the pass to show the sort of exciting places they had seen. Within my memory the old road had been widened and 'improved' in several places before the last reconstruction, and you could see, here and there, where an even older road must have gone. In the old days, before my time, the coachmen used to get their more active passengers to get down and walk the steep bits, and you used to be able to see where the roadway was scratched and scored by the skid-pans of descending carriages. There's an old mine tunnel underneath Sea Sandal and, across the pass, the Lion and the Lamb on Helm Crag—one of the sights of the district in Victorian days. In summertime the head of the pass becomes a wayside halt for campers, caravanners and motor cars, but so far it has escaped the indignity of a café and toilets. Maybe some of these things will come one day and a little more of the magic be swept away.

The pass, which is crossed by the county boundary, is a remarkable divider of the weather. Many times you drive up the Westmorland side in mist and rain to see blue skies over Skiddaw and Blencathra and cloud shadows chasing across the hills. And sometimes you drive up out of a rain-soaked Cumberland to see sunshine sparkling on the fields around Grasmere. Crossing the pass in either direction you see a completely new scene unfolded below you—the pastoral peace of the vale of Grasmere, dotted with farms and woodlands, and, on the other side, the long sweep alongside Thirlmere with Helvellyn rising steeply on the right and the ridges of Skiddaw and Blencathra straight ahead.

I was on top of the pass one weekend searching for skiable snow on a rather miserable day of dark clouds and drizzle. The upper slopes of Seat Sandal, seen dimly through the mist, looked a likely sort of place, and so we slogged up there in the rain, not very hopeful, but willing to give the weather a chance. And, high up the fellside, the drizzle stopped and, a moment later, there was a tiny vent of blue sky above Steel Fell. Within minutes a fresh breeze out of the west had swept the clouds away, so that below us we had long slopes of sunlit snow, with the road over the pass just a thin black ribbon across the gleaming white, and not a soul in sight.

TOUGH MOTORING

Slithering cautiously down Hardknott Pass one sunlit morning, just above the highest nasty hairpin on the Eskdale side, I saw a rather decrepit motor car perhaps 20 yards ahead suddenly pitch over the edge and somersault through the air down a vertical, rocky ravine. It landed among the boulders with a shattering crash and burst into flames. Fortunately there was nobody inside the motor car, and it all turned out to be merely part of a film. The vehicle's magnificently parabolic passage through the air and its crunching arrival at the foot of the gorge was being shot by a languid young man in a Norwegian sweater and yellow sandals, and several important-looking executives wearing bow ties and horn-rimmed spectacles were running perspiringly through the bracken in great excitement. Later I saw the film and noted that the frightful holocaust had taken place on the border near Gretna Green. They were only about 50 miles out.

This is the sort of thing that Hardknott takes in its stride. For something odd is always happening on Hardknott Pass—the

High Street

toughest bit of well-surfaced motoring road in the north of England, and perhaps the most formidable piece of tilted highway in the country. Certainly Hardknott is much worse than anything encountered on any of the motorable roads through the Highlands, including the very highest of them. The road from Glen Shee to Braemar, which reaches a height of 2,199 feet at the Cairnwell Pass, has only one double hairpin—the Devil's Elbow—and this should not tax the ambitious learner-driver who's had a few lessons. Even heavy coaches go over, skidding in winter between 10-feet-high banks of snow. But Hardknott has about half a dozen double hairpins on each side, and to attain its modest 1,291 feet high summit you should know how to drive. The Lecht road (2,090 feet) between Tomintoul and Braemar has no terrors, except when—as frequently happens—it is blocked by snow; and even the famous Bealach nam Bo ('The Pass of the Cattle') between Tornapress and Applecross is not so technically difficult for the motorist as Hardknott, although the last time I went over it was not so well surfaced. And all the other Scottish roads regularly traversed by motor vehicles are relatively straightforward, although there may be some brutes in the Outer Isles unknown to me. The highest road in Britain—private in its upper reaches—climbs to the 2,780-feet-high summit of Great Dun Fell in the Northern Pennines, but this is an easy ascent and so is the new skiers' road on Cairngorm.

I claim no expert knowledge of Wales, but remember in the early days of the last war taking part in a junior officers' 'toughening course' in the more mountainous sections of the principality. On one occasion we covered, on motor cycles, what was described to us as the worst bits of some international trials route, including the well-known Bwlch y Groes. The only difficulties we experienced were those of breathing, since we had to wear gas-masks, but I saw nothing through my clouding eyepieces that in any way resembled Hardknott Pass.

Nowadays I go over Hardknott in a smallish car perhaps twenty times a year, and used to drive regularly over the pass—and the neighbouring Wrynose Pass—before the war. In those days the surface was poor and after heavy storms became even worse and sometimes resembled a boulder-strewn river bed. But somehow or another we used to get up and down in our little cars. During

I

Quarries on Honister Crag

the war the passes were completely wrecked by tank exercises, but some years ago they were repaired by the three different road authorities in Cumberland, Westmorland and Lancashire—with three different surfaces. Lakes Urban District Council, for instance, used stretches of concrete on parts of the Westmorland side of Wrynose and came in for considerable criticism from the amenity watch-dogs as a result. But the twin passes are wearing well, and both sides of Cumberland's Hardknott are as well surfaced as many an important thoroughfare.

But Hardknott is still winding and steep—one in four, according to the signs at the foot, but possibly even steeper in places. There is the poignant story of the unfortunate driver of a huge Pickford's lorry—the sort of thing which blocks the traffic on busy thorough-fares. He was driving south from Whitehaven and somehow found himself at the entrance to Eskdale. When he asked a local the way to Lancaster or Manchester the farmer, either in ignorance or malice, pointed straight up the valley towards Hardknott, and, once committed to the climb, the lorry-driver had no alternative but to go on. Six times, it was said, he had to back and wriggle to get round the first hairpin, and the same process had to be repeated at almost every corner. Arrived at the top, with his arms almost wrenched out of their sockets through hauling on the heavy wheel, the driver contemplated the precipitous descent with horror, but, perhaps half an hour later, managed to reach Cockley Beck without going over the edge, although completely exhausted and in a furious temper. But his ordeal was not yet over, for he found he could not squeeze his huge juggernaut through either of the two farm gates which lay athwart the road down Dunner-dale. Before he could get through he had to take down each of the heavy gates in turn—and then replace them—and in one case it was said he had to take down a short section of wall as well—and then build it up again. Long before he reached the Travellers' Rest at Ulpha he was fervently praying he would never see the Lake District again.

I once met on the side of Hardknott the driver of a motor vehicle which I could not identify. It was a newish-looking, solidly built van without a name on the bonnet. As we stood smoking in the afternoon sunshine he told me that the vehicle was on the 'secret list' and was, in fact, the prototype of a new model which would, he said, practically cause a revolution when it came on the market. His job, he explained, was to drive it over Hardknott and Wrynose—and some of the worst roads in the North of England—every day and, in fact, the car went over these passes three times every day. There were three drivers on the job, and they took it in turns, so that the car was being driven more or less continuously throughout each twenty-four hours. I think he said they were doing this for a fortnight—or it might have been a month—and then they were going to take it for a fortnight or so on to the paved roads in Belgium. When it had had the worst pounding that any vehicle could possibly endure it was to be taken back to the research centre, where every nut and bolt, gear and shaft would be examined microscopically for wear by expert engineers. I asked him why Hardknott had been chosen for the tests. 'Because,' he said, 'this is the toughest bit of road in the north of England, and perhaps in the whole country.' When I pressed him further—and by this time he probably knew as much about Hardknott as anybody—he told me that in his opinion the stiffest bit of the whole route—and therefore perhaps the stiffest in the country—was the very first steep section and corner on the Cockley Beck side going up. This is the place where the wise motorist gets into bottom gear and stays there until he is near the top.

There are no particular tricks about climbing Hardknott—you can get up in the smallest car if you take it carefully. Hearses go over regularly. The secret, I think, is to keep the revs at a nice speed—but not too fast, for this will give you wheel spin on the corners, and you will thereby lose traction. Take the corners as wide as possible—if you cut them close you will find them even steeper than one in four.

A few years ago a sporting gentleman of 83 wrote asking whether I thought he and his companion, who was a year or two younger, could get over the pass in an old, long-wheel-base Alvis. The ambition of their lives, he explained, was to see Hardknott Fort, but for sixty years they had been constantly thwarted. I thought they could do it and wrote telling them so, but unfortunately, after vanquishing Wrynose in fine style, they were defeated half-way up the Hardknott zigzags. 'The car could have done it,' wrote the gallant old gentleman, 'but not the driver.' However, the following year I had the pleasure of driving them over and taking them around the fort.

Any day in summer you will find drivers in difficulties on Hardknott—sometimes because they have not changed down soon enough, and now and again through fright. Sometimes a car goes over the edge and down the fellside, but the number of serious accidents is remarkably low. The farm-tractor at Cockley Beck is quite often in demand by people who have, voluntary or otherwise, taken to the bracken. The Eskdale side of the pass was 'improved' a few years ago so that there is now more room to pass, although the corners are as steep as ever. The number of gates annoyingly across the route from Ambleside to Eskdale has also been reduced from five to two, one having been taken away, another replaced by a cattle grid and a third generally left open. But the old man still sits on his bench beside the gate at Fell Foot, carefully closing it after each car goes through, even if the next vehicle is only 50 yards away. A pleasant enough way, perhaps, to earn an honest copper.

The Romans took a slightly different way over Hardknott than the line of the present road, but this exciting piece of English highway has changed very little—except in surface—from the smuggling days when Lanty Slee and his friends carried their contraband over the pass and had their nightly scuffles with the excisemen.

THE SMUGGLERS' WAY

For thousands of year the passes of Wrynose and Hardknott, in some form or another, have been a walkers' short cut through the hills. Today they have degenerated into a testing place for motor cars. Of course the modern road over the passes provides much the most convenient way from Westmorland into Eskdale and the Cumberland coast, but I do wish clumsy, novice drivers would keep off these twisting hills and learn to drive on less steep gradients.

It is about twenty-three years now since these passes were 'improved' and reopened to vehicular traffic following their closing during the war so that drivers of Bren gun-carriers could go about their lawful occasions in peace and quiet. Wrynose Pass was not closed to civilian traffic until March 1945, by which time the need for Bren gun-carriers had diminished considerably, but the public had been moaning at the Ministry of War Transport for at least, two years before that. When the Bren gun-carriers had finished with Wrynose the road was in no better fettle than when the Brigantes went this way, and in places it looked as if it had been bombed. But the Government paid for the whole work of reconstruction.

The estimate of the Lakes Urban District Council for the work, which began in the autumn of 1946, was £4,556, but in the end they spent about £500 less than this—a reversal of the usual story in these days of rising costs. In a way, it seemed a pity that the money saved could not have been used for the repair of the summit section. This was not touched—until about fifteen years ago—as it was not supposed to have been damaged by the young soldiers of the Keswick Army Driving and Maintenance School.

While the Westmorland authority were repairing their side of Wrynose, the Lancashire and Cumberland authorities were tackling the other side and Hardknott Pass, and the result did not suggest there had been much collusion. Cumberland plumped for a tarmacadam surface over the one-in-four gradients of Hardknott, Lancashire temporised with a loose, gravelly surface, while Westmorland went all out for stretches of concrete which gave their section of the road something of the appearance of a long strip of toothpaste. And in between the Lancashire and Westmorland sections there was this 'no man's land' on Wrynose summit which had a surface like a rocky river bed. The situation had its humorous side. Somewhere on the Lancashire side, I think it was, you passed a notice—although I suppose you shouldn't—which read 'Road Unfit for Motor Cars'. You then continued on to the summit of Wrynose, where you came upon several more notices (erected by another authority) which instructed you to engage bottom gear, take the greatest care and so on.

I don't know who drove the first car over these two passes, but he must have been quite a bold man, for even in my younger days it could be quite an exciting journey around those loose, rocky hairpins. I believe that a car went over the two passes from

Ambleside to Eskdale with a Kendal photographer on board at
the end of the last century. In those days, or perhaps later, cars
for this sort of work were fitted with a contraption at the back
which could be lowered to assist the brakes if you missed your
gear or the car conked out on a nasty gradient.

We can only guess the age of these old roads. More than 2,000
years ago—long before the Romans—the wild hunters in these
hills knew Wrynose and Hardknott as their only way east and
west through the mountains. Perhaps the fishermen from the
Duddon estuary would meet the shepherds from the Ambleside
grazing lands and the iron smelters and spear makers from the
woods of Yewdale and Hawkshead along the road. And there
would be battles up there in the hills, high above the dancing
waters of the Brathay.

It was the Roman engineers who developed the road and made
it part of their great highway from the ports of West Cumberland
to Ambleside, Kendal and the south or over the fells east of
Windermere to the fertile Eden valley. Perhaps they did not
follow the exact line of the present road, for it has even changed
slightly in my memory, but the route must have been substantially
the same. So that the trade caravans to and from the old port of
Ravenglass could be guarded, the Romans built stations or forts
along its length, and today you can still see the remains of the
Hardknott fort, and another in fields at Ambleside, while there
was probably a third, south of Kendal, nestling in a crook of the
River Kent.

But the Wrynose road did not die with the Romans, but rather
grew in importance, all goods for export going by this steep ladder
through the fells, to be later sold by barter for goods from Bristol
and the southern ports. This was also the smugglers' route and
most of the old tales of Wrynose are tales of the packhorse days,
of laden ponies, their hooves tied with straw, trotting over the
passes at night and desperate men creeping through the bracken.
At Fell Foot, on the Westmorland side of the pass, stood the last
house on the road, and it was in this lonely spot—formerly an inn
—that the smuggling men used to meet to exchange stories and
contraband. Behind this old house, which carried the arms of
Fletcher Fleming over the door, you will find a curious terraced
mound. Historians say that here, on the main highroad east to

west and at the meeting place of passes to the north and south, the Viking settlers used to meet for their parliament.

The Three Shires Stone is supposed to mark the point on the summit of Wrynose where the three counties meet, but the actual intersection is, I think, some little distance away, and the stone is more correctly a Lancashire boundary mark. It is said that there used to be three stones at the exact point and that you could contrive to be in the three counties at once by placing your feet on two of the stones and your hands on the third. The Lancashire boundary runs along the River Brathay to its source on the summit and then, a short distance farther on, along one of the sources of the Duddon. Cumberland and Westmorland are separated by the indeterminate ridge which drops down from Pike o' Blisco.

Wrynose Pass is one of the most picturesque ladders into the clouds in England—especially on the Westmorland side. It climbs the steep fellside, for all the world like a corner of the Khyber Pass, with magnificent views of the Langdale Pikes to the right and the gullies of Great Carrs and the Coniston fells to the left. And to descend the pass on a peaceful summer's evening, with the sunlight still glinting on Little Langdale Tarn far below and thoughts of a long cool drink in the village inn, can be—even for the motorist—a pleasant ending to a day in the hills.

THE HIGHEST PASS

Every year thousands of people walk over the fells from Langdale to Wasdale or Borrowdale—or in the opposite direction—and believe they have been over Esk Hause, the highest pass in Lakeland. But while I would not want to shatter any illusions, it is almost certain they have neither been over Esk Hause nor over Lakeland's highest pass, but have crossed a lower pass, which, although it must be the most trodden mountain highway in the district and has been in use for 1,000 years, still has no name. Let me say at once that whenever I go this way I always say I am going over 'Esk Hause', for it would take too long to explain myself otherwise—but at least I know that this is inaccurate.

To thousands of Lakeland visitors—and to residents, as well— Esk Hause is the highest point of the track between Angle Tarn and Sprinkling Tarn and is marked by a low, ruinous wall-shelter in the form of a cross. Ever since people began to walk the Lakeland fells, perhaps 200 years ago, they have stopped at this point on their way up Scafell Pike, or on their way from one valley to another, to eat their sandwiches, get their wind or admire the view, and for centuries before that the shepherds and the foxhunters did the same thing. The place has always been loosely known as 'Esk Hause', and for generations has had a reputation for being a nasty place in misty weather; but the real Esk Hause is not traversed on the walk between Langdale and Borrowdale, is at least 300 yards away, more than 100 feet higher and a different pass altogether.

The real Esk Hause, the highest pass in Lakeland at 2,490 feet, is the gap between Esk Pike and Great End, and runs almost at right angles to the popular highway. It is the pass between Eskdale and Borrowdale, but is not used to anything like the extent of the misnamed 'Esk Hause'. The maps of the Ordnance Survey have always shown the pass in the correct place, and the energetic M. J. B. Baddeley of the famous *Thorough Guides*, who died more than sixty years ago, got it all right—but generations of fell-walkers have generally got it all wrong. Their 'Esk Hause' is the shallow depression between the real pass and Allen Crags, and is 2,386 feet high, which makes it not the highest pass in Lakeland but the third highest, Sticks Pass, between Thirlmere and Ullswater, reaching 2,420 feet above sea-level.

Indeed, the popular 'Esk Hause' has really no connection with the Esk at all, so that the misnomer is particularly confusing, but any attempt to give the pass another name would not get very far. So I'm not really tempted to try to rename it, for instance, Allen Hause. It wouldn't sound right, and might cause even more confusion. And, as I have said, whenever I go this way I always say I've been over Esk Hause—unless I'm talking to an expert on the district.

Mr. Baddeley, of course, knew the place well and is meticulous, as always, in his instructions to walkers. I suppose more walkers have been lost on 'Esk Hause' in bad weather than on any other pass, and the commonest trap is to land down in Eskdale when one is seeking Wasdale, Borrowdale or even Langdale. Years ago there used to be a signpost near the ruined wall-shelter, but the winter gales—and perhaps greedy camp-fires—hastened its destruction. I think it has been replaced on occasions, but has never lasted long and, if turned round by jokers as sometimes happened, was worse than useless. An indication, scratched on the rocks, could be of use, but, as old Mr. Baddeley wrote, eighty years ago: 'The only safeguard is to bear in mind that the ups and downs hereabouts are considerable, and to arm oneself with map and compass.' He also makes the sensible point that all the streams from the 'Esk Hause' highway eventually lead down into Borrowdale, and that walkers between Wasdale and Langdale who find themselves working up an easy slope to the south are off the route and making for Eskdale.

But there were none of these difficulties when I was on the pass one August day—a windless afternoon of humid heat, but clear distant views and no possible chance of going wrong, even had it been my first visit. I have known the place for more than forty years, and most of my memories are of wet, wild or misty days, for this is one of the wettest spots in England. Three of us once camped by Angle Tarn in a cloudburst and spent the night holding down the tent and the following morning in drying out our sleepings bags. I remember, too, once walking over the pass on a very black night after a late evening's climbing on Great Gable. We had looked forward to the night walk back to Coniston, for we had torches and much youthful energy, but both the torches petered out in Rossett Gill and we had a long, tiring descent in the darkness, finishing up, exhausted, in the early morning hours in the hay in the Wall End barn.

This recent August day, however, Angle Tarn, which so often looks a black pool under the shadow of Hanging Knott, was sparkling in the sunlight and friendly rather than menacing. I had come from Wythburn, which is perhaps an unusual cross-country walk and rather tiring, since much of the way is trackless and through bogland. Another trying feature of this walk to Esk Hause and back is that it involves the ascent of High Raise twice in the same day, but this is a particularly fine mountain for views, and from the summit you can see the whole of your route to the pass, about 5 miles away. To plot an interesting route, losing the minimum height, proved a pleasant exercise, but I found that the dry summer had not had much effect on the bogs at the back of

Rossett Crag, or in the Wythburn valley. Indeed, to reach the 'Esk Hause' track after so many miles of quelching through tussocks seemed almost like coming on to a motorway after a drive along farm lanes.

I met the first people of the day's walk while I was having a sandwich by Angle Tarn—two brown-skinned youngsters stripped to the waist. 'Are we all right for Esk Hause?' they asked, but it wasn't the time nor the place for long explanations. 'Straight on— about a quarter of an hour,' I told them. After all, it was near enough—even if they *did* want the real Esk Hause.

AUGUST HEATWAVE

There were a couple of brief showers of rain in August 1968 that barely damped the ground, but these were the only breaks in a month of perfect weather. Indeed, this was our best summer for years, so that all the hay was in, the hedgerows trimmed, the fell sheep clipped and the farmers with time to spare for the dale shows by the beginning of August. The district teemed with visitors queueing for cafés, buses, boats or parking spaces, but the fells were still lonely—and silent, with the becks stilled and hardly enough wind to stir the brackens, let alone whistle through the crags. We returned to Scafell one weekend and walked to the shadowed crag up the dusty ladder of Brown Tongue, stripped to the waist and shoulders burning. Far below, Wastwater danced in the morning sunlight, and straight ahead, left of the roof-tree of Mickledore, climbers were spaced out on the warm, crinkled slabs of Pikes' Crag, and their laughter came ringing down into the corrie. High up to the right more serious work was afoot among the overhangs of the Flake Crack, and we could pick out the white helmet of the leader as he tried, time after time, to struggle up the exhausting lay-back. The rope hung far out from the crag and high above the screes. It was tiring to look up so steeply, so we scrambled up to the crag for our own, more modest, climb and, some time later, descended and ran down to the valley. There was only one pool in the Lingmell Beck big enough for our purpose—perhaps 3 feet deep and a dozen feet across—but it served, and we emerged, after the first shock, like giants refreshed. Which was the better, after so warm a day—the bathe or the long, cool drink that followed in a quiet Eskdale garden, heavy with the scent of roses—I cannot now remember.

8

Days of Long Ago

MOUNTAINS ON HORSEBACK

The accepted method of attaining the summits of the Lake District mountains at the end of the last century—and for more than 100 years before that—was on horseback. Indeed, this form of 'mountaineering' was common enough up to the First World War. The ride up Scafell was one of the regular pony excursions last century, and an old guidebook of mine lists the tariffs for the various ascents—for example, Fairfield, 6s.; Helvellyn, 7s. 6d.; Skiddaw, 6s.; Scafell, 10s. This was the charge for the pony, and you paid extra for the guide—in the case of Scafell another 10s. But a guide would take charge of several ponies without extra charge, and sometimes you could get a guide for less than the pony. Apparently, however, these charges did not include refreshments for man and pony, but these would not be very exhorbitant, and I've no doubt you could ride in comfort and safety to the top of Scafell and back for about 25s.

But before the First World War lovers of the open air were beginning to use their legs a little more, and almost beginning to look down their noses at people who went up mountains on horseback. 'For those who are unequal to the fatigue of ascending the mountains or crossing the more rugged passes,' states a Lake District guidebook of about fifty-five years ago, 'ponies and guides are available at moderate charges.' Gradually the old pony tracks fell into disuse so far as their original purpose was concerned, although people walked up some of the zigzags—but cut the corners coming down.

You can find these tracks all over the Lake District—up Dollywaggon Pike, for instance, or towards the Helvellyn range from Keppel Cove, or high above Eskdale—all of them well-graded paths choosing the easiest ground and making height slowly but steadily. As walkers' paths, except to a tired party, they are rather boring, and few people bother to use them coming down. Many of them are now overgrown and little used, and some are forgotten. Even the sheep prefer their own trods.

The late Mr. Timothy Tyson, the little Grasmere bootmaker who climbed almost every mountain in Britain and knew more about the Lake District than almost anybody else, once told me that Johnson Thompson, the Grasmere guide, was even taking people up Helvellyn on horseback about fifty years ago. He believed the last person Thompson took riding in the hills was the Queen of Holland. 'Parties from Ambleside often used to come with their guides and horses to ride up Scafell,' wrote Mr. Tyson to me. 'The ascent from the Burnmoor side would be no trouble at all, but the Pike itself is more difficult, although a horse has been ridden over Scafell Pike from Wasdale to Langdale and on to Ambleside. I know, because I used to lodge with an elderly Ambleside man called Tom Jackson. When he was younger he had planned with another Ambleside man to be the first to take a saddle horse over the Pike itself, but while they were thinking about it another man did the ride. He was a visitor—a German, I think. Of course, horses were going over Esk Hause from Dungeon Ghyll to Wasdale regularly, and Wilson Youdell has told me he often made three trips a week. So all this mountain riding was an everyday occurrence up to the First World War, and it's not many years ago since one of Tommy Dickinson's Clydesdales took up the material to build the Ordnance Survey column on Helvellyn top.'

Long before people used horses and ponies for the pleasure of riding up the mountains, packhorses were the normal means of transport across the fells. The early traders travelled with their strings of ponies right across Lakeland, and some of the routes went over passes like Hardknott and Wrynose. Along these old trails, where in places you can see how the hoofs have worn tracks through the rock, went the monks, the drovers, merchants with silks and fineries, the miners with their lead, silver and graphite, and the smugglers with their whisky hung in panniers or salmon newly poached from the Duddon. These old routes still remain —Moses' Trod across the 'back' of Great Gable is one example, and there are scores of others—and the old packhorse bridges spanning the becks are still to be seen.

It was a woman who made perhaps the most famous Lakeland ride in history—Mrs. Radcliffe, a novelist who wrote *The Mysteries of Udolpho* and rode up and down Skiddaw in 1794. She engaged a guide, procured horses, 'accustomed to the labour', and set off up Latrigg with her eyes missing nothing of the scenery. This was quite a bold adventure for a woman, for Skiddaw was still regarded as a fearsome mountain and there was not yet a track to the top. The guide led the way 'through many curvings among the heathy hills and hollows', but the horses panted at the slowest walk, and it was necessary to rest them every six or seven minutes. As they climbed, the air became 'very thin' and the steep places more and more difficult, and as they neared the summit they went along a ledge above a precipice 'scarcely wide enough for a single horse'.

I can't picture where this could have been, but we must allow for a little exaggeration from a woman novelist taking part in a mountain adventure that few men would have tackled at that time. She thought it 'dreadful' to look down sharp ridges of rock at Bassenthwaite Lake far below, but she spent some time on top, despite the wind, and afterwards wrote several hundred words about the view. She could see the Scottish hills and the Isle of Man and thought she could see the 'German Ocean' (presumably the North Sea) as a thin line of mist. Strangely enough, in those far-off days when people were still frightened of mountains, she met an old man on top. He was a farmer from one of the dales below, but, she wrote, 'so laborious is the climb', that although he had passed the whole of his life within sight of the mountain, it was his first ascent.

In the summer of 1966 the national newspapers made great play of the fact that a man and a woman had just ridden ponies to the top of Scafell, suggesting it was something new or remarkable. This was by no means the case, but it is interesting to note that ponies seem to be coming into their own again, to some extent, in the Lake District. Pony-trekking centres and riding schools are springing up in many places, and young people are discovering a 'new' way of getting out into the hills. And when they were rebuilding the wall shelter on the top of Helvellyn in October 1969 pack-ponies were used to take up some of the sand—just as they would have done 100 years ago.

COACHING DAYS

The old, romantic Christmas cards seem to be going out of favour, but I had one last year that seemed to typify exactly the Lakeland Christmases before the turn of the century. It showed snow-covered hills on a frosty morning, an old farmhouse at the end of a winding road and, in the foreground, a coach and horses with the coachman handing down the Christmas parcels. Christmas in Lakeland must have been something like this years ago, and I am a little sorry that I never saw the Royal Mail come jingling up the dale on a Christmas morning. The coach lamps shining through the mist, the rattle of hooves and harness, and the jolly music of the coach-horn must have made a brave show— a bit of Old England that has gone for ever.

Undoubtedly, the coaching era was one of the most colourful periods in Lake District history, and the arrival of the Christmas mail in the villages one of the exciting events of the year. But coaches are not really ancient history in our part of the world, for they were in regular use in Lakeland long after they had disappeared from the rest of England. I can remember the old Lakeland four-in-hands and have met some of the old stage-coach drivers, and you can still see many of the old coaches, beautifully kept with shiny lamps and polished bodywork, in stables and garages in several parts of the district. Many years ago I travelled as a youngster to Grasmere sports in a four-in-hand, and a slightly eccentric friend of mine was still taking his brougham and horses across Windermere ferry just after the last war.

It has often been said that the last horsed run in Lakeland was 'The Buttermere Round', but Brown's Motors of Ambleside were running horse coaches up to the outbreak of the last war, and the Keswick and Ambleside companies took their horses off the road about the same time. When you consider that it was only in 1948 that the first passenger-carrying, double-decker bus made the journey along the main highway from Kendal to Keswick it is remarkable to recall there were still four-in-hands operating in Lakeland round about 1940.

Up to a few years ago there were still several old men alive in Lakeland who used to drive the Royal Mail over Dunmail Raise on the main Kendal-to-Keswick highway. One of them was Teddy Gardner, of Windermere, who died in his nineties within the past ten years or so and was driving a four-in-hand in Jubilee year—1887. Teddy wasn't at all pleased about the coming of the double deckers—'They'll be terribly dangerous and, anyway, they won't look nice,' he said—but then he had been annoyed, years before, about the introduction of the first small buses into Lakeland, and one can understand his attitude.

Seventy years ago Teddy was a coach-driver for Mr. Richard Rigg, of Rigg's Hotel, now the Windermere Hotel, who, because he held the contract for the Royal Mail, dressed his drivers in official scarlet. Teddy also wore a white top hat and check trousers and carried what in those days must have been almost his badge of office—the well-known 'Yard of Tin', the coaching horn with which coachmen used to clear the road ahead. He once showed me his horns, beside shining spurs, horse-shoes, polished hooves and other mementoes of the old days. Riggs started their service along the main road through Lakeland with victorias, broughams and landaus in 1847. For the service over Dunmail Raise they carried eighteen people on top and four inside, but in the winter months they cut out the Raise and just travelled between Windermere and Grasmere.

The history of coaching in Lakeland is a colourful, exciting story extending over more than 200 years. Before 1750 goods were mostly carried by packhorse, and it is said that 354 of them used to pass through Kendal every week. It was perhaps because the state of the roads had so hindered the King's troops in 1745 that the turnpike roads were built and travel became easier. Stage wagons from London to Kendal in place of packhorses began in 1757, although it is reported that a post-chaise was first kept in Kendal in 1754. A coach called 'The Flying Machine' was on the Kendal-to-Carlisle road in 1763, and Penrith became a great coaching centre, continuing to be so until long after the opening of the railway.

Dry stone walling

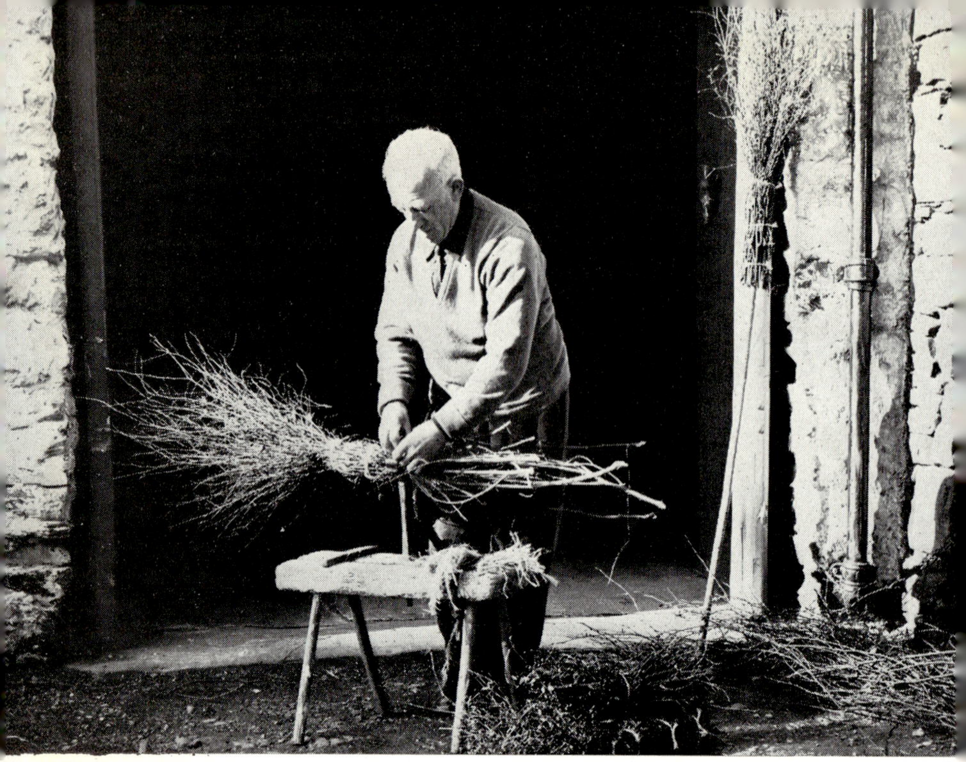

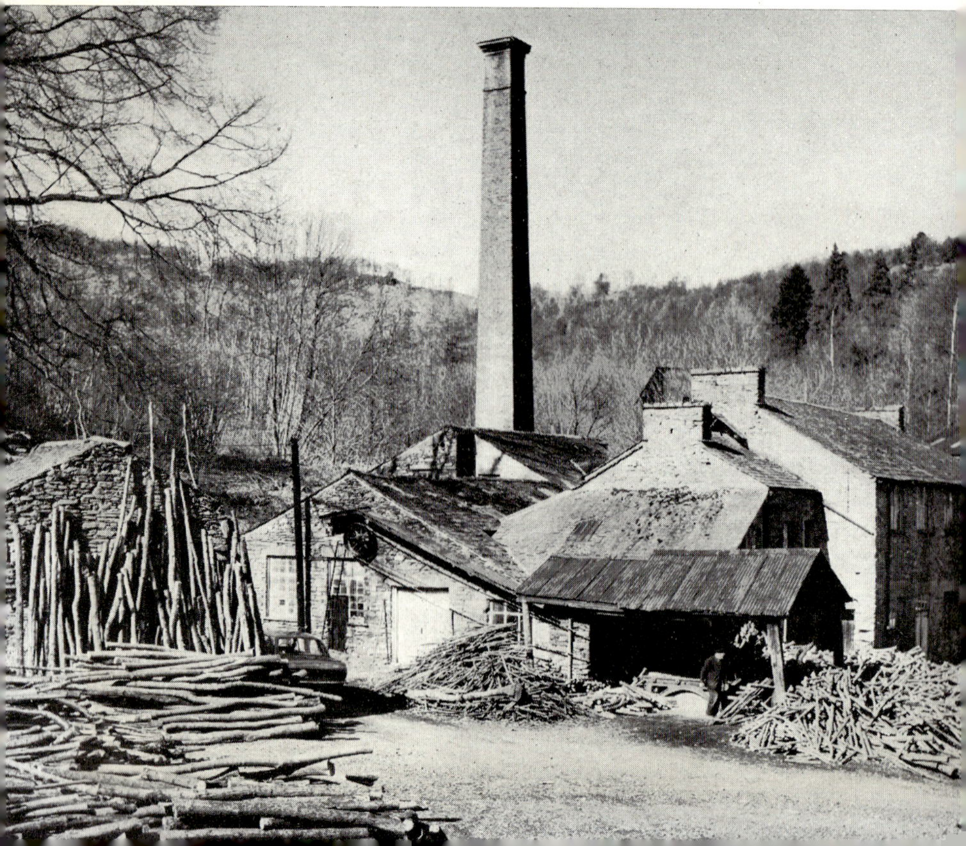

The coming of the railways swept away the coaches in most parts of England, and the invasion of the motor buses completed the end of an era—except in Lakeland. The Buttermere Round, a four-in-hand, used to leave Keswick at 10 a.m., and, after stops for refreshment for men and beasts, arrived at Buttermere, by way of Honister Pass, about one o'clock. The return journey was by way of Newlands, and the coach, with up to twenty-three passengers on board, was back in Keswick before six. The drivers in the last days were either Joe Scott or Bill Richardson, and they wore, if I remember rightly, blue coats with yellow facings and grey top hats.

The Lake Hotel Coaches Ltd. of Keswick was perhaps the oldest coach company in the country, while Brown's Motors of Ambleside carried on their horse coaches after they had become mechanised. Bill Richardson of Keswick died in about 1949—about ten years after his last run on the Buttermere Round—and the last of his gallant old horses died in about 1952 at the age of 33 years. Perhaps he was the very last of the coach horses of the Lake District. Brown's claimed to be the last coach owners in Lakeland, and their runs over Kirkstone, to Tarn Hows and Coniston and the round of the Langdales continued up to thirty years ago. Some of their old coaches are still in existence. The last man to handle a four-in-hand out of Ambleside was the late Mr. Tom Faulkner, and his brother Stan drove a one-horse gig with the Hawkshead mail when he was only 12 and took his first pair of horses over Dunmail when about the same age.

The Round of the Langdales left Ambleside every morning at 11 a.m. The route was by way of Little Langdale, Blea Tarn pass, Dungeon Ghyll, Chapel Stile, Red Bank, Grasmere and back to Ambleside, and the horses used to trot back into the square by half-past five. The charge was about 5s. 6d. or 6s. per passenger, and in 1910—according to an old guide in my possession—4s. The driver had a white top hat. He would hold the four reins in his left hand and his long whip in his right and describe the various points of interest along the route. At one time before the First World War something like 100 horses were stabled at the Salutation Hotel, Ambleside, and the stage coach used to change horses at the old toll bar at the foot of Dunmail Raise, where a toll had to be paid.

K

Besom making at Outgate
Bobbin mill at Finsthwaite

The stage-coach drivers wore their red coats with brass buttons and included such well-known local characters as Johnny Green-bank, Will Tom Nicholson, Tom Fiddler, Bobby Smith, Dick Smith, George Ewart, Bobby Park and Nathan Smith. About ninety years ago the drivers on the Keswick run didn't get a wage, but received a shilling for each passenger, with tips on top. The drivers on the Honister run used to reckon to pick up £100 between Easter and Whit, which was good money in those days. One of the best known of the Penrith drivers was Thomas Ivinson, who handled the Ullswater coach-and-four and had fifty-three years service with the Siddle family. Twice a day he picked up passengers at the steamer pier at Pooley Bridge and used to say that he saw more Americans in a week in those days than he saw later in twelve months.

Undoubtedly these old Lakeland coachmen—coachees, as they were called—were characters, men used to hard weather and hard living, men of wit and personality, and men who took great pride in their horses and their vehicles. Their equipment was always kept brightly polished even in the worst weathers, and each man had his own waxes and polishes to make his turnout, if possible, better than all the others. The dalesfolk could tell the time by the sound of the coach horn as the mail came pounding along the roads, and it must have been a thrilling sound, with far more poetry and music about it than the honk of a modern motor-car horn.

Best of all must have been the sound of the Christmas mail with the coaches packed full of presents and greetings and crowded with holidaymakers up for a few days in the fell country. And no matter what the weather, the coachmen would get through, often through deep snowdrifts and blinding blizzards, with extra horses added to the team, and a postillion riding with the leaders. These were days of indifferent roads in Lakeland, but the horse mail, would come plunging in and out of pot-holes and swinging round the icy corners with a confidence born of long experience of horses and coachmen. I am told that it was about 1784 when the Christmas mail first started to go by coach instead of by postboys and mounted couriers, and later there grew up a great tradition of punctuality. No matter what happened, the mail must get through on time.

A coachman who collected his mails late had to make up time on the next stage, and the Carlisle-to-Glasgow coach is said to have averaged 11½ miles an hour. The Edinburgh mail took forty hours to cover the 400 miles to London, and the villagers set their clocks by the minute of the coach's passing. If a coach got stuck in a snowdrift or overturned in a ditch it was the responsibility of the guard to ride on with the mailbags into the storm. More than 100 years ago the guard and driver of one of the Scottish mail coaches perished on the moors above Moffat, struggling on foot through the snows with the mail bags on their shoulders until they could struggle no more.

Many stories of the old coaching days have been passed down. I like the one about the Royal Mail coach returning from Keswick which collided on Nest Brow with a pony-chaise, knocking the pony and the vehicle through a wall. The driver of the pony-chaise picked himself up, dusted himself down and said very solemnly, 'I shall have this matter thoroughly investigated,' whereupon the driver of the mail, reining in his fractious team, whispered to his companion, 'Good God, it's Master Wordsworth.' And later the driver confessed, 'I nivver heerd a body swear gladlier, for at first I thowt we'd kilt the poit.'

MINING IN THE HILLS

For more than 300 years the great open chasm of Simon's Nick in the fells above Coniston has been a menace to benighted travellers, sheep and dogs, and down the centuries there have been many terrible tragedies in its black depths. The fencing, a year or two ago, by voluntary wardens, should make it safe for some time, but it seems strange that the job should have had to wait for volunteers when it should have been tackled long years ago by those who made their fortunes tearing the heart out of these old hills. Simon's Nick is only one of dozens of shafts, caves and levels that pock-mark the Coniston fells, and, like many of the others, it was hacked out by the German miners who came to Coniston in about the year 1600 when the first Queen Elizabeth was on the throne. Almost certainly Simon was one Simon Puchberger, who was said to be in league with the devil and perished in the shaft, but not before he had made a fortune out of the copper he was working.

The German 'invasion' of Lakeland happened just over 400 years ago, and it started in the Keswick area. Mining prospectors combing the Cumberland valleys took back to London encouraging reports of copper, silver and even gold in the Lakeland fells, and the Queen and some of her noblemen became interested. In 1561 they formed the Mines-Royal Company, with the Queen as patron and some of her principal courtiers as leading shareholders, and engaged Bavarian mining experts to work the mines, Bavaria being the foremost mining country of the day. Some of the surnames of Cumbrian families may date from this peaceful invasion, for after some opposition from the locals, the Germans and the Austrians—who were, after all, bringing employment and prosperity to the district—were accepted into the local community, many of them marrying local girls. A few years ago I was ski-ing in the beautiful Tyrolean village of Alpbach, which used to be a mining area, and discovered that half the inhabitants seemed to have the surname Moser. There are also old-established Lakeland families with the same name, and there could be a distant connection.

For a time Keswick was the Dawson City of this seventeenth-century 'gold rush', and it was not until about forty years later that the Germans moved to Coniston, where mining was already a traditional local craft. It has been said that the Romans, and even the British tribes before them, might have mined in the area, and certainly the monks had bloomeries, or iron-smelting works, around Coniston in the Middle Ages. Agricola told his soldiers that Britain produced 'gold, silver and other metals, the booty of victory', and Postlethwaite, the Lake District mining authority, once wrote: 'There is some reason to believe that copper has been wrought at irregular intervals for about 2,000 years.' W. G. Collingwood has written that the Germans, whose monopoly finished with the outbreak of the Civil Wars, began work by digging down into any outcrops they found, and had a lot of early trouble with flooding, which had to be drained by tunnelling. These tunnels had to be hacked out by the 'stope and feather' method of splitting the rock or by softening with fire, and must have entailed slow and laborious work. As a result, they were made as small as possible—rather coffin-shaped, just big enough for a man to squeeze through—and you can still find many of these tunnels on the lower slopes of Coniston Old Man, Wetherlam and around the Copper Mines Valley.

I believe the very earliest of the German workings were up Red Dell Beck, within half a mile of the mine buildings that are now a youth hostel. At one time you could go down into these workings by rickety ladders and along slippery gangways to a depth of something like 1,500 feet below the surface, but this has long been impossible, and the unseen depths are flooded. A fall here would be irrevocable.

There are the remains of other ancient workings under Kernel Crag, by Levers Water, near Low Water, at the foot of Grey Crag and dozens more around Wetherlam. Then there was the Three Kings mine above Tilberthwaite—Caspar, Melchior and Balthasar, the names of German miners and of their patron saints—and many more, some of them difficult to identify nowadays. There must be at least 100 shafts, caves, tunnels and levels around the Coniston fells, and many of them were worked by the Germans.

Of course, the mining continued long after the Germans had gone, one of the companies even driving its tunnels and shafts underneath the bed of Levers Water, which provided the water supply for some of the mines, notably Paddy End, about half a mile west of the youth hostel. In the early nineteenth century, when the Coniston copper mines were at their peak of prosperity, several hundred men and boys worked there, and the mines were making between £30,000 and £36,000 a year. In the 1870s the Coniston mines began their slow decline, partly because the great depths that had been reached made it increasingly difficult and uneconomic to work them, and also because of lowering prices through new deposits found overseas and the substitution of iron ships for wooden ones covered in copper.

Finally, the mines which had prompted the opening of the branch railway line to Coniston had to be abandoned, and all that are to be seen today are the spoil heaps, the ruined buildings, the open shafts, the tunnels and the watercourses. More than half a century of exposure to the elements has failed to cover up the eyesore of Copper Mines Valley, and the happiest thing that could happen to this once lovely corner would be for it to be flooded to make a reservoir. True this is a valley of old traditions, and there is romance to be found among the rocks if you know where to look; but the scars of the long search for mineral wealth in these fells will always remain, and Simon's Nick or some other shaft could still claim its victims.

A few years ago there was talk of mining again for copper in the shadow of Coniston Old Man and also perhaps in the Newlands valley. The Coniston Copper Mines Valley is a derelict area in need of either clearing up—which would be enormously expensive—or being given a new lease of life, but Newlands remains almost completely unspoiled. True, you can spot where the old workings were if you know where to look, and you can still see the old pony tracks, but not many visitors know that the Germans were mining here in Elizabethan days, and Newlands remains one of the quietest and loveliest valleys in Lakeland. To allow mining here again, with the wonderful old track under Maiden Moor leading up to Dale Head widened into a road for lorries, would be a tragedy, and the peace and quietude of the Derwent Fells would be gone for ever.

But there is quite a good road up to Coniston copper mines—the manager's house has been a youth hostel for many years—and new workings up there might make the place a little livelier, but could hardly do more damage than has already been done. For all around you there are the remains not only of the old copper mines but also of disused slate quarries, while the fine old woods around Church Beck were cut down many years ago. At one time there was a suggestion that the Copper Mines Valley should be flooded as part of a hydro-electric scheme, and I remember thoroughly supporting the move—the only time I have ever been in favour of an artificial lake in the National Park. Such a lake would have drowned all the spoil heaps and ruins, and the dam, due to the narrowing of the neck of the valley, could have been quite small. With good taste, the appearance of this ravaged corner of Lakeland could have been transformed, but nothing ever came of the idea.

There was no Planning Board when Daniel Hochstetter and Thomas Thurland came over from Germany nearly 400 years ago to open mines and build smelting works, and I've no doubt they brought a great deal of prosperity to the area, but the Lake

District is a different sort of place today. At one time, perhaps, the exploitation of the natural resources of the district was of great importance, but today the preservation for all time of a sizeable area like the Newlands Valley, right in the heart of the National Park, is of vastly greater importance than the provision of new jobs for 100 men. The Copper Mines Valley, however, *could* be different.

AN ANCIENT FERRY

At the southern entrance to the National Park, where a block of limestone on a plinth indicates you are entering the shrine, there is, in February or March some years, a notice to inform motorists that the Windermere ferry is out of action. So that, if you are travelling by car to, say, Coniston or Hawkshead you must drive the long way round by way of Ambleside and Skelwith Bridge. The ferry is not working on these occasions because it is being overhauled, which takes place every three or four years, but pedestrians and cyclists are ferried across by motor launch. There's normally no excitement during the fortnight or so while the ferry-boat is out of action, but I remember an occasion several years ago when passengers in the motor launch had all sorts of adventures.

There was a lot of fog about at the time—Windermere is especially prone to fog, especially in the mornings—and on several occasions the launch was hopelessly lost. Once it nearly ran aground on Belle Isle, and there were occasions when it had to be guided across by shouts from the shore. More than once it was dark when the passengers set foot on dry land, and the launch even had to be navigated across the 600 yards by compass. On one occasion the launch found itself down at Ramp Holme, and another time when the pilot found he was approaching High Cunsey he had almost to feel his way back along the 'nabs and neuks' of the Lancashire shore. 'Much worse than being lost in a fog at sea,' said the ferryman, accustomed to handling a craft which pulls itself along on chains, after two or three such hectic crossings. 'You've plenty of space to move about in at sea, but on Windermere you never know what you're going to hit next.'

Even with the normal ferry boat on its chains, the crossing of

Windermere in fog can sometimes be awkward. Occasionally the ferryman has to stand on the prow of the boat so that he can see the shore in time, and there have been times when the ferryman has thought he has landed when he has still been a yard or two off shore. Nowadays, lights on the jetties are useful, but they can't be seen in the thickest fog.

Down the centuries there have been many excitements on the Windermere ferry. The late Mr. Bruce Dixon of Sawrey, who must have travelled on it thousands of times, once told me he remembered an occasion when the ferry boat lost one of the wheels round which the wire ropes ran, in the middle of the lake. They could not get the boat back to Ferry House—the way they were going—because of the wind, but managed to crawl back to the Bowness side by all the passengers and crew leaning over the side and pulling with all their might on the wire ropes. Mr. Dixon also remembered being taken across—when the ferry was laid up —in one of the huge rowing boats that were in use before the introduction of the steam ferries. There were two oarsmen, but the passengers had to work their passage as well. The only work passengers may be called on to do nowadays is to shout for the shore when there's fog about and they're in the motor launch, but there have been complications when nobody could be sure whether the answering shouts came from the Westmorland or the Lanca-shire side. In Wordsworth's time the boatman, it is said, used to be guided across the lake on a foggy day by a bell hung in the trees and, occasionally, by the musical voice of his daughter calling from the shore.

The worst disaster that has ever overtaken the Windermere ferry—or any other boat on the lake, for that matter—was the oft-quoted one of 19th October 1635, when forty-seven passen-gers, many of them members of a wedding party, and eleven horses were drowned. There are many versions of this dreadful tragedy, one of them being that the date was 1746 and that seven horses were drowned, another one escaping by swimming ashore. Some stories say the entire wedding party, most of them Kendal folk returning from a wedding at Hawkshead Church, were drowned, but a record in the Grasmere Parish Register refers to 'one that escaped'.

There is a local legend that William Sawrey and Thomasina

Strickland, who were married at Hawkshead Church on 18th October of that year, were drowned, but this has not been confirmed, and an account published the following year suggests that this was not so. This old account tells how the bride's mother and brother were drowned, but makes no mention of the bridal pair. Besides the wedding guests, the boat is said to have been crowded with carriages and horses, which, 'together with the roughness of the water and extremity of weather occasioned this inevitable danger'.

The old report goes on: 'Launch'd had they scarcely to the middle of the water, being scarcely a mile broad, but the Boat, either through some pressure of weight which surcharged her, or some violent and imperious windes and waves which surprised her, with all her people, became drench'd in the depths. No succour, no reliefe, afforded by God's definite Will had so devised . . . .' And the following year there was another fatal accident at the ferry, and, for all I know, several more in later years. In those far-off days the ferry was across a much wider part of the lake, the old landing place on the Furness side being nearly half a mile farther down the shore, at a point where the Sawrey road drops steeply to the lake.

We can only guess at the age of the Windermere ferry. In some form or another it might have existed since towns like Kendal first had their markets and fairs, and it was certainly in use as long ago as 1575. In those days a rent of 6s. 8d. a year was paid to the Lords of Graythwaite Manor for the right to ferry across the lake, and the monks of Furness Abbey, who owned Hawkshead and had boats on the lake, might at one time have held the ferry rights. Towards the end of the seventeenth century the ferry rights were held by the Braithwaites of Braithwaite Fold, and later they came into the hands of the Curwens, who owned Belle Isle. When Mr. Bruce Logan took over the tenancy of the former Ferry Hotel in 1880 he first paid rent for the ferry rights, and later, when he purchased the ferry boat, bought the rights as well. Later the Joint Ferry Committee took over the rights on lease, and when the Freshwater Biological Association turned the hotel into a science laboratory the committee bought the ferry rights for, I think, £5,000.

In the old days the return toll for the ferry was one penny per person, and there was a fearful commotion in 1699 when they tried to raise the toll. But the toll has often been increased down the centuries, although there's been no change now for several years. The present toll of 6*d*. for foot-passengers and cyclists—for either a single or a double journey—is supposed to be a concession to the locals, as is also the charge of 8*d*. for a horse, or 5*d*. each for up to half a dozen sheep, calves or pigs (with an extra penny for each additional two or less). A flock practically needs an accountant on the job. But the tolls for vehicles are much steeper —3*s*. 10*d*. return, for instance, for a largish car, and 7*s*. for a coach— and you have to pay 6*d*. for every passenger additional to the driver.

The Windermere ferry, they say, has existed 'from time beyond the memory of man', and in its long history has gathered around it many tales. Nearly everyone must have heard of the ghostly Crier of Claife—the passenger who calls for a boat and haunts the ferryman to his death—and there are many ghostly tales associated with the Lancashire shore. There is one, for instance, of a phantom boat with terrible sights on board, and you may still hear strange stories around Sawrey way of mysterious lights, weird cries and ghostly faces at cottage windows. They say that at one time no boatman would cross the lake in the dark, but to most people, especially visitors, the Windermere ferry is no more than a happy holiday experience—a pleasant trip across the lake on an unusual craft, an exciting morning's run for the kiddies.

IN THE SEVENTIES

Nearly 100 years ago when visitors went about the Lake District by horse-drawn coach, and hired guides and ponies if they wanted to go up a mountain, there was talk of running a railway up the Winster valley to Bowness—to bring Lakeland closer to the Midlands. 'It is quite beyond our comprehension', wrote an Oxford scholar, Herman Prior, about that time, 'why a railway is not now constructed up that valley, and so provide the shortest, by far the most beautiful, and the most convenient approach from the Midland counties.' How the wheel has turned full circle in less than 100 years!

This is just one of a host of fascinating items that can be culled from a study of Prior's 350-page pocket guide to the Lake District —undated, but I think published in the late 1870s or early 1880s. The little book, small enough to go into a waistcoat pocket but so closely printed that, set out, it would make a very large volume indeed, came out some years before the first of the long series by Baddeley, and contains even more assorted information. When it was written Wordsworth was in his grave beside the Rothay, Ruskin in residence at Brantwood, Dr. Arnold's daughter in her father's house of Fox How under Loughrigg, rock-climbing as a sport had hardly begun, and it cost 5s. 6d. for bed and breakfast in the best hotels at the height of the season. Servants, added Mr. Prior, 'are charged for in the bill at one shilling and sixpence a day'.

You could hire a one-horse conveyance for the day for a pound, and hire a driver for 6s. Boat hire, 'for an entire day', was 5s. for the craft and 5s. for the boatman, but it was 10s. a day for a mountain pony and the same for the guide, 'although one guide will take charge of several ponies'. 'Tourists undertaking any of these ascents', explained Mr. Prior, 'usually travel as far as possible by carriage, thence continuing the journey with the guides and ponies previously arranged for.'

But despite this general dilettante attitude to the mountains, Mr. Prior himself seems to have done his fair share of rather rougher exploration. Although Haskett Smith, the 'Father of British mountaineering', had not yet made his first climbs—or possibly was just starting—Mr. Prior gives detailed directions, together with a drawing, for the ascent of Pillar Rock by the easy way. He adds, however, that this is 'the most hazardous of the two or three risky ascents in the district . . . for he who scales Pillar Rock literally carries his life in his hands'. Mr. Prior also explains how to ascend Broad Stand and Mickledore Chimney on Scafell—still regarded by modern guidebook writers, and rightly so, as rock climbs and therefore to be avoided by the ordinary tourist.

Manchester had not tapped Thirlmere when Mr. Prior was writing his guide, and he describes the lake as 'of the rarest beauty if properly seen, which is not from the Keswick road'. He also writes of the 'exquisitely finished Hawes Water'—generations

later to become Manchester's second Lake District reservoir—
that it was difficult to imagine anything 'which more completely
satisfies the eye'. He thought the best mountain-top view was from
Great Gable, and many people will still agree with him.

Mr. Prior didn't like the spire of St. Mary's Church at Ambleside—nor have some other people—and thought that Bowness
was 'too much hemmed in', especially when the 'cheap trippers'
were about. He then goes on: 'It should be understood that by
"Bowness" we mean the old village at the bottom of the hill. All
the rest is Windermere, and we are disposed to think that, not
very many years hence, there will be a considerable town, with
the latter name, extending between the railway station and
Bowness Bay.' And, of course, he was right.

Nearly 100 years ahead of a suggested Lake District festival
centre and the thoughts of many of us about the problem of the
wet day, Mr. Prior declares with emphasis:

> The important centres of the Lake District suffer very much from
> the want of promenading resorts for the summer and autumn
> evenings and—more important still—for the wet days which will
> occur. At present, if the weather breaks, there is absolutely nothing
> to be done but playing billiards and staring at the rain through the
> window, which soon tries the patience of all but enthusiasts, and
> those few who rather enjoy a drenching, and off they go to the train.
>
> We altogether and emphatically dissent from the notion that so-
> called innovations as promenading and concerts ruin the 'unsullied
> natural loveliness' of the district. Nothing of the kind would be done
> by them, no more than the once-condemned graceful line of smoke
> from the funnels of the steamers has made Winander Mere any less
> attractive. Steam has done its part, but the wet days and long
> evenings still want an antidote.

Mr. Prior was still calling the lake, Winander Mere, and other
old spellings of his include Grass Mere, Ulls Water, Styx Pass
and Walney Scar. He found 'an absence of any push or spirit'
about Coniston—'except when the coaches arrive from Ambleside
and Windermere'—and writes with some honesty about the
tourists in Grasmere being taken on trips to the churchyard to
see the poet's graves—'when they would sooner be drinking
bottled porter at Brown's'. Of Kentmere he remarks that the mere
had been drained some years earlier by the owner, for the sake of

the agricultural produce of the few acres of bog that had been left. 'It is sufficiently palpable', writes Mr. Prior, 'that while he was spoiling the valley, in a picturesque sense, he was not himself getting much pecuniary advantage.' He was not to know that many years later a prosperous industry was to be established in the swamp, winning valuable diatomite from the bogland.

Mr. Prior was not carried away by the charms of Keswick as a town, although admitting that he would begrudge its short-comings being replaced 'by nineteenth-century improvements'. He is not, however, very specific about his criticisms, contenting himself with a passing reference to 'its quaint stuccoed, town hall, its long monotonous street, its square, stone-coped windows and its pitched pavement, over which the wooden shoes of the youthful population clatter like a charge of cavalry'.

Borrowdale, however, he considered the loveliest valley in Lakeland, and Langdale the next best, but adds: 'When the English Lake District Association has succeeded in getting a carriage road over the Stake Pass the two finest valleys in England will be connected. . . . Enthusiasts should contribute their mites and influence towards the carrying out of this desirable work, which would not be so costly as might at first appear.' One can only be eternally grateful that the English Lake District Association did nothing of the kind and that Mickleden and Langstrath remain undefiled. Wasdale Head, thought Mr. Prior, lacked good accommodation and what there was he found 'humble', although he agrees the scenery was magnificent. But no mention of the famous Auld Will Ritson who was either at the inn at the time or living in retirement in the valley, and no reference whatever to rock climbing.

Although some of Mr. Prior's observations may not appeal to all, I find it interesting to browse through this very thorough work, with its references to a Lakeland that has long since passed. Certainly, Herman Prior was an honest man who spoke his mind, a man with a vast knowledge of the district and, unquestionably, a great love for its hills and dales. 'Very little work goes to waste in it,' he tells us. 'It is so small, and so closely packed with hill and dale that you escape the "dull bits" altogether.'

ONE WAY HOME

There are many ways home from Wasdale—the very heart of the sanctuary—and one of them takes me through the lovely wooded country of the Furness Fells, well away from the tourist traffic and comfortably set between the mountains and the sea. Here, indeed, is an area—if you except the spreading new forests just to the north and the occasional beautifully built conversion of farm or cottage—where little has changed since my boyhood nearly fifty years ago and where the old-world charm of the fell country our grandparents knew still remains. The hilly lanes still wind—mercifully 'unimproved'—through the woods where we used to go blackberrying and nutting, the old crafts continue in smithy or woodshed, the deer and the badgers live in the thickets, pails clink in dairies and sheepdogs sleep in the sun, and there's always the sweet smell of woodsmoke in the evenings. One day we left the Wasdale hills when the sun was still shining on the snows of Scafell, passed the gulls wheeling over the stubble near Santon Bridge and took the lonely Bootle Fell road down to the Duddon and into boyhood haunts, where we once knew all the best farmhouses for a glass of milk. Over the years the main roads have changed, but once in the byways we could have been back in the days when bed and breakfast at High Cross was pricey at 6s., and where you could get ham and eggs at Rusland for half a crown. The white-washed farmsteads looked just the same, the woodlands where we went adventuring have been left alone, but we came back to 'civilisation' at the cafes and the new bungalows around the foot of Windermere.

9

The Flavour of Lakeland

THE DALESMAN'S TONGUE

Although I live in Westmorland and mix to some extent with the dalesfolk, it must be quite a time since I last came up against the real, unadulterated Lakeland dialect. Everyday dialect words like 'yak', 'lonnin', 'seesta', 'fashed', 'laikin', 'fettle' and 'nobbut', of course, one hears often enough, but I'm thinking of the sort of mouthful that would baffle most middle-aged people, even those born in the area. The truth, of course, is that dialect is rapidly dying out, and it is really only the old people—and not very many of them—who know it well. For a real dialect speaker, spurning normal English and sticking to the words he learned at his mother's knee, can be almost unintelligible, even to those born in the Lakeland counties, while those from the cities and towns would probably never understand one word he was saying.

The Lakeland Dialect Society, which celebrated its silver jubilee five years ago, realises, of course, that this standardisation of speech is inevitable; but the fact makes the very existence of this sort of society increasingly important. Lakeland is changing rapidly, and more and more of its regional characteristics are disappearing or being fused into a general English pattern. But much of the charm of Lakeland depends upon these characteristics —dry-stone walls, building styles, local sport, old customs, to mention just a few—and one of the most individualistic of them is the native speech. For a broad Lakeland dialect cannot really be understood in the adjoining counties of Lancashire, Yorkshire,

Northumberland and Durham. It belongs to the fell country and to nowhere else.

And yet, to be precise, it should be explained that there is really no native language of the Lake Country, but rather many different dialects. In the north of Cumberland and around Carlisle, for instance, the speech is not greatly removed from Lowland Scots, while in West Cumberland it is a rougher tongue, with perhaps a smattering of Tyneside, and certainly of Irish, about it. In the western dales, however, the speech is higher pitched and broader, and the pure Westmorland tongue rather softer and almost sing-song. Furness folk, too, have their own rich tongue, but the important thing is that all these dialects are part and parcel of the same basic Lakeland tongue, and all have their origins in Old Norse or Scandinavian. Many families who have lived in the dales for hundreds of years are descendants of the Vikings, and it is from the Vikings that much of the old dialect stems. Surely, then, this is a heritage, well worth preserving, and this is the job the Lakeland Dialect Society is pledged to do.

Ranged against them—although not, of course, deliberately— are the road engineers who are each year bringing the Lakes nearer to the cities, the so-called affluent society, new methods in education, television, the planners, to some extent, and even writers like myself, whose work makes the district better known and, inevitably over the years, more cosmopolitan.

And it's not only the local speech that is disappearing; the local names, too, are tending to disappear from the village shops, while in most of the towns the integration is almost complete. Time was when you'd find parts of the Lake District almost entirely peopled by Edmondsons or Braithwaites or Tysons or Porters, but those days are long past, and you are nowadays just as likely to find Joneses, Smiths or Robinsons in a Lakeland village as you are to find Grisedales or Grahams.

I have long thought that the richest Lakeland dialect comes from the western dales, and if asked to put my finger on the very centre of it all, I think I would plump for Eskdale. For in this dale, and in other places well away from the main roads, you can still hear the real Lakeland tongue, full of strange words, a sort of clacking rhythm and a high-pitched lilt that give it almost a musical flavour. It is a kindly tongue, honest and downright, well thickened with

The Winster valley

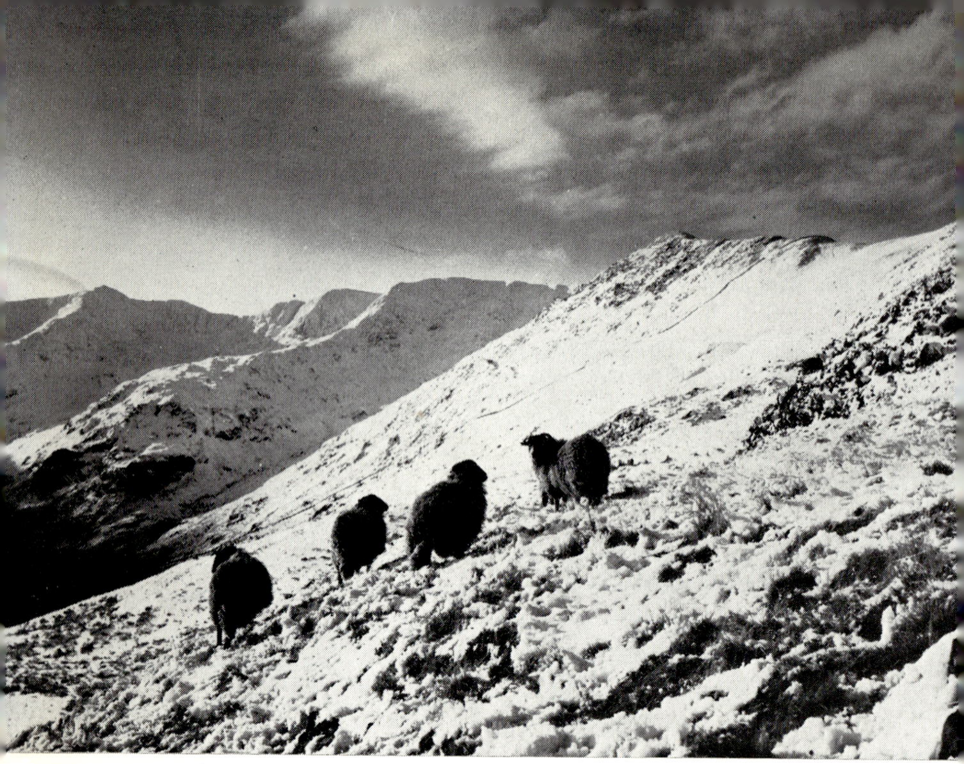

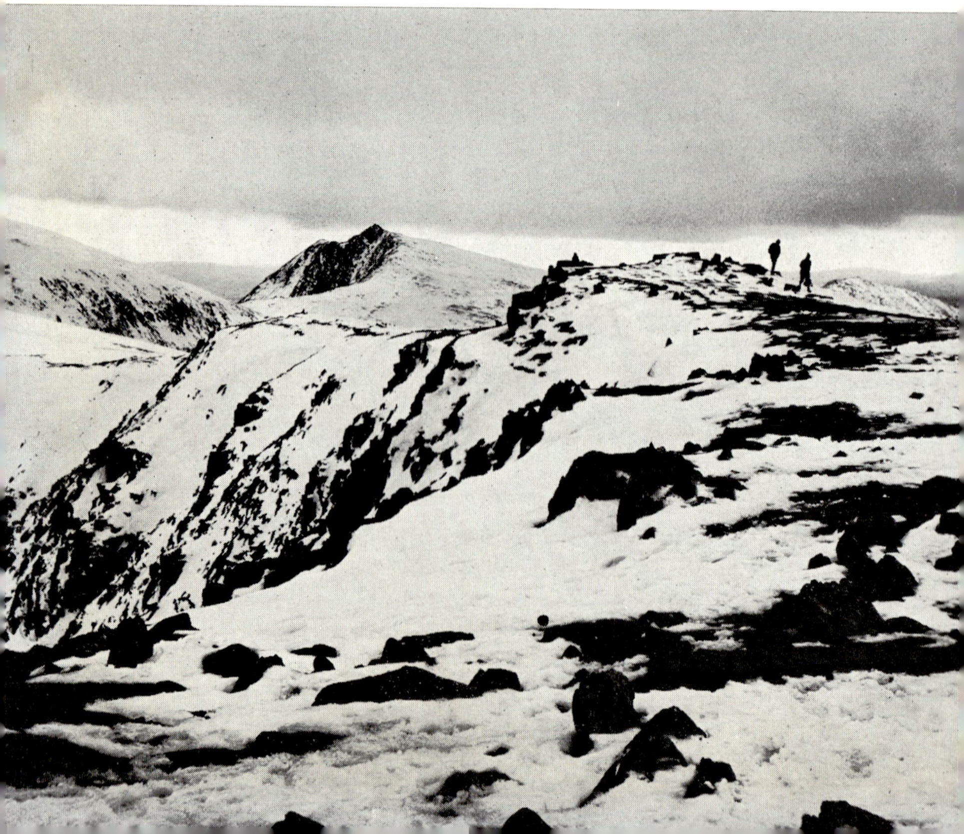

such expressive words as 'traepsin', 'moiderin', 'bledderin' or 'saezzlin'.

One readily noticeable feature of the Lakeland tongue is that the dalesman will always make two syllables out of one, if he can —'me-ad', for made, for instance, 'be-ast' for beast and 'ste-an' for stone. But it is also a particularly economic and terse tongue, so that the dalesman does not need to waste words to make his meaning clear. One or two well-chosen words can convey to the knowledgeable as much as a couple of sentences in more formal English.

You can't, of course, take a piece of ordinary English and 'translate' it into Cumbrian, merely by altering the words into dialect: the whole thing has to be thought out again in the Lakeland idiom. Cumbrian is not really a written tongue, although the Lakeland Dialect Society encourages the writing of dialect essays in schools. For the writer is merely trying to reproduce with letters the sounds that he knows, and the results can differ vastly, so that a piece of dialect writing can look like double-Dutch. Tape-recording would appear to be a more successful method of preserving the dialect, for dialect writers are unlikely ever to agree on a vocabulary.

Among the dialect writers in the 200-odd membership of the Lakeland society was the late Mr. William Sanderson of Keswick, who contributed a remarkable piece of research on local bird names to the jubilee journal. For some common birds he produced several names, for instance, the Bessie blakelin, the yalla yowderin or the yalla yorlin for the yellowhammer. Blakelin refers to the colour, 'blake' meaning pale yellow as in the expression 'blake as May butter'. For the blue-tit he gave Tom tit, Tommy-tee and Tommaty-taa; while there is willy-wicket for the sandpiper, beck Bessie for the dipper and the descriptive flecky-flocker for the chaffinch. Some familiar birds, said Mr. Sanderson, are given Christian names as well as surnames, including Cuddy hoolet (or ullet) for owl, blue Tommy (blue-tit), Johnny-ma-crank (heron), blue Jack (fieldfare) and laal Jacky for the jack snipe. The dipper is a Bessie-dooker, and the reed bunting, Bessie blackcap. Sometimes, too, there are Jinnies and Nannies, and occasionally Peggy. For the swift, Mr. Sanderson produced no fewer than five local names—clavvers, clavverhawk, black martin, deevlin and kill-

L

Below Striding Edge
Walkers on Great Carrs

deev'l—while he found seven for the fieldfare, besides blue Jack—fell throstle, blue felty, blue wing, grey bird, pigeon felty, blue black and felfoe. And a mistle-thrush can be a shreely, a shrite, a churr-cock, a shraily, a shrailicock, a fell-throstle, a moonten throstle, a shillcock or a shilapple, although in some parts of Cumberland a shilapple can be a chaffinch. So you can see how complicated a tongue Cumbrian can be.

Mr. Sanderson gave dozens more names for birds, but produced only one for the cuckoo, which has always been known throughout the area as a gowk. Although why 'gowk', which means a stupid person, for a bird which is clever enough to foist its offspring on to unsuspecting and unpaid baby sitters was just as incomprehensible to Mr. Sanderson as it is to all of us.

I hope that despite the new motorways and the opening up of the dales, that the Lakeland Dialect Society can continue its important work, and I commend to it as a task for its next twenty-five years the compilation of a complete vocabulary—before it's too late.

A year or two ago a most interesting piece of research into dialect in the Furness area was carried out at two local schools. The aim was to find out—in this age of television, radio and the general speaking of an approximation to standard English—how many dialect words out of a list of 150 were known to the pupils. Fifty juniors, aged from 7 to 11 years, at the Kirkby Ireleth village school on the edge of the fells tried the list, the average number of known words working out at only fifteen. All the children knew 'fell', 'gob', 'moider', 'hagging' and 'lug', thirty-five knew 'clarty', thirty-two 'girn' and 'scrow', while thirty children knew 'lonning', 'moudiwarp' and 'neb'. The children seemed mostly familiar with words used probably by older people in scolding them. Forty years ago, when I knew Kirkby as a young man, most people in the area spoke dialect—the basically Icelandic tongue which had probably been used almost unchanged for 1,000 years, passed down by word of mouth.

The list of 150 words was also tried by eighty pupils from a comprehensive school at Ulverston, but these youngsters of an average age of eleven years only knew an average of seven words out of the list. Only four of the youngsters knew more than twenty words, and one of them didn't know any at all. But many Ulverston children spoke dialect in my younger days. The best-known dialect words for these Ulverston children appeared to be 'clout', 'clarty', 'docking', 'clod' and 'clat'. Sixth-formers at the same school also attempted the list and did rather better, the scholars in one form apparently knowing an average of thirty-seven words.

It is interesting to note that a Furness family living in the area tried the list and did very much better. Grandfather, aged 82 years and brought up in Coniston, knew 104 of the words, while his son knew 109. The grandson, however, a science student at London University who had previously lived at Barrow, knew only fifty-eight of the words. I tried the list myself and got just over 100, falling down on such words as attercrop (spider), dinnel (to tingle), eggin (mating), giversum (greedy), kysty (dainty), reckling (last of a litter) and waffy (tasteless). With a lifetime's residence in the area I should have done better, but I don't suppose my children, who went to school in the district, know more than three or four dozen of the words. And their children may hardly know any.

Older Lakeland folk will remember the Grasmere dialect plays, which were a feature of Lake District life for many years. Something like thirty of these plays were written by Mrs. Rawnsley, wife and later widow of the celebrated Canon H. D. Rawnsley, and I remember talking to her in the 1950s about them. In the days when she was writing the earliest of these plays no public vehicles went over Dunmail Raise to Keswick during the winter months, and later a conveyance made the journey only twice a week. You could not even get from the railway terminus at Windermere to Grasmere by public transport after two o'clock in the afternoons. People, therefore, stayed in the dales and had little contact with the outside world, and they spoke the dialect of their fathers and grandfathers before them. The first Grasmere dialect play was written by Miss Charlotte Fletcher, daughter of the Rector of Grasmere and a great-grand-daughter of a close friend of Wordsworth. She felt that the people of Grasmere wanted something to cheer them up during the long winter months, and she also thought there was a great instinct for dramatic expression in the district which required proper direction. The play was called *The Dalesman*, and it was produced in about 1893.

From about that time the Misses Simpson took an increasingly active interest in the project, and from the year 1900 Miss Eleanor Simpson, who later married Canon Rawnsley, wrote all the plays, her sisters co-operating with her in the production. Miss Fletcher left the district, but two more of her plays—*A Daughter of the Dales* and *The Testing of John Truman*—were also produced.

Every year, apart from the war years (1915–19) and 1923 when Mrs. Rawnsley was ill, there was a dialect play at Grasmere, and the last of them all, *A Will and a Way*, was played in 1937. After that, with the threat of war in the air and the death of several administrators and performers, the Grasmere dialect plays, always held in late January or early February, came to an end, and it seems unlikely they will ever be revived.

The last play I saw was *The Mistress of Mosshead* in 1934. This play, like other popular ones, was played several times, the first time being in 1911. Dipping into the play at random, I find delightful lines like these: 'I'se yan 'at likes to set a time for my eatin' and a', and stick til't, but men foak's allus behint, trailin'; or, 'I want nowt wi' a wife. I maun't ga and hankell mysel in a briar bush like a feckless hog to rue it a' my days after'; or even 'T'house isn't seam spot sin' Matilda cum'. I can nivver mannish to please her. I reckon if I was to say t' watter ran doon-bank she'd threap doon thump 'at it run up-bank. She's terr'ble reedan and contradictious.'

The plays were most carefully produced, and every effort was made to ensure that every syllable was correctly pronounced. For some of the principal characters this sometimes meant attendance at up to fifty rehearsals. In the very earliest days the plays used to be given in the village school, then in the old drill hall, and, from about 1905, in the Grasmere Hall or 'New Hall', as it is still called. The plays never moved out of Westmorland, and only once moved out of Grasmere, that being in about 1907 when *Pace-Egging Time* was given at Milnthorpe. Up to £400— the record is £419—used to be collected every year, performances used to run for about a week, and the money was always given to charities. Costumes, scenery and so on were either borrowed or made. Today their successors, the local amateurs, the Grasmere Players, have an excellent reputation and in 1970 performed Wordsworth's only play, *The Borderers*, during the bicentenary celebrations. But, for the most part, they keep off the dialect.

THE VIKING HERITAGE

Every fell, crag, wood, beck, farm and nearly every field in Westmorland has its own name, but nobody knows them all nor what they all mean. Some of the names may be known only to a handful of people, and many will one day disappear. Several have disappeared already. But the really fascinating thing is that every name has a meaning, deliberately thought up by somebody hundreds of years ago, and behind many of the names lie stories with their origins buried in the very beginnings of our history. Everybody knows the familiar names—Windermere, Langdale Pikes, Kirkstone Pass, Fairfield, Loughrigg, Kentmere and so on —and some of us who live in these parts may know a few hundred of them, and be able to guess at the meaning of several. But two volumes on Westmorland names, published three or four years ago by the English Place-Name Society, examine thousands and dig out some sort of a meaning for most of them.

Inevitably, these rather formidable volumes totalling more than 600 pages are works for the scholar. What is required for the average reader is a much simpler work, giving the derivation of perhaps a thousand or so of the principal or more interesting place-names of Westmorland interwoven with the history of the county from its earliest days. For Westmorland, perhaps the wildest and least spoiled county in England and, with Cumberland, the most Norse in its origins, is not only a most fascinating county to explore but, equally, the perfect study for those interested in the meaning of things, the stories behind the names.

Perhaps half the place-names in Westmorland—it may be more —can be traced back to the influence of the Viking raiders, and the fine Scandinavian names can be found on every fell and dale and in scores of hamlets. Indeed, much of the dialect is basically Norse, so much so that it is said that a local farm lad, finding himself in Norway during our wartime exploits there, was able to make himself understood with his own dales tongue. And to one fortunate enough to live in this lovely county it is satisfying to be aware of its links with such a splendid, individualistic country as Norway, and to realise that the Vikings named the farm over the hill and knew these woods and fells.

It is realised that these volumes are definitive works, intended to provide authoritative material for the student and scholar, yet I would have welcomed an attempt to relate the vast mass of the facts to the exciting story of the county. For instance, a great deal of rather dull information has had to be given—the derivation, say, of thousands of field-names—and yet several things have been missed out. I can't, for example, find out why Dollywaggon Pike, which always conjures up so many fanciful scenes, is so named—although some possibilities are quoted elsewhere—nor can I find the meaning of the strangely named Willie Wife Moor. And the likely story of how John Bell's Banner came to be so named does not seem to be included. John Bell was almost certainly the Rev. John Bell, curate and schoolmaster of Ambleside, who lived from 1553 to 1620. Banner is the old word for boundary, and since at one time the parishes of Windermere, Grasmere and Patterdale met on the top of Caudale Moor, it is probable that the summit or thereabouts became known locally as the limit of the sphere of Mr. Bell's ministrations, this being before the days when Ambleside became a separate parish. There would, of course, be other John Bells—a fairly common local name—and another suggestion is that the name could have had a hunting derivation—the place where John Bell had to try to turn the quarry during a hunt.

Now and again, Mr. Bruce Thompson of Troutbeck, a local authority, is quoted as supplying interesting points, and these serve to lighten the meal and make it rather more digestible. For instance, he recalls a local tale that Brothers Water might have been named from two brothers drowned in a skating accident which seems at least more interesting than the official derivation. And then, elsewhere, Mr. Thompson reports there is good fishing in Angle Tarn, that whooper swans regularly come for the winter to Elterwater, that a burial place was found on the top of Kirkstone Pass when the inn was built in 1840 and much more besides.

Incidentally, I find the quoted derivation of Kirkstone Pass a little confusing. The name is said to refer to 'some remarkable stones near the gorge of the pass' and to mean 'church stone', which is fairly obvious. But surely the name almost certainly refers to a particular rock at the head of the pass which is shaped on top exactly like the roof of a church, although there is no reference in the works to this rock.

They are not the sort of books you can read through, but are ideal for reference or for dipping into at random. You can, for instance, read how the various Kendal streets came to be named. Finkle Street, it is suggested, might come from a local word 'to cuddle' and to have originally been Love-lane. Captain French-lane was named after an ex-Parliamentary officer who took part in the Kaber Rigg plot of 1663, while Stramongate is derived from 'straw-man'—a man who dealt in straw. Branthwaite Brow is derived from a word meaning 'steep clearing', while Strickland-gate was the road leading to Strickland Ketel, a parish to the north of the town.

Or you can study the names of some of the mountains of West-morland. There are Fairfield, 'a level piece of ground' on the top of Rydal Head; Kettle Crag, 'the crag of the cauldron or bubbling spring'; Caudale Moor, 'the cold valley'; Stybarrow Dodd, 'the steep path on a rounded hill top'; and many more.

One chapter deals with the names of the islands on Windermere. Belle Isle, formerly The Holme and then Long Holme, was purchased in 1781 by Isabella Curwen and has since been known as Belle Isle. Ramp Holme was formerly Berkshire Island, named after its then owner, the eighteenth-century Earl of Suffolk and Berkshire, while Hen Holme is 'waterhen island'. Lady Holme is named after 'the lady chapel of Tholme', and Skirtful Crags is an allusion to the Devil dropping his load of stones from his apron or skirt.

The books place the beginnings of the Viking invasions in the tenth century. Many of these Norwegians came from Ireland, where they had arrived about fifty years earlier, and they settled extensively in parts of Westmorland. Viking archeological objects have been found at Casterton, Witherslack, Kentmere, Orton and Ormside, as well as Viking crosses at Burton, Kirkby Stephen, Ravonstonedale and Lowther. But mostly it is the thousands of place-names with a Scandinavian origin that have given Westmor-land and the Lake District its distinctive Viking flavour. Everyday words like dale, crag, gill, band, thwaite, beck and many, many more all have Scandinavian origin, and many local place-names and surnames have the same root.

FORGOTTEN WESTMORLAND

How many Westmorland folk can remember those Sunday mornings more than sixty years ago—before I was born—when the local gentry drove to church in their carriages, each bearing its owner's crest and each coachman wearing a tall silk hat with a cockade in the side. There were the Bensons from Hyning, the Gandys from Heaves—Mrs. Gandy always gave a lift to old Bella Eccles, from Levens, who received her alms bread after the service—the Walkers of Brettargh Holt, the Bagots from Levens Hall, the Argles from Eversley, the Swindlehursts from Hincaster House, the Rogers Shaws from Greenside, Mrs. Keighley from Preston Patrick and Miss Constance Holme from Owlet Ash.

The stables at the Blue Bell Inn and at the 'Eagle and Child' at Heversham were full of horses on these Sunday mornings not so very long ago, when Westmorland was a very much different place from what it is today. The roads, for instance, were surfaced with broken stones crushed by a heavy steam roller, and the dust so covered everything in dry weather that householders saved their used water to settle it. So little traffic passed along that the children could play their marbles, whip and top, shuttlecock, hoops or 'booleys' in the middle of the roadways.

This peep into Westmorland village life at the beginning of the century is taken at random from a particularly valuable and unusual book about the county published by the Westmorland Federation of Women's Institutes in 1957. The book was called *Some Westmorland Villages* and consisted of extracts from village histories compiled by nearly fifty Women's Institutes in the county. As Appleby, the county town of Westmorland, is one of the very few towns in the country with a population (about 1,700) small enough to have an Institute, its story is included, as also are the stories of Dent and Howgill, which, although situated in Yorkshire, have their Institutes affiliated to the Westmorland Federation.

It is interesting to read about the old salt industry of Arnside and to find out that as long ago as 1829 the only sea-washed parish in Westmorland was already a holiday resort. Regattas used to be held there in the summer, one of the contests being for home-made

Hardknott Pass, looking to Wrynose Pass. Summit of Red Screes.
(Overleaf) *Patterdale.   Ice floes on Low Water.*
Kentmere reservoir.   Ill Bell from Troutbeck.

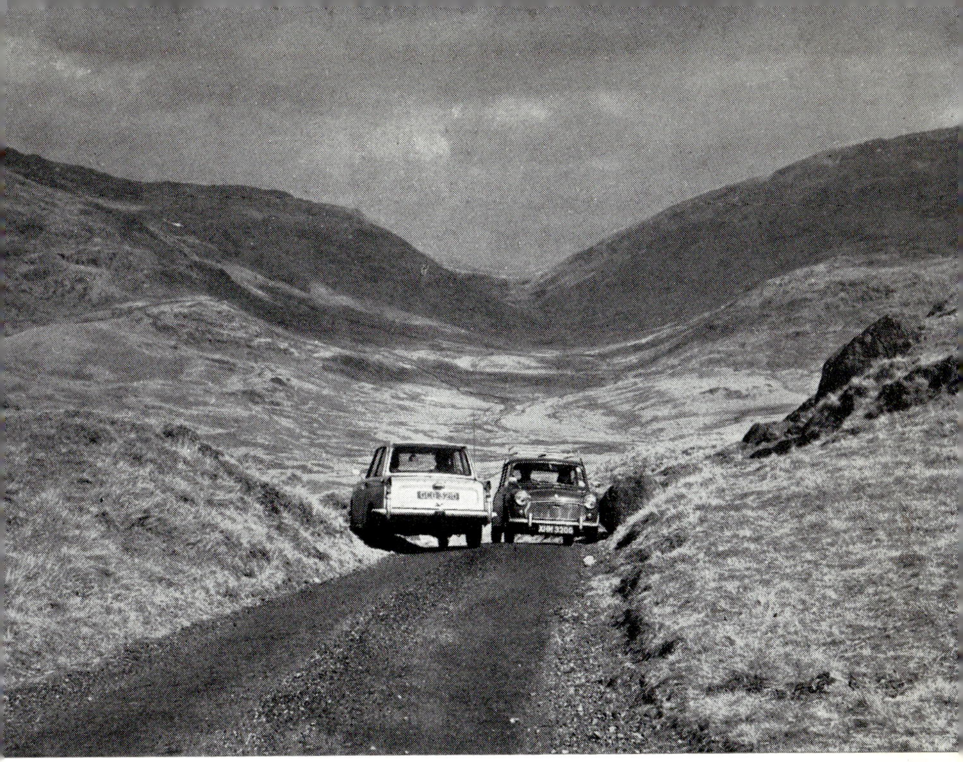

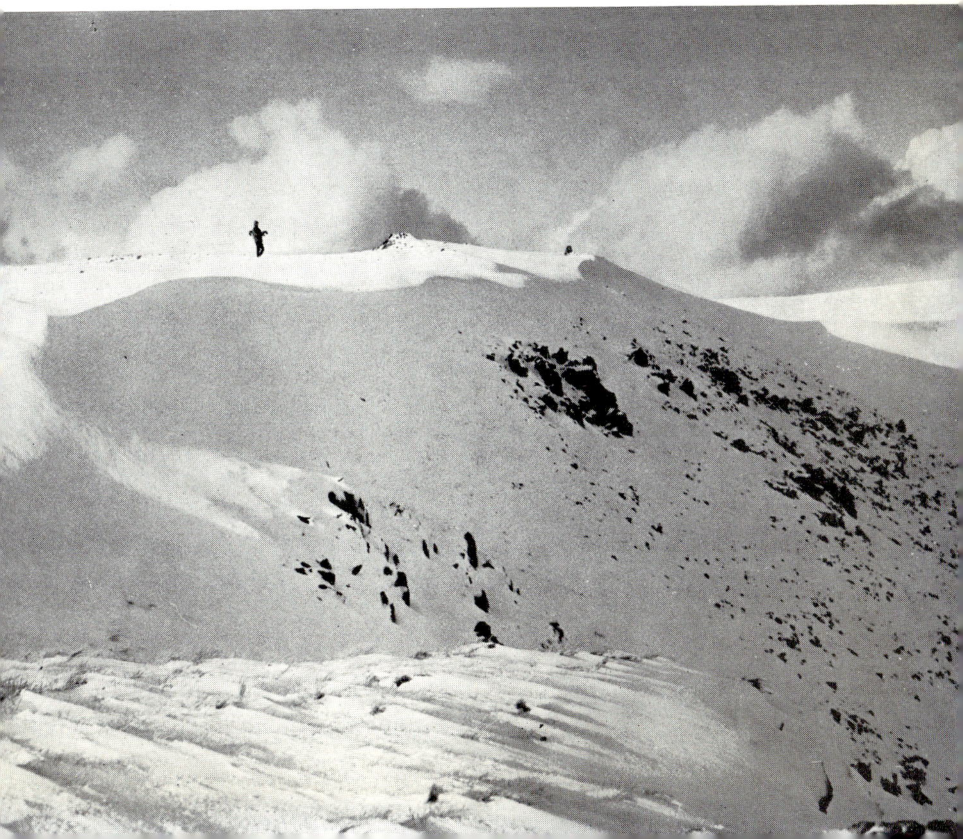

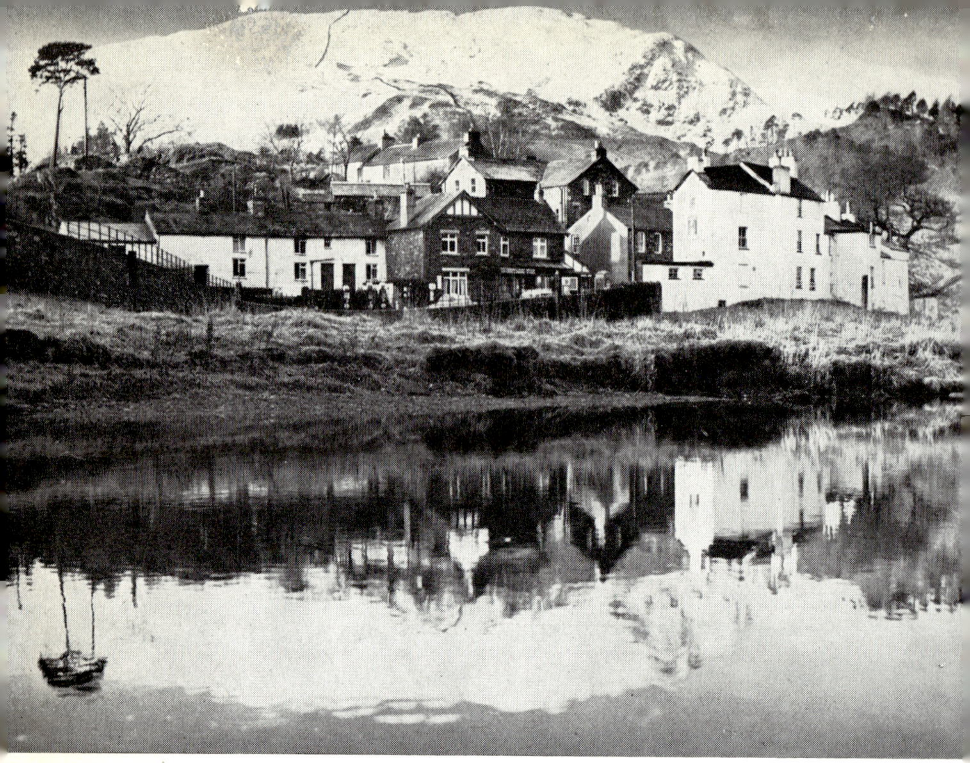

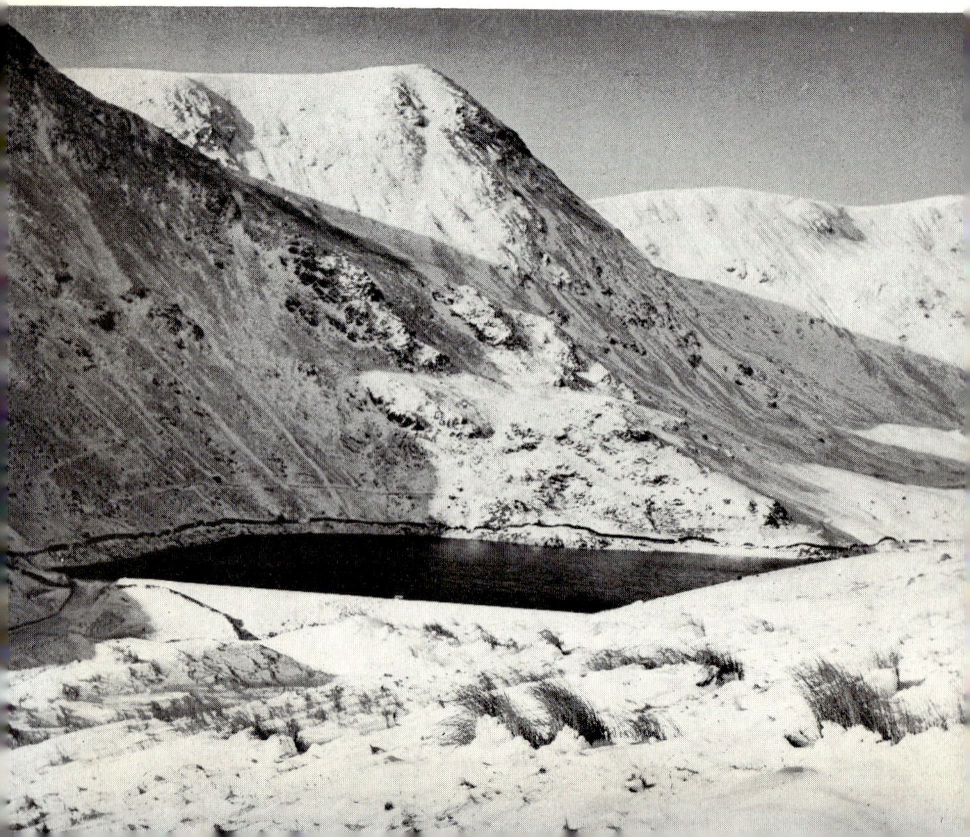

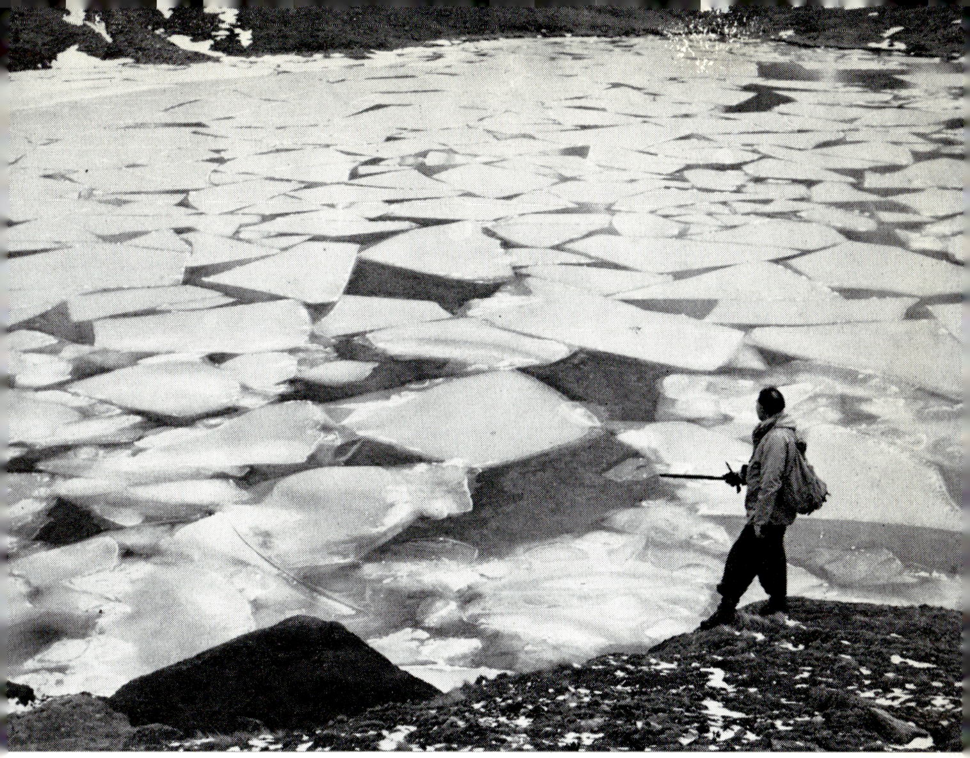

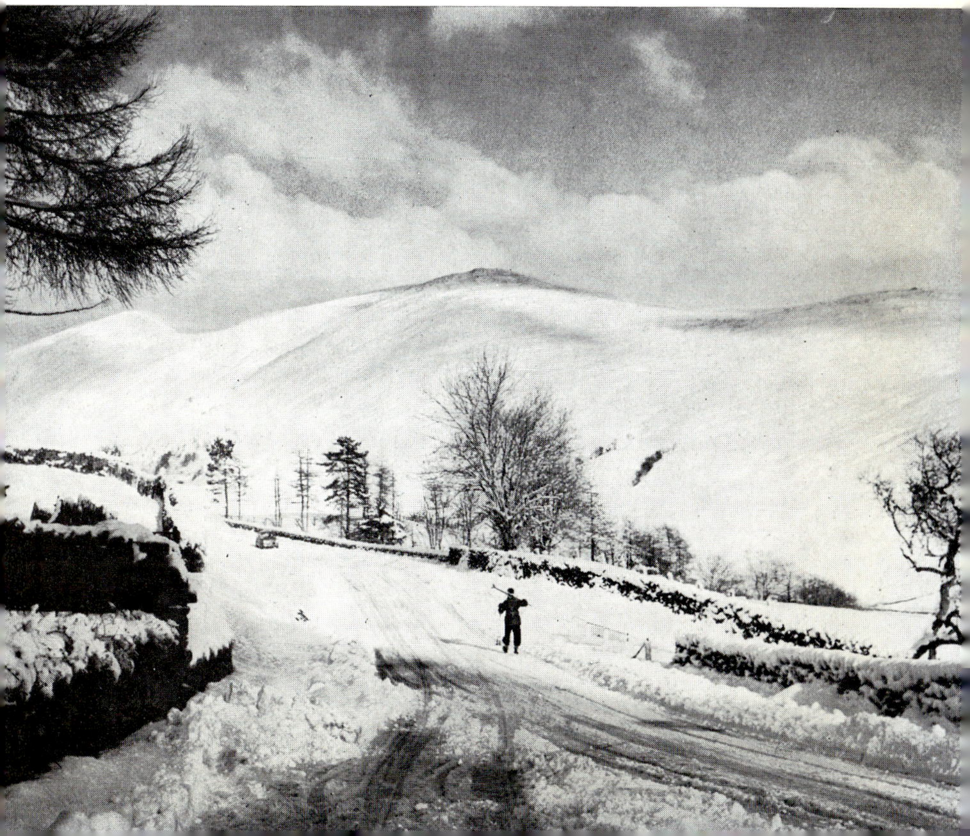

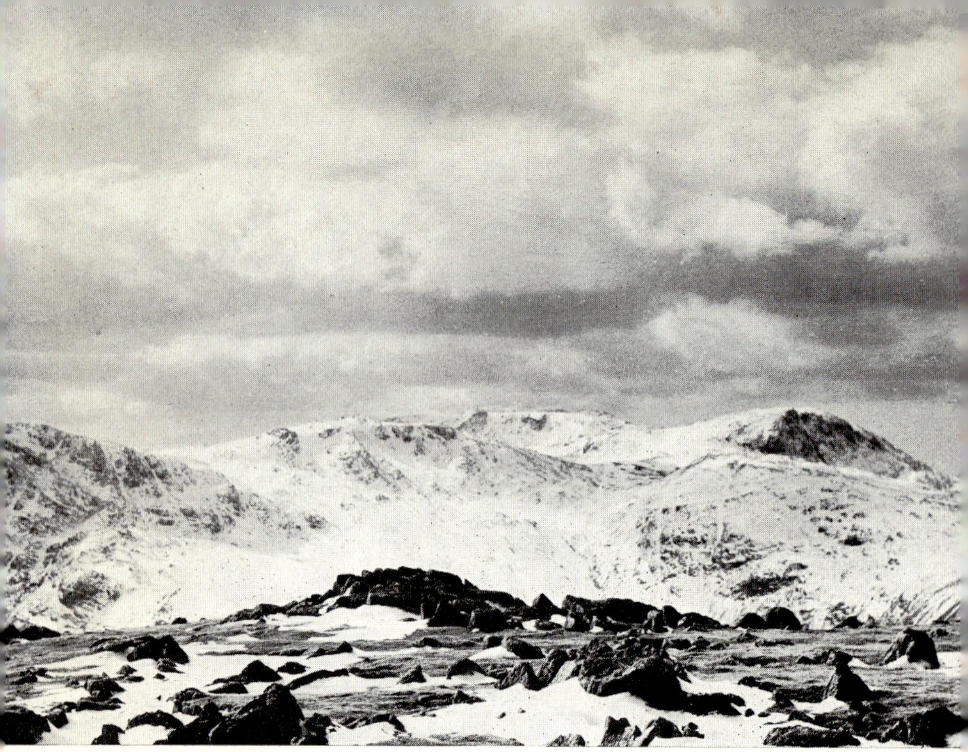

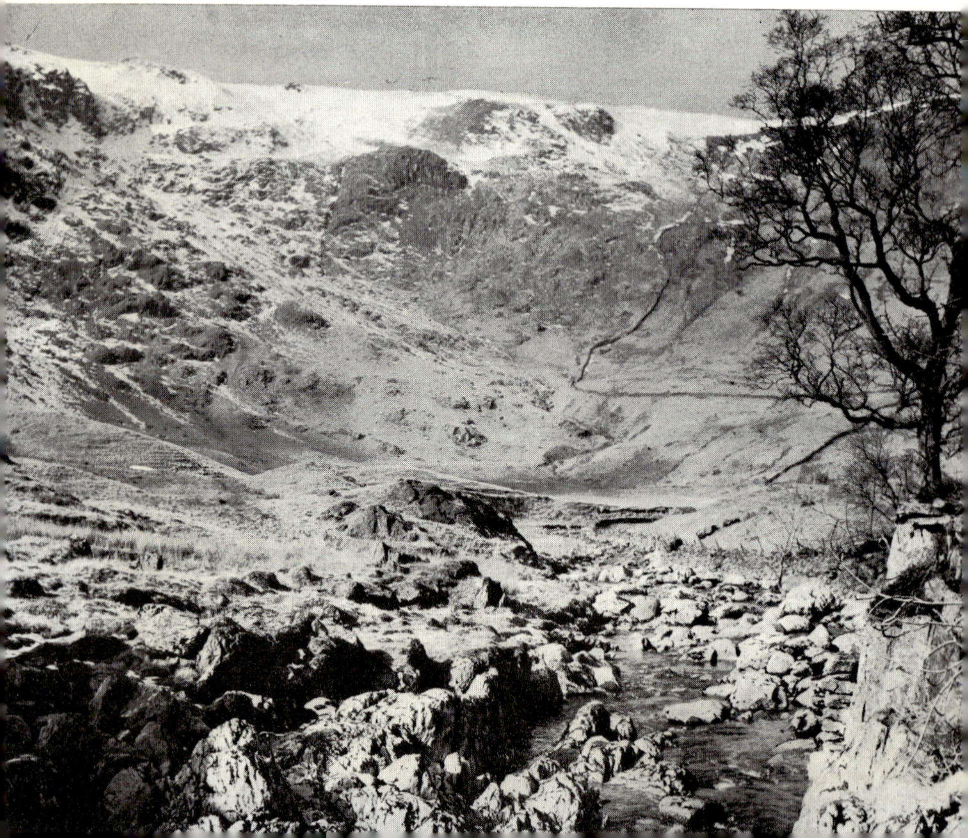

boats in the shape of tubs which often capsized. It is 113 years since the building of the viaduct, which was first made of wood.

When the Wordsworths lived at Town End, Grasmere—they never called their home Dove Cottage—they used to put their letters under a barn-door for Fletcher, the carrier, to take to Kendal. In the late nineteenth-century the carrier left Grasmere at 2 a.m., reached Kendal about 9 or 10, and, having collected his load for the return journey, set out at 1 p.m. and arrived in Grasmere about 8 p.m.

Mr. Rigg of the Windermere Hotel drove his first coach from Windermere to Grasmere in 1847. Every coachman had his 'yard o' tin', a copper coach horn, which he sounded on rounding Penny Rock or coming down the Raise into Grasmere. There was no coach over the Raise in winter. In the late nineteenth century the coach office was Miles Dixon's shoe shop at Kirk Allans, where tickets could be bought for 3*d*. a mile.

There was no milk delivery in the average Westmorland village sixty years ago, and the children used to take a milk-can to the farms for their supplies. The farmers' wives wore long skirts, pinned up over striped petticoats, and pretty, patterned, frilled cotton bonnets. The doctor travelled by pony and gig, and the district nurse cycled around in all weathers. German bands used to visit some of the villages, as well as Italian barrel-organ grinders with a performing monkey dressed in red jacket and skirt. There were also performing bears on chains travelling from village to village, with their owners getting coppers for their performances.

One of the chapters records that the bill for completely furnishing the Old Dungeon Ghyll Hotel, Great Langdale, in 1897—carpets, furniture, cutlery, china, etc.—amounted to £226. Today it would cost several thousands. It is also recorded that the funeral expenses of the famous old Eskdale and Ennerdale huntsman, Tommy Dobson, who died in harness in Langdale in 1910 at the age of 83, was £6 8*s*. 6*d*., including conveyances and coffin. The cortege left Langdale and went by way of Wrynose and Hardknott passes to Eskdale, the journey taking four hours. Last century Langdale School had 150 scholars and all had to walk to school—mostly in clogs.

Milnthorpe had its 'shouters' until comparatively recent times—men, accompanied by a fiddler or accordion player, who went

From High Raise, looking west
Head of Swindale

round the village on Christmas and New Year's Eve, greeting the occupants of each house by name, calling out the time and passing on seasonal greetings. Next day they called for their reward. Travelling tailors, making the round of Westmorland villages in 1880, charged 3s. 6d. for making a suit or two pairs of trousers from the householder's own material. A jacket and waistcoat cost 1s. 3d., but it cost half a crown, oddly enough, merely to have a jacket mended.

Fifty years ago the food eaten in Westmorland villages (according to the New Hutton authoress) was very plain, consisting chiefly of catcake, oatmeal porridge and skim-milk cheeses, called 'wangy' cheese, meaning it was tough. There was a mincemeat of raisins, currants, peel, spice and a good amount of the very fat mutton, with sugar, and the whole covered with a rich crust. At Easter time there was 'feg Sue', which consisted of figs stewed in beer and flavoured with spices. A herb pudding made out of the young leaves of snakeweed, mixed with egg and oatmeal, was also very popular. A hundred years ago eggs were sixpence for thirteen and butter about 10d. a pound.

Staveley children, both boys and girls, wore clogs every day (except Sundays) seventy years ago, and I suppose the children of other villages did the same. The clogs had wooden soles and kept the feet dry. Most boys wore rather wide knee-breeches, and girls always wore pinafores and long frocks, with their hair long and tied in a ribbon. Boys' hair was allowed to grow without being cut. When the children met any of their 'betters' (on Sunday) the girls would drop a curtsy and the boys would salute.

Broom growing in abundance in the Winster district was used for making the famous Kendal Green dye. Woad supplied the blue, and the broom a yellow, which combined to make the green. Coal-mining was carried on at Casterton as early as Charles I's reign, and a mine on Casterton Fells continued in operation until about 100 years ago, Colliers Lane being a present-day reminder. The first time a motor car was used at a Warcop wedding was in October 1909, while nine years later the first aeroplane landed in the parish. A Mrs. Scott of Waterside, Levens, the book recorded, possessed the very gun that her great grandfather, a Mr. James Spicer, used when he fought at Waterloo.

FAIRIES AND GOBLINS

You and I may not believe in fairies, or phantom black dogs or water spirits, nor would we eat a roast mouse if we wanted to cure ourselves of whooping cough, but not so very long ago there were many people living in Westmorland and the Lake District who did. Just over seventy years ago an historian wrote that faith in the 'little folk' had not died out in the Lake Counties, and that occasionally, even in those days, the dairymaid might be seen furtively putting a pinch of salt in the fire at churning time 'so that t'fairies mayn't stop t'butter frae comin'. And even today, when we talk lightly of space travel and other marvels, there are old country folk in Westmorland whose parents believed that the best way to cure warts was to rub them with a piece of stolen beef.

Several years ago a careful, scientific investigation into all these folk-lore survivals and many more was carried out in the southern part of the Lake District. Later, the learned members of the anthropology section of the British Association listened with interest to a treatise on the old folk-lore remedies of Westmorland, and we read in the newspapers the next day that to tie a frog round the patient's neck was one of the best ways of tackling whooping cough. I am now given to understand that passing the patient three times under the belly of a donkey (or brood mare) was just as good a cure; that an excellent remedy for warts was to rub them with a black snail; that string tied round a finger would stop nose bleeding; that a pair of pigeon's feet carried in the pocket cured toothache; and that the wearing of kippers inside the stockings was the rather smelly, but certain, answer to rheumatics.

My informant in all these matters—and many more—was Professor Edward M. Wilson, son of a former Mayor of Kendal, who has made a hobby of the study of folk-lore, and sent out questionnaires on the subject to country folk in Westmorland and North Lancashire. These people included schoolmasters, clergymen, farmers, blacksmiths, gentry and labourers, and from their replies he was able to publish carefully documented papers covering a very wide range of folk-lore subjects.

I have referred to one or two of the hundreds of reported folk-lore 'cures' about which Professor Wilson talked to the scientists, while his published paper dealt with beliefs about fairies, phantom black dogs and funerals and water spirits in southern Lakeland. One authority on the subject, writing of Westmorland fairies just 130 years ago, claimed that although once 'plentiful', they were then extinct. He described these fairies as beings 'between men and spirits. They had marriages, reared children, lived in caves, followed occupations, and, in particular, churned their own butter. They were considered perfectly harmless, capable of being visible or invisible at pleasure, and generally of small stature.'

Another writer, in 1899, speaks of farms in Little Langdale being regularly visited by fairies of the 'house-goblin class', whose principal occupation seems to have been churning butter after the family had retired for the night. Near the Forge it was apparently common to find bits of butter scattered in the wood, no doubt dropped in their morning flight. It is also said the 'little folk' used to steal from the stalls in Ambleside market.

One local fairy story given to Professor Wilson had been first told by the grandfather of his informant, and it is said that the incident is supposed to have happened about 1855. Coming to the four-lane ends on the Kirkby Lonsdale–Lupton road one night, an old farmer, named Michael Black, found a dry-stone wall across the road. A 'little gentleman' offered to make him a way through the wall if he would give him a pound of butter, and the farmer, agreeing, eventually got home in the early morning hours, minus his pound of butter. And when his son went along the road the next day there was the butter on the top of the wall.

Fairies were supposed by some people to have hindered the construction of a bridge at Shap when the Lancaster–Carlisle railway was being built more than 100 years ago, but one informant places their 'last appearance'—in Martindale at any rate—as about the end of the eighteenth century. Apparently one Jack Wilson of Martindale was crossing Sandwick Rigg on his return home one evening when he saw, in the light of the moon, a large company of fairies. As he drew closer he saw a ladder reaching from them into the clouds, and he watched the little folk scamper up aloft and disappear. The grandson of the man who last saw the fairies, himself an old man, always swore the story was true.

The 'brownie' of the Lake Counties—he lived in farmhouses and was known as Hob thrush, Hobthrust, Throb thrush or Hob —was firmly believed in by many people, and farmers used to leave porridge, milk and oatcake for him. Professor Wilson was told by one informant that less than eighty years ago there was a man living in Brigsteer—not far from the 'Fairy Steps'—who believed in fairies.

Many reports of phantom black dogs and funerals were collected by Professor Wilson. They include stories of ghostly animals on Stainmore, on the road between Kendal and Burneside (this is a headless phantom), at Channel Hall, Endmoor and on Bela-side Hill, between Bentham and Milnthorpe (each night at twelve o'clock, and also headless). Then there is 'Kell Bank Dobby', another mastiff-goblin near Kirkby Lonsdale, and similar ghostly forms at Shap and Sedbergh.

More than one informant has written of the belief that if you went into the churchyard at midnight on St. Marks' Eve you would see the ghosts of all who would die during the year, and it is reported that before anyone dies at one Old Hutton farm a coffin appears in the air above the farmyard. A woman in white, according to another correspondent, walks in Dallam Park, near Beetham, before a death, and at Ingmire Hall there was supposed to be a ghostly coach-and-four.

Tales of water spirits in the lakes and rivers are legion—particularly around Hawkshead and Esthwaite Water, where the spectres appear to have been particularly gruesome—and in the area of the professor's survey there are Boggart Bridge, Coffin Bridge and Boggie Well—all with stories attached. One of the best known water bogies of the North-west was Jinny Greenteeth, who lived in stagnant pools and frightened little children; but there were many more. After all this it is quite a relief to discover that witches disappeared from the Lake District a long time ago.

THE NEW FORESTS

The biggest change in the landscape of the Lake District during a lifetime has been brought about not by the roads, the reservoirs and the buildings but by the trees. The appearance of whole valleys, Ennerdale and Grizedale among them, and Dunnerdale in part, has been completely altered, bare hillsides in the Lorton Fells and in several areas to the north-west of Keswick newly clothed in dark green, and big tracts of land in the Furness Fells and around Wasdale and Eskdale taken over by the foresters. This landscape revolution began soon after the formation of the Forestry Commission just over fifty years ago, and after a slow beginning gathered in momentum, until today the commissioners are planting in something like one-fifteenth of the area of the National Park. In a sense the Lake District, in places, is going back thousands of years to the days when woodlands carpeted the mountainsides or to those later times when great forests and deer parks sprawled across the northern counties—except that the new trees are different. It is not the traditional oak and ash, beech and birch that is being planted in thousands today but spruce, larch and pine—trees from distant lands that make a quicker, more economic, crop, but may not immediately fit into the scenery. But the days when the Forestry Commission made many enemies by their blanket coverage of conifers planted in hideous straight lines have now passed with the mellowing of their plantations, their opening up of rides and footpaths and liberal planting of hardwoods, their agreement to keep out of the dale heads and to consult with amenity interests at every stage, their encouragement of wild life and their splendid work in reviving one of the district's traditional industries. And when a cairn on Whinlatter Pass was unveiled in June 1969 to commemorate the Commission's fifty years most people were happy to give them credit for a good job now perhaps half completed.

10

Looking to the Future

Many people—including hundreds, or even thousands, living in or around the Lake District—are only happy when they are living in the past. To them, the present is a dull, unexciting time, and the future just not to be thought about. The great days, they say, were the days of long ago, and nothing that has happened since then is particularly interesting or important. Perhaps this is why we are so interested in such things as rush-bearing festivals, the proceedings of the Ambleside Bond for the Prosecution of Felons or, for instance, the annual 'Mayor making' ceremony at Troutbeck—events which might have had some significance 100 years or more ago, but which today are merely quaint survivals. We seem to be hanging on to the past like grim death, and I've no doubt we will continue to do so. Perhaps in Langdale in 100 years time they will be performing some sort of solemn masque in commemoration of the electricity controversy, or—who knows? —of the quaint days when visitors were allowed to drive their cars up the valley.

It is not merely that we are living in the past; we seem to be doing so to an increasing extent. Rush-bearing festivals attract bigger crowds then ever, the bondsmen of Ambleside are today more numerous by far than at any time in their history, while the new Mayor of Troutbeck is nowadays toasted by more people with more beer and whisky than in the days when the job was important. A touch of old Lakeland—with a couple of good hunts thrown in—is a sure catch for the townsman and the television cameras.

Like thousands of others, I am content to live in the past—to some extent, at least—although ready to admit I may be wrong. For instance, the Lake District was at its best—for me—between thirty-five and forty years ago, and it will never be quite the same again, but much older people will recall with greater nostalgia the days of sixty or more years ago.

It is, I think, interesting to speculate where this preoccupation with the past might lead. Obviously, the country outside the Lake District will develop during the next fifty or 100 years to a vastly greater extent than it will inside the National Park, so that, increasingly, Lakeland will become a very special sort of area. And therein lies a danger—the danger, freely hinted at a few years ago, that Lakeland might become some kind of a Red Indian reserve. You can see what I mean. Fifty years from now counties like Lancashire and Durham might be a network of tremendous wide speedways at different heights above the ground with aerodromes—or whatever they will be using then—as thick on the countryside as filling stations are today. No doubt life will be going on there at a great pace, but only five minutes away by atomic air taxi there will be the English Lake District, not greatly different than it is today.

Nowadays, they crowd to Troutbeck to watch the ancient 'Mayor's Hunt'; in fifty or 100 years' time they might be flying up from London to watch the dalesmen ploughing or milking cows. It will be all so different from the fast, efficient world outside. If we can get quite worked up today about a piece of dry-stone walling, how much more exciting it will appear in 100 years' time when all the walls in the outside world are made of synthetic iron, or plastic, or unbreakable glass. It might, indeed, be worth while—you can hear some people saying—to stay in the past, so as to cash in on the future. Old shippons, dingy bar parlours, quaint tumble-down farmhouses, shepherds in flat caps and heavy boots, and golden-haired children selling wild flowers, will all have their values. 'Come and see how the wild Lakelanders live,' will run the advertisements. 'Nature in the raw in the last corner of Olde England.' Remember, we might be only five minutes away from London. They might pop over for an hour to see what sheep look like. All this, of course, would be the very worst thing that could happen to Lakeland, but when I see shepherds with crooks posing for photographs or phoney 'olde worlde' trash offered for sale in the shops I begin to wonder whether the rot has not already set in.

Lakeland is not likely to change during the next 100 years to anything like the same extent as its surroundings, but there *will* be changes. No doubt, the very centre of the district will be much the same as it is today, but how do we know there will not be some sort of radio device on the tops of the mountains so as to give the best possible pictures on colour television—or whatever the equivalent might be in those days. Just the same as we have had public enquiries about bringing electricity to the valleys, there may be—in fifty years' time—similar arguments about radio-repeater stations on mountain-tops to bring the ordinary amenity of three-dimensional colour television to the poor, benighted dalesfolk.

It is unlikely there will be any more trees in the mountainous heart of Lakeland, but farther out from the centre there may be largish forests—as there were a few hundred years ago. Forests may become more important and sheep less, although by then some method will probably have been discovered of dealing effectively with the bracken menace, and there will be much more grazing land. If, on the other hand, bracken continues to defeat the scientists and engineers, it will, no doubt, have spread over the whole of Lakeland, and there will be nothing much else to see.

Fifteen years ago I wrote, despairingly, that in fifty years' time most of the lakes would have become reservoirs—part of some national water grid—and that fishing, boating and bathing on these lakes would be prohibited. I thought, however, there would still be some unspoiled lakes left in Scotland. Today I am not so pessimistic. Despite the gloomy predictions of the Water Resources Board, I do not expect any greatly increased use of Lake District water in the future, and certainly not the creation of new lakes as reservoirs, as was, for instance, threatened in the Winster valley. Public opinion against desecration is now so well organised that projects of this kind are unlikely to have much chance of success. Relatively minor schemes calling for some measure of control over lake levels might get through, but I expect to see more emphasis on schemes for taking water from the mouths of rivers and also, of course, for bringing down the cost of desalination. With the schemes for tapping Ullswater and Windermere still as

M

I write (in mid-1970) under construction and some controversy in the air about taking supplies from Bassenthwaite Lake, I can hardly go so far as to assume that these will be the limits in the use of our lakes for water, but I do believe that major developments are unlikely. While public access to, for instance, the existing reservoirs of Haweswater and Thirlmere will be improved.

We can, I think, assume that there will be considerable control in the future over the use of the lakes for fast motor-boating and water ski-ing—activities which tend to interfere with the enjoyment of the majority—and I am sure that the smaller lakes and tarns will certainly remain protected in this way. Car-parks and caravan parks—especially around the perimeter of the National Park—are certain to multiply, and no doubt there will eventually be helicopter or aircraft landing grounds. But even if the worst happens to Lakeland and it becomes a place like Niagara Falls, there will still be quiet places in the hills—save for the photographers in the helicopters—where the buzzards soar, the becks twinkle among the rocks and the sun gilds the crags in the evening. Windermere, perhaps Ullswater and even Borrowdale may not be quite the same as they are today, but, for those who seek it, there should still remain something of 'the silence that is in the starry sky, the sleep that is among the lonely hills'.

But the biggest problem, of course, facing the National Park is the problem of people and motor cars. England's principal sanctuary for peace and quietude is in danger of being ruined—not only because of over-popularity but rather because it is too easily accessible. The sanctuary is becoming a cock-pit. By the time this book is published the Westmorland motorway will have been completed and the Lake District will be within an easy day's journey—there and back—of the Midlands. And some of London's millions might be tempted to try Lakeland for the occasional weekend. Car ownership in this country has doubled within a few years, and by 1980, it has been stated, there will be an average of one car to every family. How can a small area like the Lake District possibly cope with the expected flood?

The answer, I believe, is straightforward although exceedingly difficult to apply, and even revolutionary. The National Park will have to be closed to traffic—not all of it, and not all the time, but certainly the best parts and certainly during the holiday season, and perhaps at weekends. Not this year and not next year, and perhaps not for several years to come, but I believe some restriction on vehicular entry into the inner dales will *have* to come some time—perhaps sooner than we realise.

For if a priceless national heritage is being ruined by the motor car there seems only one solution—the gates will have to be shut. Just as they're shut by the Forestry Commission in Ennerdale, which, despite its conifers, could nearly claim to be the least spoiled of the major valleys of Lakeland. And this is by no means the pipe-dream of a fanatic, the wishful thinking of a narrow-minded preservationist. For I have good reason to believe that this sort of ultimate solution is being actively considered by those concerned, up to government level. It should be realised that although you can cram Blackpool or Morecambe to bursting point and keep everybody happy, the Lake District depends for its survival as a sanctuary on the presence of a reasonable minimum of people and man-made objects in the landscape and a comparative absence of noise and tumult.

But you can't stop people going to Lakeland simply by talking about the menace of mass tourism, and many would argue that motorists have as much right to the area as mountaineers. For some the problem seems simple. 'More and more people,' they say, 'are coming to Lakeland. All right, we must give them better, wider and faster roads.' And so the main roads through the Park are being widened and straightened, and once-quiet places like Ambleside and Keswick are tending to resemble refuelling points on race-tracks. Already the main highways through the National Park are becoming speedways and commercialism colours the popular places. But let us, at least, have some quietude in the remoter corners. You can't plant trees in some of these daleheads or pitch tents or site caravans or use coloured tiles—why should you be able to clutter them up with cars? They still manage to keep cars away from some of the best bits of Switzerland; might not something like this be possible in some of our still unspoiled places?

When it was suggested a year or two ago that it might not be a bad idea to try out a pilot scheme banning all but essential cars from Langdale on some autumn weekend, the idea was greeted with a great howl of protest from the valley and from other parts of the Lake District as well. A great deal of nonsense was written about the suggestion at the time and there was a lot of confused thinking, but I am quite satisfied that some day something like this might have to be tried out. Possibly the idea was a little premature, but you can't launch into traffic-control schemes that interfere with the freedom of the motorist without most careful study and experiment, and this was all that was implied. Obviously, you can't ban vehicles in every dalehead or right through the summer, nor can you ban *all* vehicles. But I will be very surprised if a start on some form of traffic control in one or two valleys—perhaps Langdale and Borrowdale—on certain days of the year, perhaps bank holidays and some weekends, is not found necessary within the next few years. Obviously the free movement of the locals will not be affected, nor that of visitors staying in the hotels, farms, hostels or huts, while other essential traffic will also be unrestricted. But the casual motorist, just coming into the valley for the ride, would be asked to park his vehicle at the entrance to the dale and either use the public transport provided or his own feet.

And this does not seem to me to be such a terrible alternative in a National Park created for the enjoyment of fresh air and outdoor recreation. Every encouragement in the inner dales should be given to the walker and the cyclist. For is it really right that the last unspoiled parts of such a tiny precious area that could be lost in Scotland should become no more than a weekend motoring alternative to Blackpool and Morecambe?

Indeed, the time may come when the more gregarious type of visitor will have to be encouraged to go elsewhere, for the beauty of the mountains and lakes can't really be enjoyed in crowds, nor the song of the birds and the tinkle of the becks heard above the noise of speedboat and car engines. Camping and caravanning must still have their place in the park, but these should preferably be only small, wooded, secluded sites, smaller than some of those now in use, but many more of them. How much better it would have been at Wasdale Head, for instance, if a wooded site near the western end of the lake had been chosen and the head of the dale kept unspoiled. The mountains would still have been within easy reach of the campers. Years ago the climbers used to walk all the way from the railway at Seascale.

Something might have to be done to divert the traffic flood to places outside the National Park. North and east Westmorland, for instance, contain unspoiled country almost as lovely as some parts of the Lake District, yet few weekenders or holiday-makers go there, and even the indigenous population is drifting away. Such an area—and there are others in the north, some of them conveniently close to large areas of population—seem ideally suited for the intelligent introduction of tourism.

Of course, some people say that the weight of traffic will eventually solve the problem itself. Already it is claimed that these long slow queues make for safer motoring, and eventually, they say, the park will become so blocked that people won't bother to go there any more. I doubt this myself, but what's to happen in the meantime? And what a pitiful prospect—England's finest corner cluttered up with cars like Manchester in the rush hour! I hope I'll never live to see the notice 'Park full'—meaning the National Park—at the entrance to Lakeland, but it's certainly going to be filled to overflowing very soon if the problem isn't tackled realistically, and it could then be ruined for all time. I remember one Easter six years ago when there was snow, hail, high winds, thunder and lightning in Lakeland? And yet there were claimed to be queues stretching for up to 11 miles at the southern entrance to the park. So what may it be like this summer, or next year or two years hence?

I believe that the widening and realignment of the main road through Lakeland from Kendal to Keswick will, in the long run, be welcomed as necessary and wise—*providing* that it succeeds in channelling most of the traffic along this popular highway and diverting it from the narrower and more precious roads into the dales. Naturally, I would have preferred the character of the old road to have remained largely unchanged, but most of the old highway has already gone, and soaring traffic figures force certain 'improvements' upon us. Far better, in my view, to try to contain the increasing traffic along this highway and leave the winding roads into the dales untouched. After all, most visitors to the Lake District are either merely motoring, there and back, from the towns and cities or seeking out places either on or not far from the main highway. A much smaller proportion of the total explore farther afield, and of this smaller section a very small percentage indeed get out of their cars and use their legs to any noticeable extent. Recent surveys have shown this very clearly. It seems to me, therefore, that we will have to try to contain these motorists—most of them just released from fifty to 150 miles of motorway—along a decent highway—and hope that most of them will stay there. And if, in return, we could look forward to a few more years of reasonably uncluttered access into the dales the sacrifice will have been well worth while.

The ultimate aim of the road engineers should be some sort of a circular route or system of perimeter roads around the National Park, mostly using the existing highways, with the remaining network of roads, and especially the roads into the daleheads, left mostly as they are, their character unchanged. Coaches, apart from public-service vehicles, may ultimately have to be banned from all but the principal routes, parking on roadsides prohibited and towed caravans and boats restricted to certain defined routes. These sort of expedients will not, of course, solve the problem for ever, but they could give time for a breathing space and for a detailed examination into the habits of our visitors. For before the authorities are forced into such a step as the suggested prohibition of all but essential vehicles in some of the dales a great deal of research will have to be done, as well as close consultations with hotels, shops and other commercial undertakings that depend on visitors for their existence.

And, in the meantime, the casual motorist with no real interest in the Lake District apart from its happening to be a convenient goal for a day's run may have to be discouraged from cluttering up the best of the National Park. May I commend as a useful task for the English Lakes Counties Travel Association the compilation of a survey of tourism in the area which would show what proportion of our visitors come to walk, climb, fish, sail, camp or just look at the scenery and how many come merely because Keswick or Ambleside happens to be within convenient motoring distance of their homes—but have no other real interest in the district?

I believe that more hotels might well be built in the Lake District within existing community areas and that there will be a growing emphasis on the long-stay visitor, especially visitors from abroad. The area is being publicised more than ever before, and the tourist industry will increase in importance with growing wealth and leisure. It would, however, be the greatest pity if the tourist attractions common to seaside resorts and to many places on the Continent are ever introduced into Lakeland. The recent argument that the 'Sunday supplement set'—whoever they may be—accustomed to such attractions abroad, will expect and demand them in the Lake District should be most sternly resisted. Artificial attractions are completely unnecessary, and quite undesirable, in a National Park set aside as an area of unspoiled natural beauty, and people who want such facilities and entertainments should go elsewhere. Lakeland has always had the problem, for some, of the wet day, but to try solve it by the introduction of the sort of indoor entertainments commonly found in seaside resorts would be to ruin the whole atmosphere of the area.

The attraction of the Lake District lies in its traditional qualities of quietude, seclusion and unmatched mountain beauty, and there are quite enough potential visitors seeking just these qualities to ensure that the important business of tourism has a bright future. To add other attractions to try to draw people who would not otherwise come to the Lake District would be to begin the gradual cheapening of the area. Wider roads, more car-parks and caravan sites around the perimeter, these have been forced upon us; but to try to convert Lakeland into some vast amusement park—even in a restrained sort of way—would be criminal. Our grandparents came to the Lake District for what it had especially to offer—mountains, lakes, woods and solitude—and these have remained the principal attractions of the area throughout my lifetime. Bingo halls, casinos, amusement arcades, sports centres, evening entertainments and the like can all be found elsewhere, but the particular attractions of Lakeland are quite unique in this country, and must remain so, unadorned and untarnished. People will always come to Lakeland for what it is, not for what it might be if the developers had their way. You cannot gild the lily, and the highest mountains in the country, the biggest lakes and the atmosphere and traditions built up over the centuries cannot be improved by gimmickry and commercialism.

Some of the Lakeland of my youth has been lost for ever, but the best of it still remains and must be guarded more jealously than ever before. England is an overcrowded, shrinking country—

shrinking under the outward sprawl of cities and motorways. But a few small areas remain where people can breathe and look out across unscarred countryside, and one of the most important of these—in my view *the* most important—is the English Lake District. The pressures upon us during the remainder of this century will be tremendous, but all those who treasure wild places and quiet scenery should dedicate themselves to ensuring that this priceless heritage remains unviolated and the real Lakeland a sanctuary for ever.

THE END OF THE YEAR

There are fell days in the sad tail-end of every year so still and quiet that you might be looking out at a grey and faded photograph. Mist over the little towns, chimney smoke over the hamlets and the farms, with the bare, black trees just probing through the gloom, not a sound or movement anywhere, not a bird or a sighing of the wind and, high up, grey mountain snows merging uncertainly into grey skies. On one of these days I drove north out of the greyness into the red sandstone country seeking bright sunlit snows, but finding instead black ice and mountain mists. Even after a lifetime of mountain wandering I never cease to be fascinated by the changes that can be brought out by 2,000 feet of height. Down in the valley, a mild day with the smoke rising straight from the chimney-pots, but, on the mountain, rutted ice on the track, rock-hard snowdrifts, a biting wind and visibility down to a few yards. The skier, moving fast over unfamiliar terrain, wants to be able to see well ahead, but that afternoon was rather like sliding down a toboggan run at night and not knowing which way it might turn next. But even on the worst day the enthusiast gets his reward, and sure enough, it came that afternoon. First, a rush of wind and a tiny triangle of blue sky and then, suddenly, the grey clouds torn aside and flung helter-skelter across the sky, a flood of sunshine across dazzling white snows and the dale leaping upwards in warm browns and reds from far below my skis. Within seconds, a grey tunnel with a dark smudge 10 yards away that might be either a rock or a hole became a sparkling white mountain-side looking out over two sunlit counties with, curving gently downwards, a magical Christmas glideway to the valley.

Index

THATTO HEATH
BRANCH LIBRARY